RADIX LISTENING for the TOEFL iBT®

BLACK LABEL 1

TABLE OF CONTENTS

Introduction	**004**

Part A	**Basic Comprehension Questions**	
Unit 01	Main Idea	010
Unit 02	Detail	030
Actual Practice Test 1		**050**

Part B	**Pragmatic Understanding Questions**	
Unit 03	Function	058
Unit 04	Attitude	078
Actual Practice Test 2		**098**

Part C	**Connecting Information Questions**	
Unit 05	Organization	106
Unit 06	Connecting Content	126
Unit 07	Inference	146
Actual Practice Test 3		**166**

Practice TOEFL iBT Listening Section	**174**

Answer Keys & Audio Scripts	**182**

INTRODUCTION

TOEFL®: Test of English as a Foreign Language

The TOEFL is a standardized test developed to assess English language proficiency in an academic setting. By achieving a high score on the TOEFL, you will demonstrate that your skills in English qualify you for admission to a college or university where English is used as the language of instruction. Academic institutions around the world will look at your performance on the TOEFL, so whether you are hoping to study in North America, Australia, Europe, or Asia, this test is the key to your future educational career.

TOEFL Today: TOEFL iBT

The TOEFL Internet-based test (iBT) is the version currently administered in secure testing centers worldwide. It tests reading, listening and writing proficiency, and speaking abilities.

Getting to Know the TOEFL iBT: Important Points

- The test is divided into four sections: Reading, Listening, Speaking, and Writing. These are the skills that are essential for proficiency in any language.
- As well as measuring the individual skills listed above, some portions of the test require you to apply various combinations of skills in order to complete a task. Examples of such integrated tasks include:
    - listening to a passage and speaking in response to a question on the passage
    - reading a passage, listening to a second passage, and then speaking in response to a question on the two passages
    - reading a passage, listening to a second passage, and then writing a response to a question on the two passages
- In each section of the test, a tool bar is displayed on the computer screen. It lists the section and question number you are currently working on, the amount of time remaining, and has help, navigational, and volume buttons. The function buttons may differ slightly from one section to the next.
- In the Speaking section of the test, you will be required to speak your responses into a microphone. Your input will be digitally recorded and evaluated by ETS's trained scorers.
- In the Writing section of the test, you will be required to type your responses.
- There is no section dedicated to grammar, but your grammar skills will be tested indirectly throughout the test, especially in the Speaking and Writing sections.
- You will be allowed to take notes during all portions of the test, and you will likely find these notes very helpful when answering the questions.
- You can view your scores in your ETS account approximately 6 days after your test date. You'll receive an email when your scores are available, and you can access your account online or via the official TOEFL® app.

Getting to Know the TOEFL iBT: Test Format

You will take all four sections of the test (Reading, Listening, Speaking, and Writing) on the same day. The duration of the entire test is about four hours.

Test Section	Description of Tasks	Timing
Reading	3–4 passages, each approximately 700 words 10 questions on each passage	54–72 minutes
Listening	3-4 lectures, each 3-5 minutes long 6 questions per lecture 2–3 conversations, each around 3 minutes long 5 questions per conversation	41–57 minutes
BREAK		10 minutes
Speaking	4 tasks • 1 independent task – speak about personal knowledge and experience • 3 integrated tasks – read-listen-speak / listen-speak	17 minutes
Writing	2 tasks • 1 independent task – write about personal knowledge and experience • 1 integrated task – read-listen-write	50 minutes

Score Scales

You will receive a score between 0 and 30 for each section of the test. Your total score is the sum of these four scores and will be between 0 and 120.

Registering for the TOEFL iBT

The most convenient way to register to take the TOEFL iBT is online by visiting the "Register for the TOEFL® Test" section of the TOEFL website (www.ets.org/toefl). Here, you can check current listings of testing centers and schedules. It is also possible to register for the test by phone and by mail. For more information, consult the TOEFL iBT Bulletin, which can be downloaded or ordered from the TOEFL website. It is free and features important information regarding the registration process.

GUIDE TO LISTENING

For students pursuing studies in English-speaking environments, listening comprehension is an essential skill, as information will be delivered through lectures and conversations. The Listening section of the TOEFL iBT will require you to demonstrate your understanding of English as it is spoken in academic settings in North America and throughout the world. Questions in the Listening section are designed to test:

1. Your basic comprehension of a lecture or conversation, including the main idea and key details
2. Your understanding of the speaker's purpose for relating certain information and his or her attitude about this information
3. Your ability to synthesize information from various parts of a lecture or conversation in order to understand its organization and the relationships between its ideas, and to draw inferences based on it

Listening Section Content
The material you will hear in the Listening section will include academic lectures typical of a classroom setting and conversations related to student life. The speech will accurately reflect real-life spoken English, and may include the following features: polite interruptions, mistakes and corrections, hesitations and repetitions. Although many of the speakers in the Listening section will have standard American accents, some may have a regional U.S. accent or an accent from another English-speaking country.

Academic Lectures
There are two formats of academic lectures that appear in the Listening section: monologues and interactive lectures. In a monologue, the professor is the only one who speaks. In an interactive lecture, one or two students will participate in a discussion with the professor about the information he or she is presenting. The subject matter of both monologues and interactive lectures imitates what is commonly covered in introductory-level classes at colleges and universities. Lecture topics are quite varied, but no prior knowledge or expertise is required to understand the material. You will be able to answer all the questions using only the information contained in the lectures.

Conversations
Unlike the lectures, the conversations in the TOEFL iBT do not involve specific academic material. Instead, they are concerned with problems and situations typical of student life. One speaker is usually a student, and the other can be a professor, teaching assistant, office clerk, librarian, another student, etc.

Types of Questions

The questions found in the Listening section can be divided into seven categories.

Question Type	Testing Point
Main Idea	The overall content or purpose of the lecture or conversation
Detail	Important details introduced in the lecture or conversation
Function	The speaker's reason for making a specific statement in the lecture or conversation
Attitude	The speaker's attitude toward or degree of certainty about ideas in the lecture or conversation
Organization	The overall relationship between major ideas in the lecture
Connecting Content	Relationships that have been stated or clearly implied in the lecture or conversation
Inference	The speaker's intended meaning or implication in the lecture or conversation

Important Points to Keep in Mind

- You can take notes on all of the listening materials as you hear them. This is recommended, as you are not expected to memorize the material you hear.
- There will be a picture or pictures shown on the computer screen to provide context for each lecture or conversation.
- For lectures that use specialized terms, the new vocabulary may appear on a "blackboard screen" on the computer. This imitates the way a professor might write important terms on a blackboard. The purpose of these screens is to assist in your understanding of the lecture, but they do not necessarily present information related to the questions you will have to answer.
- When you see a headphone icon next to a question, it means you will have to listen again to an excerpt from the lecture or conversation before answering the question.
- There is no time limit for individual questions in the Listening section, but you must budget your time in order to finish the entire section within the allotted 60–90 minutes.
- A tool bar is displayed on the computer screen. It lists the section and question number you are currently working on, the amount of time remaining, and has help, navigational, and volume buttons.
  Keep in mind that in the Listening section, you cannot return to a question after you have confirmed your answer.

Tactics for the TOEFL iBT Listening Section

To strengthen your listening skills before taking the TOEFL iBT, it is essential to frequently expose yourself to sources of spoken English. Watching movies and television and listening to radio programs on various topics are simple and effective ways of doing this. To receive practice specifically with academic speech, check out the audio material available at libraries and bookstores. You may find it helpful to obtain a transcript of the material so you can read along as you listen.

During the test, remember to:
- make a note of new words and concepts that are presented in the lectures
- remain focused by thinking about what the speakers will likely say next
- consider each speaker's motivation and why they present certain information
- concentrate on the organization of the lecture or conversation so you can notice the difference between changes in topic and digressions
- listen for key words that demonstrate how important ideas are related to each other

HOW TO USE THIS BOOK

This book gives you instruction, practice, and strategies for performing well on the TOEFL iBT Listening Section. It will familiarize you with the appearance and format of the TOEFL iBT and help you prepare for the TOEFL test efficiently.

Each unit in the book corresponds to one of the seven question types in the Listening Section. Each unit consists of the following:
- An **Introduction** that provides basic information about the question type
- **Basic Drills** that offer short listening materials to give examples of the question type being covered and allow you to become familiar with it
- **Listening Practice** involving longer listening materials that will improve essential skills
- **iBT Practice** that provides extensive exercises
- **Note-Takings** that help you practice and improve note-taking skills for the TOEFL iBT
- **Dictations** that require a focus on accuracy, general comprehension, and special features of pronunciation while you transcribe or orally reproduce what you hear
- A **Vocabulary Review** that offers a variety of activities designed to help you review and master essential vocabulary

In addition, this book contains three **Actual Practice Tests** to help you measure your progress, and these appear after units 2, 4 and 7.

PART A

Basic Comprehension Questions

▶ **UNIT 01**   MAIN IDEA
UNIT 02   DETAIL

UNIT 01 Main Idea

Introduction

- Main Idea questions require you to have an overall understanding of the given conversation or lecture.
- These questions ask about the topic of the conversation or lecture.
- 1 Main Idea question is given for every conversation or lecture, and it will always appear as the first question for the passage.

Question Types

1. **Question forms for conversations:**
   - Why does the student go to see the professor?
   - What problem does the student have?
   - What are the speakers mainly discussing?

2. **Question forms for lectures:**
   - What is the lecture mainly about?
   - What is the main point of the lecture?
   - What aspect of X does the professor mainly discuss?

Strategy

1. Listen closely to the beginning of the conversation or lecture.
   (1) In conversations: The student's problem is usually the main idea. Identify the problem quickly at the beginning of the conversation.
   (2) For lectures: At the beginning of the lecture, the professor introduces the subject he/she will talk about.

2. You must understand the content comprehensively. As you listen, concentrate on the overall flow of the passage while you catch the major points. Writing down key words and phrases is effective.

3. Correct answers to the Main Idea questions are key words or phrases from the passage that have been reworded or paraphrased. Thus, answer choices that have the exact words and phrases from the passage are mostly likely incorrect.

Sample Question

TOEFL Listening

Professor

Now, the term "heat island" refers to urban air and surface temperatures that are higher than those in nearby rural areas. Many cities have air temperatures that are 2 to 10°F warmer than the surrounding natural land cover. What I want to talk about today is the factors that contribute to the relative warmth of cities. First… as a city grows, trees are cut down to make room for commercial development, roads, and suburban growth. As you know, plants and soil absorb heat during the day, and then carry the heat away through evaporation. Also urban areas generate more heat than other areas because of their higher populations… of course, a large population involves a lot of transportation, heating, and manufacturing. In addition to this, asphalt roads and tar roofs have absorptive properties so that heat is actually trapped in urban areas… there's little material in urban areas that reflects heat… and this is the problem.

What is the lecture mainly about?
- Ⓐ The necessity of planting trees in the city
- Ⓑ Different factors causing cities to become hot
- Ⓒ The ways of decreasing air pollution in the city
- Ⓓ Key principles in developing cities

Answer and Explanation
The professor briefly explains what "heat island" is first, then talks about the three factors that contribute in creating the "heat island" effect in cities. Thus, Ⓑ is the correct answer.

Basic Drills

1 Why does the student go to see the professor?

- Ⓐ To enroll in the design program
- Ⓑ To suggest an idea for a magazine
- Ⓒ To discuss her idea for a name card
- Ⓓ To request a change in her assignment

2 What is the main point of the lecture?

- Ⓐ A diverse range of superheroes has existed since the 1940s.
- Ⓑ There are many movies featuring new versions of old superheroes.
- Ⓒ Modern superhero films are better representing minority groups.
- Ⓓ The superheroes of today share similarities with those of the past.

3 What is the lecture mainly about?

- Ⓐ The decline of the piano's position in home recreation
- Ⓑ Effects of technological development on music
- Ⓒ Reasons for the popularity of the piano among the middle class
- Ⓓ Various home recreations before the spread of television

4 What is the student's problem?

- Ⓐ He missed an important meeting with his professor.
- Ⓑ His school orientation overlaps with his camping trip.
- Ⓒ He has difficulty in making friends at the school.
- Ⓓ He didn't get notice of the school orientation.

5 What is the lecture mainly about?

- Ⓐ The distinctive digestive system of hummingbirds
- Ⓑ How hummingbirds survive in the winter
- Ⓒ Different sources of energy for hummingbirds
- Ⓓ How hummingbirds cope with their high metabolism

6 What does the professor mainly discuss?

- Ⓐ How plants produce chlorophyll
- Ⓑ Requirements for photosynthesis
- Ⓒ Why leaves change color in fall
- Ⓓ The process of food production in plants

Dictation

Listen and fill in the blanks.

1. But these movies and similar, um... television shows have been _____ _____ _____ _____ pop culture for decades.

2. Throughout the years, however, one thing has been _____ _____ _____ _____ and TV series.

3. Today, though, the, um... the movies that are being made _____ _____ _____ _____ _____ in diversity.

4. These movies and others are bringing a, um, _____ _____ _____ _____ to traditional superhero tales.

5. The piano's secure status as the favorite form of _____ _____ began to change with the development of technology.

6. I mean, people were given options other than music performed _____ _____ _____.

7. As this instrument was not only cheap but also _____ _____ _____, its popularity spread quickly.

8. Because of this rapid flapping, these birds... hummingbirds that is... _____ _____ _____ _____ _____ and energy needs relative to their weights of any birds.

9. At night, or any other time food _____ _____ _____ _____, they are capable of slowing down their metabolism.

10. During torpor, the heart rate and rate of breathing are _____ _____ _____ ... the heart rate to roughly 50~180 beats per minute, reducing their need for food.

11. Chlorophyll is the compound _____ _____ _____ the manufacture of foods, and it so... it increases during summer when more sunlight and water _____ _____ _____ uhm... for food-making through photosynthesis.

12. But as autumn approaches and the hours of daylight and humidity diminish, _____ _____ _____ _____ _____ between the uhm... the leaf stalk and the woody part of the tree.

Listening Practice 01

SERVICE ENCOUNTER

1 What request does the student make to the manager?
  Ⓐ To switch his position
  Ⓑ To raise his salary
  Ⓒ To shorten his hours
  Ⓓ To adjust his schedule

2 What can be inferred about the student?
  Ⓐ He doesn't have any interest in cooking.
  Ⓑ He regrets joining the school jazz band.
  Ⓒ He doesn't get along with his colleagues.
  Ⓓ He is satisfied with his current job position.

Listen again to part of the conversation. Then answer the question.

3 Why does the manager say this: 🎧
  Ⓐ To explain to the student why he can't work afternoons
  Ⓑ To convince the student that kitchen work is the best choice for him
  Ⓒ To apologize for not changing the student's schedule as he wants
  Ⓓ To suggest that the student should quit the school jazz band

Dictation 01

Listen and fill in the blanks.

Student: Ms. Davidson, can I talk to you about _____ _____ _____?

Manager: Changing your hours? Peter, _____ _____ _____ the cafeteria work schedule for this month.

S: I know... but I just joined the school jazz band a few days ago and they _____ _____ _____.

M: Well, what kind of change are you proposing?

S: Well, I'm _____ _____ _____ _____ from five to nine in the evenings, Monday through Thursday. I was hoping to keep the days but _____ _____ _____ to the afternoon.

M: Sorry, we have enough lunchtime waiters already. _____ _____ _____ _____ for the breakfast shift instead?

S: Oh, I can't. I've got my Music Appreciation class at 9 am.

M: Hmmph. Tell you what... I can move you to, um, afternoons if you switch from waiting tables to kitchen prep. The pay's the same and we've _____ _____ _____ from one to five.

S: Kitchen prep? You mean chopping vegetables and stuff? Hmm... I've never thought about it. Actually I took this job because it lets me, um, _____ _____ the professors... I figured it could be helpful if I, you know, got to know them better. I don't want to _____ _____ _____ _____ _____.

M: Hmm... Peter, I don't think kitchen prep is that bad, and you wouldn't _____ _____ _____ _____ _____. And if you can't work evenings anymore, you don't _____ _____ _____ _____ _____.

S: All right, all right. _____ _____ _____. I'll switch to kitchen prep.

M: Good choice. When can you start?

S: _____ _____ from tomorrow.

018

Listening Practice 02

MARINE BIOLOGY   **SEAHORSES**

1 What is the lecture mainly about?
- Ⓐ How the species of seahorse are classified
- Ⓑ The process of a seahorse's growth
- Ⓒ What makes the seahorse a unique creature
- Ⓓ The physical differences between male and female seahorses

2 How does the professor explain the appearance of a seahorse?
- Ⓐ By gesturing with her hands
- Ⓑ By comparing it to other animals
- Ⓒ By contrasting it with the human body
- Ⓓ By naming all its organs

3 What does the professor say about the reproductive process of seahorses?
- Ⓐ Pregnancies last for just over a month.
- Ⓑ The female waits for the male to be ready.
- Ⓒ The male becomes pregnant.
- Ⓓ Only the male changes its color.

Dictation 02

Listen and fill in the blanks.

Professor: Seahorses are _____ _____ _____ _____ _____ in the animal kingdom. You've all seen pictures, if not the real thing, right? They look like... well... their heads and necks are kind of like a horse's... _____ _____ _____. Their mouths are at the end of their snout, which they use to suck in prey. And they've got prehensile tails... meaning that they can use their tails _____ _____ _____ _____... you know... like a monkey.

Besides this unique appearance, perhaps the most fascinating thing about seahorses is _____ _____ _____ _____. In this species, it is actually the males who _____ _____ _____ _____ _____ _____ _____. Interesting, huh? Okay, let me tell you about their mating process. They have _____ _____ _____ of a few days. When they meet, they change colors to sort of _____ _____ _____ _____ that they are interested. Then they grab each other's tail... kind of like holding hands... and _____ _____ _____ _____ for a few days. Finally, when the female is ready to mate she raises her snout and the male _____ _____ _____ _____ _____. Then he opens up his pouch and the female _____ _____ _____ _____ _____ so that the fertilization can occur. Then the male carries the fertilized eggs around for two to three weeks... the length of time depends on the species... but when the young are ready, _____ _____ _____ _____.

Student: Wait... but which parent _____ _____ _____ _____ once they're born?

P: Neither. The young seahorses are _____ _____ _____ _____. They simply swim off and are able to care for themselves.

Listening Practice 03

1 What is the lecture mainly about?
- Ⓐ Various applications of convection
- Ⓑ How convection works
- Ⓒ Three different forms of heat transfer
- Ⓓ How convection affects the weather

2 According to the professor, what causes the convection current in fluids?
- Ⓐ Impact of molecules
- Ⓑ Inactivity of molecules
- Ⓒ Unequal density of molecules
- Ⓓ Irregular movement of molecules

3 How does the professor explain natural convection?
- Ⓐ By providing details about its effects
- Ⓑ By emphasizing its importance over forced convection
- Ⓒ By giving an example of one of its phenomena
- Ⓓ By discussing its difference from forced convection

Dictation 03

Listen and fill in the blanks.

Professor: Last time we discussed _____ _____ _____ _____ _____... conduction and radiation. Now we're going to cover a third kind: convection. Convection _____ _____ _____ _____, which are generally liquids or gases, and transfers heat _____ _____. This, um... this movement _____ _____ _____ _____ _____ in different parts of the fluid, which is generally caused by heating.

 Let me explain a bit further. First, imagine a fluid. If we heat _____ _____ _____ the fluid, the molecules in that area will expand, reducing density. So... because _____ _____ _____ _____, these heated molecules will begin to rise. As they rise, cool molecules _____ _____ _____ _____, setting up a circulatory motion. The process repeats as the fluid is heated up again and once again begins to rise, causing heat transfer. _____ _____ _____ the movement in your heads? We call this a convection current, and you can easily observe it in the swirling action of any liquid that is _____ _____ _____ _____.

 Now, convection can either _____ _____ _____ _____. In forced convection, the movement occurs when artificial means such as a pump or a fan _____ _____ _____. Ovens and refrigerators are examples of this. As for natural convection, a good example occurs in our everyday weather. Sunlight heats the land, warming the air directly above it, which _____ _____ _____ _____ _____. The convection current created when cool air sinks, is, umm... is _____ _____ _____ _____ _____.

iBT Practice 01

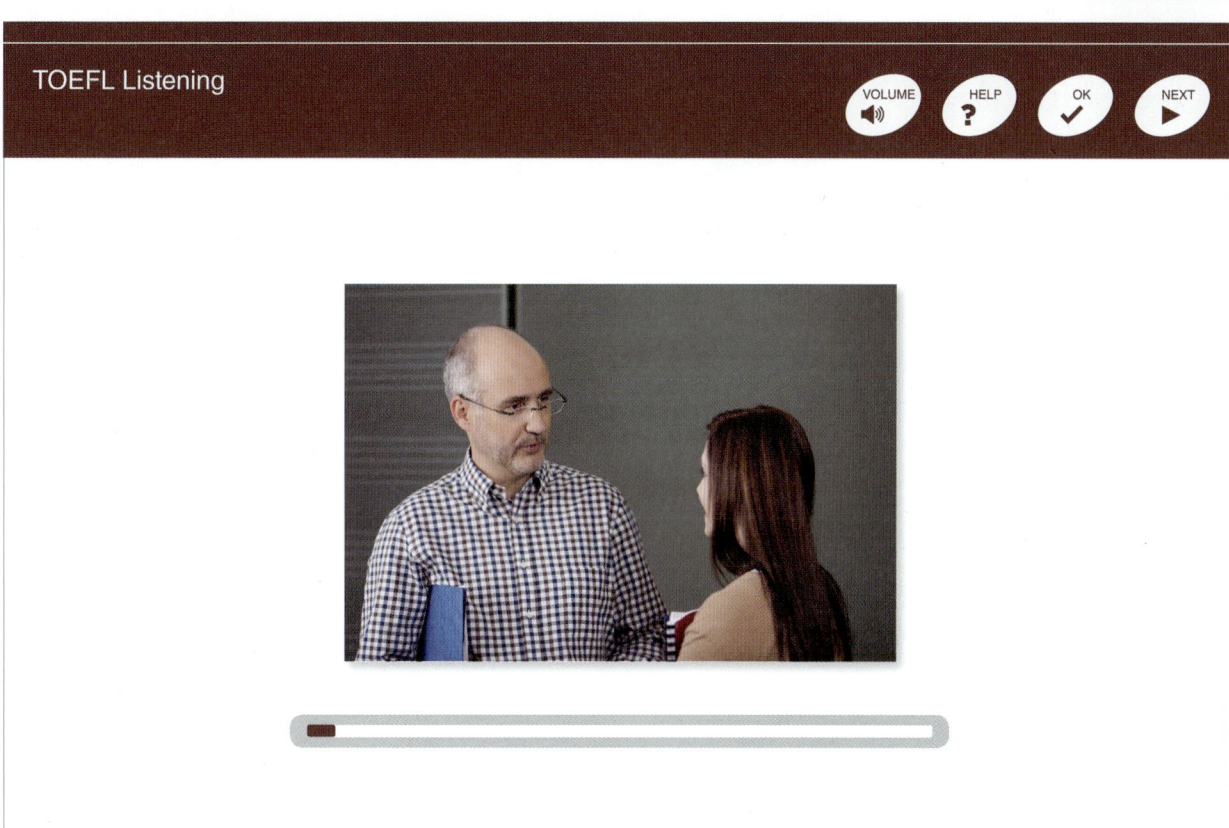

Note-Taking

TOEFL Listening

1. Why does the student go to see her professor?
   - Ⓐ To get advice on how to manage her time
   - Ⓑ To ask permission to hand in her assignment late
   - Ⓒ To talk about the outline of her report
   - Ⓓ To inform her professor that she has moved

2. What reason does the student give for taking a part-time job?
   - Ⓐ She is saving up money to go abroad.
   - Ⓑ She has to support herself.
   - Ⓒ She is the breadwinner of her family.
   - Ⓓ She has lots of free time between classes.

Listen again to part of the conversation. Then answer the question.

3. What can be inferred about the student?
   - Ⓐ She needs more credits.
   - Ⓑ She is enjoying living by herself.
   - Ⓒ She is studying hard to win a scholarship.
   - Ⓓ She has learned from her mistake.

Listen again to part of the conversation. Then answer the question.

4. What can be inferred about the professor?
   - Ⓐ He is uncomfortable with his decision.
   - Ⓑ He doesn't believe the student's excuse anymore.
   - Ⓒ He doesn't like imposing strict deadlines.
   - Ⓓ He is disappointed by the student's judgement.

iBT Practice 02

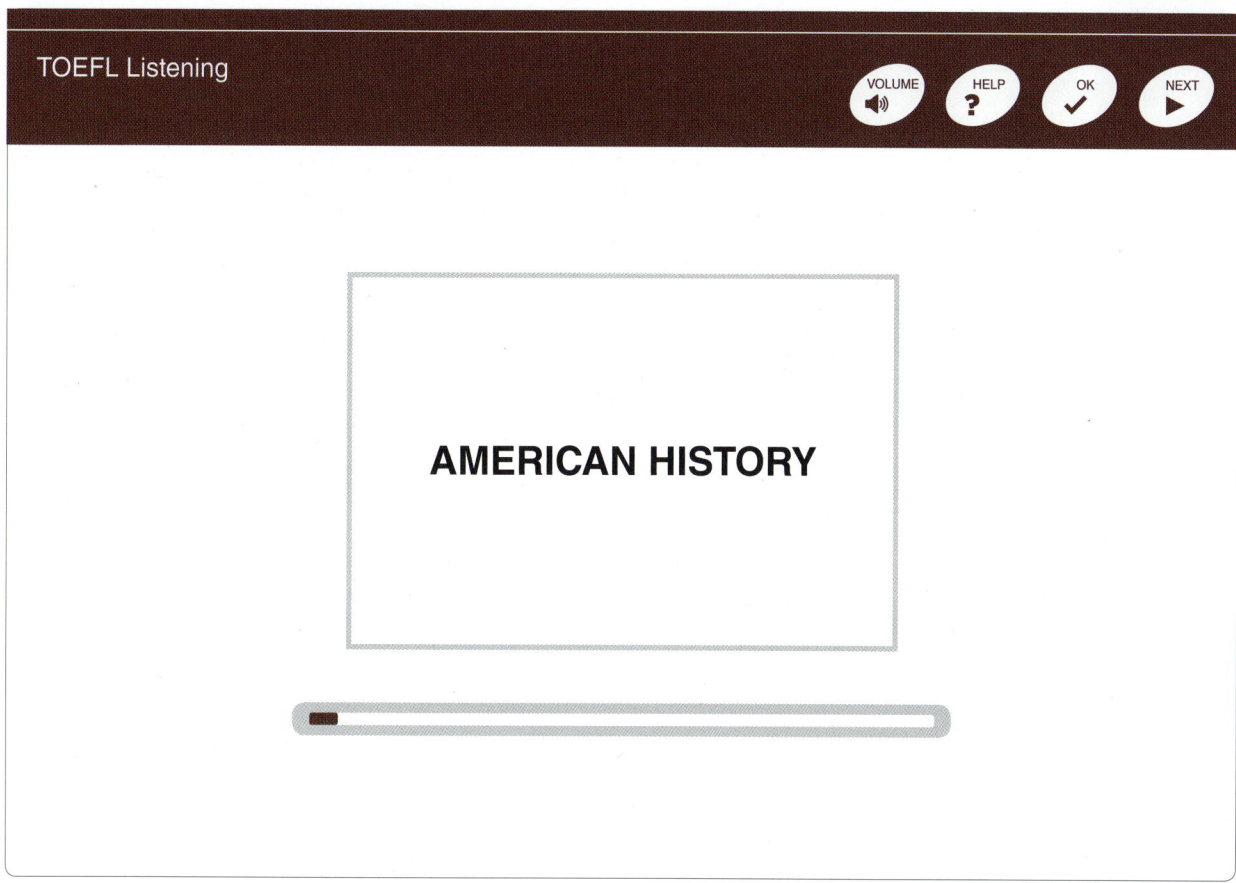

AMERICAN HISTORY

Note-Taking

TOEFL Listening

1. What is the lecture mainly about?
   - (A) Changing the legislative process during the Great Depression
   - (B) A bank panic in the 1930s and the economic policy to solve it
   - (C) Establishing new banking policy by the American Bank Union
   - (D) Effects of the "Banking Holiday" during the national crisis

2. According to the professor, what is a bank panic?
   - (A) It's when companies take out too many loans from banks.
   - (B) It's when banks can't give loans to companies due to insolvency.
   - (C) It's when individuals borrow more money than they can pay back.
   - (D) It's when people withdraw money from banks for fear of losing it.

3. Why did Roosevelt keep all U.S. banks closed?
   - (A) To raise money to help weak banks run their businesses
   - (B) To finish New Deal programs for economic recovery
   - (C) To exercise presidential power by controlling the economy
   - (D) To prevent banks from collapsing and to issue a guarantee policy

Listen again to part of the lecture. Then answer the question.

4. What can be inferred about the student?
   - (A) She casts doubt on the solution explained by the professor.
   - (B) She disagrees with the facts given by the professor.
   - (C) She is concerned about the economic situation at that time.
   - (D) She doesn't understand the effect of the bank panic.

Vocabulary Check

- [ ] urban
- [ ] rural
- [ ] contribute to
- [ ] relative
- [ ] suburban
- [ ] absorb
- [ ] absorptive
- [ ] evaporation
- [ ] generate
- [ ] property

- [ ] feature

- [ ] diversity
- [ ] groundbreaking
- [ ] protagonist
- [ ] predominantly

- [ ] domestic
- [ ] on the spot
- [ ] appliance
- [ ] phonograph
- [ ] centerpiece
- [ ] ebb
- [ ] blow
- [ ] flexible

- [ ] transfer
- [ ] mandatory
- [ ] requirement

- [ ] hummingbird
- [ ] hover
- [ ] flap
- [ ] metabolic rate
- [ ] metabolism

- [ ] hibernation
- [ ] torpor

- [ ] chlorophyll
- [ ] compound
- [ ] photosynthesis
- [ ] humidity
- [ ] diminish
- [ ] stalk
- [ ] fade
- [ ] pigment

- [ ] shift
- [ ] appreciation
- [ ] (I'll) tell you what.
- [ ] prep
- [ ] chop
- [ ] figure
- [ ] count sb in

- [ ] seahorse
- [ ] hence
- [ ] snout
- [ ] prey
- [ ] prehensile
- [ ] fascinating
- [ ] breed
- [ ] mating
- [ ] mate
- [ ] courtship
- [ ] pouch
- [ ] deposit
- [ ] fertilization
- [ ] fertilize
- [ ] deliver

- [ ] conduction
- [ ] radiation
- [ ] convection
- [ ] fluid
- [ ] density
- [ ] dense
- [ ] molecule
- [ ] descend
- [ ] circulatory
- [ ] swirl
- [ ] as for

- [ ] post
- [ ] extend
- [ ] extension
- [ ] demanding
- [ ] appreciate
- [ ] migrate
- [ ] definitely
- [ ] against one's better judgment
- [ ] grant
- [ ] let sb down

- [ ] crisis
- [ ] bankrupt
- [ ] withdraw
- [ ] panic
- [ ] go broke
- [ ] loan
- [ ] deposit
- [ ] insolvency
- [ ] collapse
- [ ] legislation
- [ ] act
- [ ] go bust

Vocabulary Review

A Choose the correct word for each definition.

> compound   humidity   hover   descend   fade   loan

1. an amount of money that is borrowed: _____
2. to gradually lose color: _____
3. to stay in the same place in midair: _____
4. a substance made up of two or more elements: _____
5. the amount of moisture in the air: _____

B Choose the best word or phrase to explain the underlined word.

1. If you grant something, you _____ it.
   - Ⓐ pay
   - Ⓑ allow
   - Ⓒ block
   - Ⓓ extend

2. If your confidence ebbs, it becomes _____.
   - Ⓐ flexible
   - Ⓑ weaker
   - Ⓒ prehensile
   - Ⓓ strict

3. If something is dense, it is _____.
   - Ⓐ easily recognized
   - Ⓑ built a long time ago
   - Ⓒ overly decorated
   - Ⓓ made of closely-packed particles

4. If something is mandatory, you _____ do it.
   - Ⓐ have to ask to
   - Ⓑ may choose to
   - Ⓒ can't
   - Ⓓ must

C Choose the best word or phrase to complete each sentence.

1. If you're looking for someone to take part in the game, you can _____.
   - Ⓐ go bust
   - Ⓑ let me down
   - Ⓒ count me in
   - Ⓓ give a big hand

2. She _____ her baby in the car because she couldn't get to the hospital in time.
   - Ⓐ punished
   - Ⓑ delivered
   - Ⓒ pursued
   - Ⓓ grabbed

3. He had to go _____ because his debt was more than he could pay back.
   - Ⓐ bankrupt
   - Ⓑ insane
   - Ⓒ wild
   - Ⓓ private

4. When fall comes, bears go into _____ for the winter.
   - Ⓐ conduction
   - Ⓑ insolvency
   - Ⓒ hibernation
   - Ⓓ courtship

D Choose the correct word to complete each sentence.

1. I'm going to ask my professor for a(n) _____ because I need more time. (convection / extension)
2. I did my best. As _____ the outcome, I can only leave it to fate. (for / to)
3. After years of living beyond her means, she finally went _____. (broke / panic)
4. He is good to have around in times of _____. (crisis / torpor)
5. Against my better _____, I agreed to help them. (investment / judgment)

E Choose the word that is closest in meaning to the underlined word.

1. I thought the documentary was <u>fascinating</u>. I learned a lot.
   - Ⓐ realistic   Ⓑ inaccurate   Ⓒ legislative   Ⓓ interesting
2. I couldn't see her any longer because she <u>transferred</u> to another school.
   - Ⓐ enrolled   Ⓑ changed   Ⓒ responded   Ⓓ applied
3. Windmills are used to <u>generate</u> electricity.
   - Ⓐ distribute   Ⓑ enhance   Ⓒ produce   Ⓓ replace
4. If you don't accept credit cards, I will have to go to the bank to <u>withdraw</u> some cash.
   - Ⓐ take out   Ⓑ put in   Ⓒ borrow   Ⓓ refund
5. It is important to get plenty of <u>fluids</u> when you are ill.
   - Ⓐ fruits   Ⓑ rest   Ⓒ pills   Ⓓ liquids

F Choose the word that is the opposite of the underlined word.

1. The bad press caused sales to <u>diminish</u>.
   - Ⓐ expand   Ⓑ swirl   Ⓒ stop   Ⓓ collapse
2. I prefer <u>urban</u> areas because there are more things to do.
   - Ⓐ diverse   Ⓑ coastal   Ⓒ rural   Ⓓ exotic
3. She works in a <u>predominantly</u> male environment.
   - Ⓐ intentionally   Ⓑ minimally   Ⓒ mistakenly   Ⓓ oppressively

PART A

Basic Comprehension Questions

UNIT 01 MAIN IDEA
▶ **UNIT 02** DETAIL

UNIT 02 Detail

Introduction

- Detail questions ask about the key details mentioned in the conversation or lecture.
- Sometimes, these questions ask whether a piece of given information is true or false.
- Occasionally, these questions require 2-3 correct answers.
- 2 or more questions are given for each passage.

Question Types

1. Question forms that require one correct answer:
   - According to the professor, what is the problem with the X method?
   - Which of the following is NOT mentioned as X?

2. Question forms that require two or more correct answers:
   - What are the key features of X mentioned in the lecture? Click on 2 answers.
   - According to the professor, what are the reasons for X? Click on 3 answers.

Strategy

1. Identify the conversation or lecture topic right away. Then take notes, focusing on information related to the main topic as you listen.
   (1) For conversations: The content of conversations usually consists of possible solutions for a student's problem or concerns. So, when you listen, concentrate on the solutions being suggested.
   (2) For lectures: Questions ask about information strongly related to the main topic rather than about secondary or trivial details. Definitions, examples, reasons, results, features, etc. are usually used to support the main idea.

2. In most cases, answer choices that have the exact words or expressions given in the conversation or lecture are incorrect. Generally, correct answer choices paraphrase information from the conversation or lecture.

Sample Question

TOEFL Listening

Professor

Alright, class. So, last time we talked about the honeybee's social order. Today we're going to talk about their communication. Honeybees are known to have different ways of communicating... such as dancing and using chemicals or odors. We... uh... we're going to focus on their dancing, today. Right, honeybees dance to communicate and uhm... we can understand it as their body language. Let's see how it works. When worker bees return to the hive having successfully found food, they perform a kind of dance to share information about the location of the food. Other bees, called dance attendees, they... uhm... observe this dance and infer the food sources. When the food is nearby, honeybees dance in a round shape, kind of like a big circle. And for more distant food, they perform the waggle dance, which looks like a figure of eight.

According to the professor, why do honeybees dance?
- Ⓐ To attract mates
- Ⓑ To entertain worker bees
- Ⓒ To warn of dangerous situations
- Ⓓ To inform other bees of where food is

Answer and Explanation
The professor is talking about the honeybee's dancing as a way of communication. The question is answered by the professor when he says, " ~ they perform a kind of dance to share information about the location of the food." The best answer choice is Ⓓ.

Basic Drills

1 Why does the man have to pay a fine?

- A Because he broke an appliance in his dorm
- B Because he didn't follow traffic signals at the intersection
- C Because he didn't return books to the library by the due date
- D Because he parked in a space reserved for off-campus students

2 What does the professor say about Keith Haring's art?
Click on 2 answers.

- A It focused on modern problems.
- B It was designed for rich people.
- C It was brightly colored.
- D It was large in size.

3 What does the professor say about the whale shark's eating behavior?

- A It filters its prey through its gills.
- B It only uses one part of its teeth to eat.
- C It becomes fierce when eating.
- D It can go without eating for several weeks.

4 Why didn't the student get the notice about the bill?

  Ⓐ Because she was too busy to check her email
  Ⓑ Because she has changed her email address recently
  Ⓒ Because the notice went to the wrong student
  Ⓓ Because the employee forgot to send the notice

5 What aspect of the education system of his time did Dewey criticize?

  Ⓐ He didn't like the content being published in school textbooks.
  Ⓑ He believed the "great books" of his day were too old to be useful.
  Ⓒ He disagreed with how students were forced to focus on memorization.
  Ⓓ He thought too many skills were being taught in a single classroom.

6 Why did some Impressionists paint at the same time on a different day when painting outdoor scenes?

  Ⓐ To show the change in nature itself on different days
  Ⓑ To ensure their paintings accurately depicted the effects of light
  Ⓒ To reflect their different feelings toward nature
  Ⓓ To refine what they painted on a previous day

Dictation

Listen and fill in the blanks.

1. Like other artists from the movement, Haring's primary goal _____ _____ _____ _____ _____ _____ high art and low art.

2. Basically, Haring wanted to _____ _____ _____ _____ _____.

3. It was another way of making sure his work _____ _____ _____ _____ _____ to the general public, not just wealthy art lovers.

4. On average, whale sharks are around 25 feet long, but _____ _____ _____ _____ _____ 40 feet long.

5. I guess it sounds like a _____ _____ _____ _____ _____.

6. And the interesting thing is… it's a filter feeder, so it eats _____ _____ _____ _____ from water.

7. After closing its mouth, the _____ _____ _____ to filter the nourishment from the water.

8. As an educator John Dewey _____ _____ _____ and beliefs.

9. _____ _____ _____ _____ of his day was that students passively received information _____ _____ _____ _____ and predigested by teachers and textbooks.

10. Dewey… uhm… he argued teaching should emphasize _____ _____ _____ _____ _____.

11. So, the principal aim of Impressionist artists _____ _____ _____ _____ a visual image and record the brief effects of light.

12. Impressionist painters _____ _____ _____ _____ _____ _____ the light and its variations.

13. They were very interested in _____ _____ _____ _____ _____ in different weather and at different times of the day.

14. You know, even when they painted the same natural scene, the painting _____ _____ _____ _____ _____ _____ according to the change of light.

Listening Practice 01

OFFICE HOURS

1 Why does the student go to see his professor?
- Ⓐ To decide on a topic for his report
- Ⓑ To borrow some books for his research
- Ⓒ To ask for advice on the report he is working on
- Ⓓ To get an explanation of what makes a good academic essay

2 What is the problem with the student's paper?
Click on 2 answers.
- Ⓐ He just lists a lot of information.
- Ⓑ He hasn't found enough information.
- Ⓒ He focuses on too many aspects of the topic.
- Ⓓ He doesn't present his own ideas.

Listen again to part of the conversation. Then answer the question.

3 Why does the professor say this: 🎧
- Ⓐ To encourage the student in his upcoming work
- Ⓑ To express her satisfaction with the student's report
- Ⓒ To provide useful sources for the student's research
- Ⓓ To emphasize the importance of time management

Dictation 01

Listen and fill in the blanks.

Student: [knocking] Excuse me, Professor Duncan. I made an appointment with you today _____ _____ _____ _____ _____ ... umm... about endangered species. Did you have a chance to look at my report?

Professor: Yes, _____ _____ _____ _____. You were looking at endangered elephants in Africa.

S: Right...

P: Well... it seems you've _____ _____ _____ _____ _____ finding information... I can see diverse data...

S: Well, I thought _____ _____ _____ _____, the better the report.

P: Hmm... that's true. To write a good report, it's necessary to have enough information. But there's a more important aspect you should pay attention to. That's _____ _____ _____ _____ _____ _____ about your report.

S: I see. Please go ahead.

P: All right. This report is _____ _____ _____ _____ of the information you found. But I don't see your personal ideas. I want you to _____ _____ _____ _____ _____ by reflecting your thoughts. Simply summarizing it is not sufficient.

S: I'm confused. Could you tell me _____ _____ _____ _____ _____?

P: Okay. I mean... _____ _____ _____ _____ the information, you should classify and organize the data _____ _____ _____ _____ _____ African elephants to be endangered, and... what else?... yes, how the situation can be improved. But it should _____ _____ _____.

S: I see. Actually, I didn't pay much attention to putting my ideas into the report. I've got a lot of work _____ _____ _____.

P: Yes, but you already have enough sources for your report. _____ _____ _____ _____ to revise them.

S: I guess not. Thank you for your help.

Listening Practice 02

1 What is the lecture mainly about?
- Ⓐ The characteristics of Minimalist art
- Ⓑ The social background of the Minimalism movement
- Ⓒ Difficulties in appreciating Minimalist art
- Ⓓ Differences between Abstract Expressionism and Minimalism

2 Why does the professor mention the common conception of art?
- Ⓐ To emphasize the importance of reflecting emotion in art
- Ⓑ To indicate the attitude of people toward Minimalist art
- Ⓒ To explain how difficult it is to reflect feelings in artwork
- Ⓓ To illustrate how Minimalist artists were different in expressing emotions

3 What does the professor say about Minimalist artworks?
- Ⓐ They are colorful and complex.
- Ⓑ They reflect various feelings of artists.
- Ⓒ They emphasize the depiction of an object itself.
- Ⓓ They express their themes by symbolizing subjects.

Dictation 02

Listen and fill in the blanks.

Professor: The next movement in the art world we're going to consider is Minimalism. As the name suggests, Minimalism is... or _____ _____ _____ _____ other types of art. Minimalist artists _____ _____ _____ their work to the smallest number of colors, shapes, and lines, _____ _____ _____ _____ Abstract Expressionism.

Student: Was there a particular reason for that?

P: Well... Minimalist artists wanted to, essentially, _____ _____ _____ _____ _____. I mean... they rejected the idea that art should reflect the personal expression of its creator. Now the uhm... the common conception of art is that it _____ _____ _____ of the real world such as a landscape or a person. Or perhaps... perhaps that art reflects an experience such as an emotion or feeling. However, with Minimalism, artists consciously _____ _____ _____ _____ _____ and avoid abstract representation. Their aim was to... to kind of _____ _____ _____ _____ the viewer based only on what was in front of them. So Minimalist art did not refer to _____ _____ _____ _____ _____. For example, color... if used, was non-referential. Dark colors represented only dark colors and not some deeper emotional or philosophical mood. Basically, with Minimalism, _____ _____ _____. Minimalist artists didn't feel that _____ _____ _____ _____ _____ _____ simple forms they were creating a poorer experience for the viewer. _____ _____ _____, they believed that they were creating the possibility _____ _____ _____ _____ _____ _____ _____ between the viewer and the work.

Listening Practice 03

ENVIRONMENTAL SCIENCE

1 What is the lecture mainly about?
- Ⓐ The weak points of the recycling process
- Ⓑ The importance of generating less waste
- Ⓒ The difference between reusing and recycling
- Ⓓ The need to distribute more public trash cans

2 According to the professor, why aren't our recycling efforts succeeding?
- Ⓐ Because there are too many products that cannot be recycled.
- Ⓑ Because people didn't get involved with them soon enough.
- Ⓒ Because we are still producing the same amounts of waste.
- Ⓓ Because recycling everything is too much of an inconvenience.

3 What can be inferred about the professor?
- Ⓐ He believes that recycling is a waste of time.
- Ⓑ He disagrees with experts' opinions on the topic.
- Ⓒ He favors composting over recycling and reusing.
- Ⓓ He supports the idea of living a zero-waste lifestyle.

Dictation 03

Listen and fill in the blanks.

Professor: It should _____ _____ _____ _____ to anyone in this room that our planet is facing an unprecedented crisis, one that is being caused by our unrestrained consumer lifestyles. _____ _____, we are, um, we are drowning the Earth in our trash. There was _____ _____ _____ _____ when people were confident that boosting our recycling efforts would be the answer, but, unfortunately, they were incorrect. Don't _____ _____ _____, recycling is, is, um... well, it's essential. But as long as we keep generating the same enormous levels of waste, all of our recycling efforts _____ _____ _____ _____ in the end. The bottom line, according to many experts, is that we need to start creating less waste, and that's where the concept of "zero waste" _____ _____ _____. It refers to the type of lifestyle in which absolutely no trash is created—in other words, we personally use, reuse or recycle everything we purchase or create. This might sound daunting, maybe even impossible, but you need to understand that it's, it's really just _____ _____ _____ _____ _____. Even if we don't reach it, simply by foregoing plastic cups, paper towels, and things like that, we can become part of the solution _____ _____ _____ _____ the problem. It's not like it's some kind of great inconvenience to use reusable mugs and cloth towels after all. Imagine _____ _____ _____ _____ _____ you don't even have a trash can, because... well, because you don't need one. Because everything you buy can be either recycled, composted or washed and reused. It's an interesting concept, and one _____ _____ _____ _____.

iBT Practice 01

TOEFL Listening

Note-Taking

TOEFL Listening

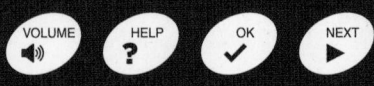

1. Why does the student visit the post office?
   - Ⓐ To change her home address
   - Ⓑ To pick up her forwarded mail from Spain
   - Ⓒ To send a package to her friend in Spain
   - Ⓓ To inquire about post office services during her absence

2. What does the clerk suggest the student do about her magazine subscription?
   - Ⓐ Ask her friend to pick the magazines up
   - Ⓑ Forward the magazines directly to Spain
   - Ⓒ Have delivery temporarily stopped
   - Ⓓ Change over to an online format

3. What can be inferred about the student's plans after her semester abroad?
   - Ⓐ She will travel Spain for a while.
   - Ⓑ She hasn't made up her mind.
   - Ⓒ She is going to look for a job in Spain.
   - Ⓓ She is going to take summer courses.

Listen again to part of the conversation. Then answer the question.

4. Why does the clerk say this: 🎧
   - Ⓐ To explain how to send international mail
   - Ⓑ To recommend an alternative plan
   - Ⓒ To express to the student how boring his job is
   - Ⓓ To indicate he can help the student with her mail

iBT Practice 02

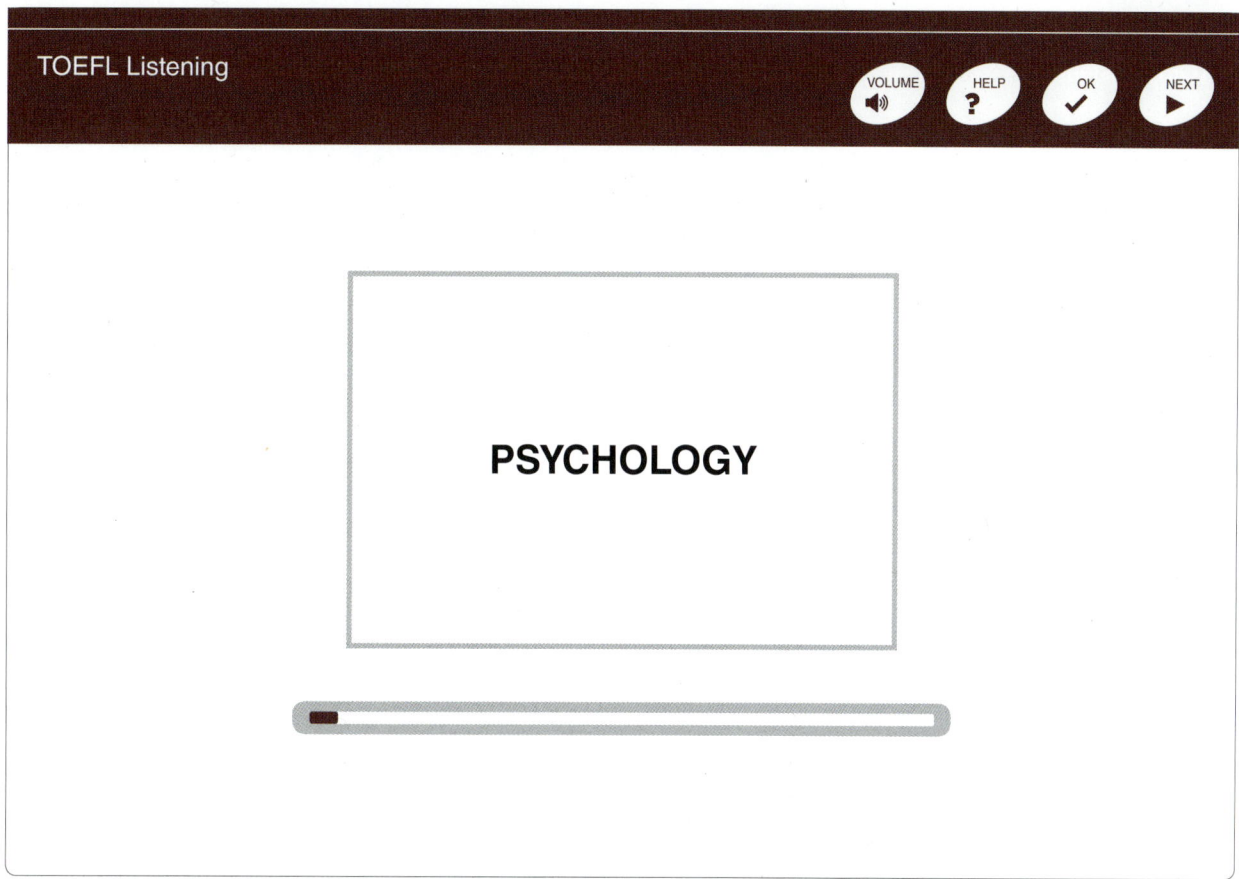

Note-Taking

TOEFL Listening

1. What is the lecture mainly about?
   Ⓐ The potential side effects of placebos
   Ⓑ The ethical controversy over placebo effects
   Ⓒ The possible explanations of the placebo effect
   Ⓓ The various uses of placebos in drug companies

2. What does the professor say about placebos?
   Ⓐ They are effective when taken with actual medication.
   Ⓑ They are currently used for testing new medicine.
   Ⓒ They damage the brain when overused.
   Ⓓ They are useful for treating mental disorders.

3. Which of the following is NOT mentioned as a factor of the placebo effect?
   Ⓐ A chemical change occurring in the body
   Ⓑ Illnesses naturally going away
   Ⓒ A physical reaction to a combination of medicines
   Ⓓ A shift in symptom interpretation

4. What is the professor's attitude toward placebos?
   Ⓐ He is impressed with their strong power over patients.
   Ⓑ He believes they work on patients temporarily.
   Ⓒ He is interested in applying them to developing a new medicine.
   Ⓓ He is doubtful about the scientific basis of their effects.

Vocabulary Check

- [ ] odor
- [ ] attendee
- [ ] waggle
- [ ] figure

- [ ] buck
- [ ] dorm
- [ ] reserved

- [ ] blur
- [ ] accessible
- [ ] cartoonish
- [ ] contemporary
- [ ] retail

- [ ] predator
- [ ] decent
- [ ] organism
- [ ] krill
- [ ] tissue
- [ ] gill
- [ ] nourishment

- [ ] disconnect
- [ ] slip one's mind
- [ ] prior
- [ ] penalty

- [ ] revolutionize
- [ ] dominant
- [ ] practice
- [ ] passively
- [ ] predigest
- [ ] genuine

- [ ] Impressionist
- [ ] objectively
- [ ] glance
- [ ] put emphasis on
- [ ] variation

- [ ] draft
- [ ] endangered
- [ ] go through
- [ ] diverse
- [ ] enumerate
- [ ] revise

- [ ] strive
- [ ] rejection
- [ ] consciously
- [ ] objectify
- [ ] invoke
- [ ] literal
- [ ] referential
- [ ] pare down

- [ ] unprecedented
- [ ] unrestrained
- [ ] drown
- [ ] boost
- [ ] generate
- [ ] enormous
- [ ] amount to
- [ ] the bottom line
- [ ] come into play
- [ ] daunting
- [ ] forego
- [ ] compost
- [ ] ponder

- [ ] semester
- [ ] forward
- [ ] subscribe to
- [ ] subscription
- [ ] periodical
- [ ] put ... on hold
- [ ] access
- [ ] in advance

- [ ] hypochondriac
- [ ] soothe
- [ ] autonomic nervous system
- [ ] trigger
- [ ] painkiller
- [ ] neurotransmitter
- [ ] in kind
- [ ] coincidence
- [ ] in the fullness of time
- [ ] ineffectual
- [ ] wax and wane
- [ ] perceive
- [ ] perception
- [ ] regression
- [ ] alternatively
- [ ] tingle
- [ ] indigestion
- [ ] unverified
- [ ] physiological
- [ ] spontaneous
- [ ] alter
- [ ] indisputably

Vocabulary Review

A Choose the correct word for each definition.

> enumerate physiological daunting literal predigest accessible

1. having to do with the physical or chemical processes of the body: _____
2. to make simple for easy understanding: _____
3. to list one by one: _____
4. able to be reached or approached: _____
5. tending to make people afraid or less confident: _____

B Choose the best word or phrase to explain the underlined word.

1. If something has variations, it has several _____.
   - Ⓐ advantages
   - Ⓑ facilities
   - Ⓒ competitors
   - Ⓓ versions

2. If something slips your mind, you _____ it.
   - Ⓐ fail to analyze
   - Ⓑ are confused about
   - Ⓒ are obsessed with
   - Ⓓ can't remember

3. If you do something consciously, you are _____ it.
   - Ⓐ fond of
   - Ⓑ good at
   - Ⓒ aware of
   - Ⓓ afraid of

4. Something that waxes and wanes _____.
   - Ⓐ ceases
   - Ⓑ fluctuates
   - Ⓒ soars
   - Ⓓ decays

C Choose the best word or phrase to complete each sentence.

1. She works very hard. She is _____ to graduate with honors.
   - Ⓐ resisting
   - Ⓑ adjusting
   - Ⓒ pretending
   - Ⓓ striving

2. If you don't follow the instructions, there will be a(n) _____ of two points.
   - Ⓐ penalty
   - Ⓑ aspect
   - Ⓒ draft
   - Ⓓ disposal

3. If something is _____, it has never happened before.
   - Ⓐ unprecedented
   - Ⓑ invoked
   - Ⓒ revised
   - Ⓓ disconnected

4. Constant _____ of his proposals had discouraged him.
   - Ⓐ perspective
   - Ⓑ rejection
   - Ⓒ practice
   - Ⓓ subscription

D Choose the correct word to complete each sentence.

1. Please _____ this email to everyone in your address book. (access / forward)
2. Please let me know in _____ if you will be attending. (advance / kind)
3. This is _____ the best way to proceed. No doubt about it. (indisputably / alternatively)
4. If you describe someone's behavior as _____, you mean that it is extreme or intense. (unrestrained / endangered)
5. He went _____ the paper and made some corrections. (through / throughout)

E Choose the word that is closest in meaning to the underlined word.

1. I have to write a report on an important historical figure.
   - A document
   - B site
   - C character
   - D evidence

2. The announcement triggered a series of events that led to the ultimate demise of the company.
   - A reflected
   - B eased
   - C altered
   - D caused

3. No one was prepared to forgo their lunch hour to attend the meeting.
   - A remember
   - B sacrifice
   - C change
   - D hurry

4. The child's behavior is the result of ineffectual parenting.
   - A abusive
   - B failed
   - C violent
   - D decent

5. Microsoft remains the dominant company in the computer industry.
   - A leading
   - B prior
   - C unverified
   - D referential

F Choose the word that is the opposite of the underlined word.

1. He made a genuine apology. I think you should forgive him.
   - A planned
   - B thoughtful
   - C fake
   - D spontaneous

2. TV allows you to be entertained passively but the Internet is interactive.
   - A simply
   - B actively
   - C intensively
   - D significantly

3. Try to consider the issue objectively. Look at the facts.
   - A literally
   - B diversely
   - C subjectively
   - D specifically

Actual Practice Test

Listening Section Directions

This section measures your ability to understand conversations and lectures in English. You will listen to 1 conversation and 2 lectures. You will hear each conversation or lecture only one time. After each conversation or lecture, you will answer some questions about it. The questions typically ask about the main idea and supporting details. Some questions ask about a speaker's purpose or attitude. Answer the questions based on what is stated or implied by the speakers.

You may take notes while you listen. You may use your notes to help you answer the questions. Your notes will not be scored. If you need to change the volume while you listen, click on the Volume icon at the top of the screen.

In some questions, you will see this icon: 🎧 This means that you will hear, but not see part of the question. Some of the questions have special directions. These directions appear in a gray box on the screen.

Most questions are worth one point. If a question is worth more than one point, it will have special directions that indicate how many points you can receive.

You must answer each question. After you answer, click on **Next**. Then click on **OK** to confirm your answer and go on to the next question. After you click on **OK**, you cannot return to previous questions.

Actual Practice Test 01

TOEFL Listening

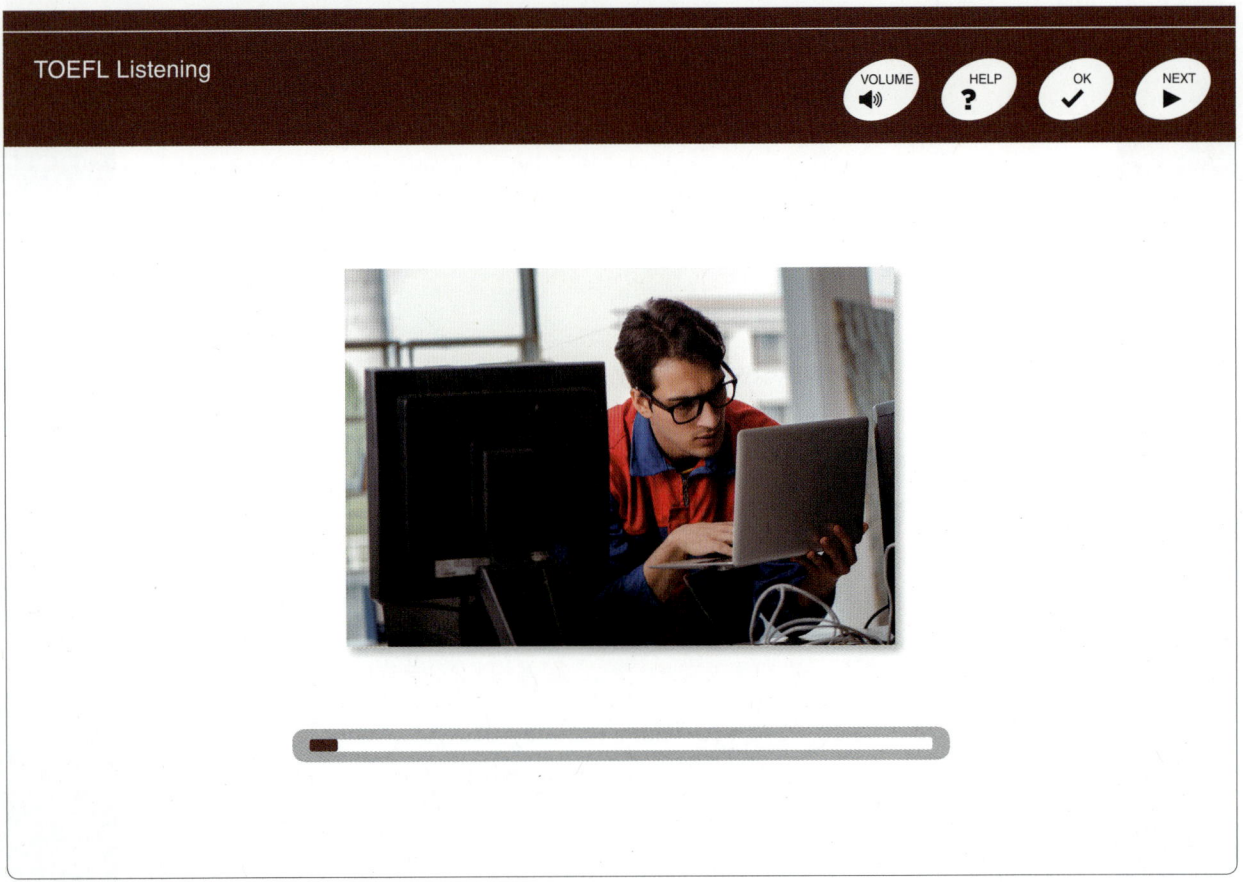

Note-Taking

TOEFL Listening

1. What is the student's reason for visiting the computer shop?
   - Ⓐ She has an issue with a laptop she rented.
   - Ⓑ She needs an update on an ongoing repair.
   - Ⓒ She is trying to find a specific model of laptop.
   - Ⓓ She wants to have her broken laptop examined.

2. What happened to the student's current laptop?
   - Ⓐ It was exposed to extreme temperatures.
   - Ⓑ Its keyboard got wet recently.
   - Ⓒ Its screen stopped showing an image.
   - Ⓓ It refuses to download a certain app.

3. How will the employee contact the student?
   - Ⓐ Stop by her residence
   - Ⓑ Give her a phone call
   - Ⓒ Send her a text message
   - Ⓓ Email her school account

Listen again to part of the conversation. Then answer the question.

4. Why does the employee say this:
   - Ⓐ To imply that the issue is only a minor one
   - Ⓑ To determine a possible cause of the problem
   - Ⓒ To explain the reason for the delay in the repairs
   - Ⓓ To find out if the student has previously contacted him

Listen again to part of the conversation. Then answer the question.

5. What can be inferred about the student?
   - Ⓐ She doesn't fully trust the employee.
   - Ⓑ She is only taking one or two courses.
   - Ⓒ She does not live on or near the campus.
   - Ⓓ She has rented a laptop many times before.

Actual Practice Test 02

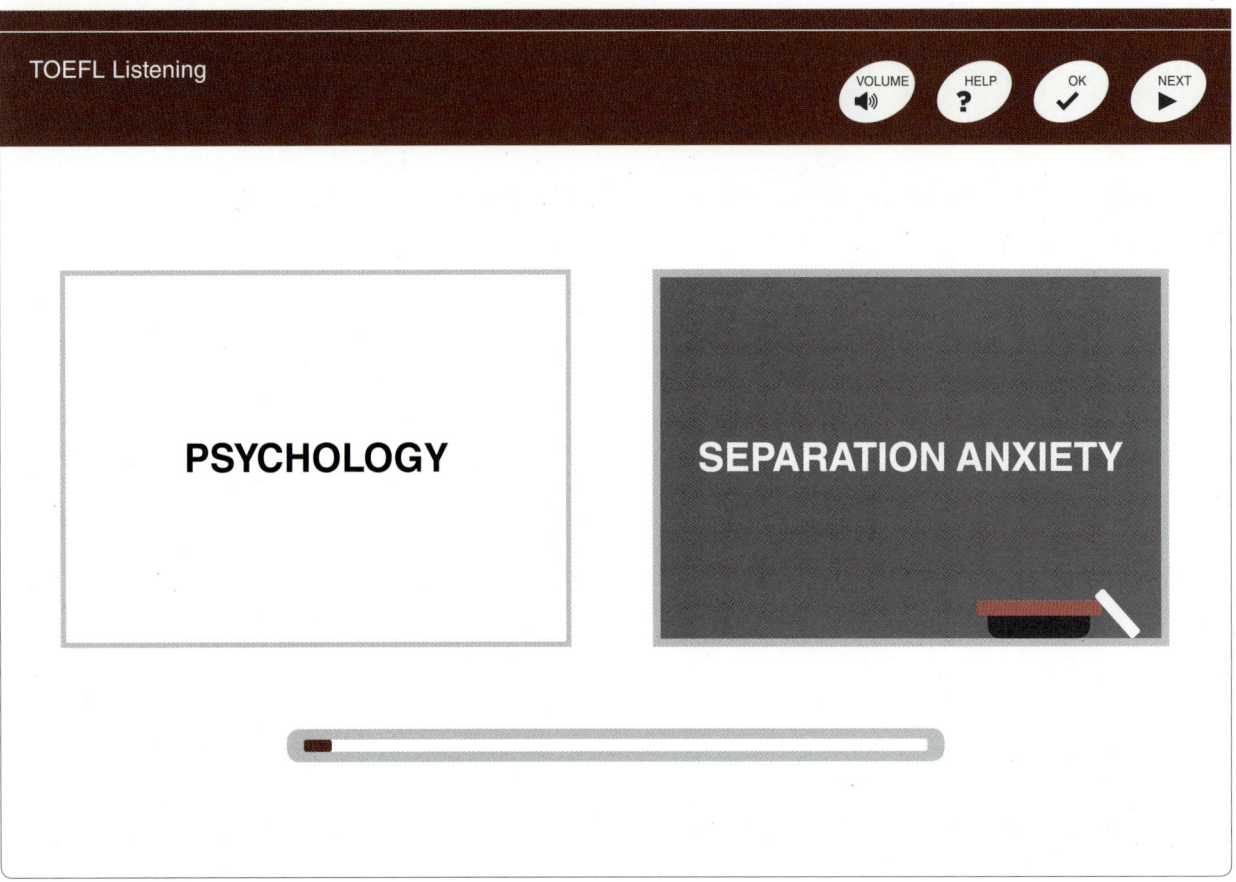

TOEFL Listening

6. What is the lecture mainly about?
   - Ⓐ Causes of separation anxiety disorder
   - Ⓑ The stages of cognitive development
   - Ⓒ Methods of dealing with separation anxiety
   - Ⓓ A developmental phase that young children go through

7. How does the professor introduce the concept of separation anxiety?
   - Ⓐ By referring to a discussion from a previous class
   - Ⓑ By giving a definition from a psychology textbook
   - Ⓒ By comparing it to other types of anxiety
   - Ⓓ By describing a possible real-life situation

8. According to the professor, what are babies under six months old unable to do?
   - Ⓐ Remain apart from their parents
   - Ⓑ Recognize different people
   - Ⓒ Begin cognitive development
   - Ⓓ Accept people they don't know

9. What does the professor say about separation anxiety disorder?
   - Ⓐ It is a common problem among children.
   - Ⓑ Most children can overcome it naturally.
   - Ⓒ It is a serious psychological condition.
   - Ⓓ It is usually the parents' fault.

Listen again to part of the lecture. Then answer the question.

10. What can be inferred about the student?
    - Ⓐ She does not believe what the professor is saying.
    - Ⓑ She has not learned about cognitive development.
    - Ⓒ She does not understand the professor's point.
    - Ⓓ She has not experienced what the professor is describing.

Listen again to part of the lecture. Then answer the question.

11. Why does the professor say this:
    - Ⓐ To help the students comprehend the child's point of view
    - Ⓑ To explain a problem with parent-child relationships
    - Ⓒ To emphasize the importance of a concept of time
    - Ⓓ To ask the students about their memories of childhood

Actual Practice Test 03

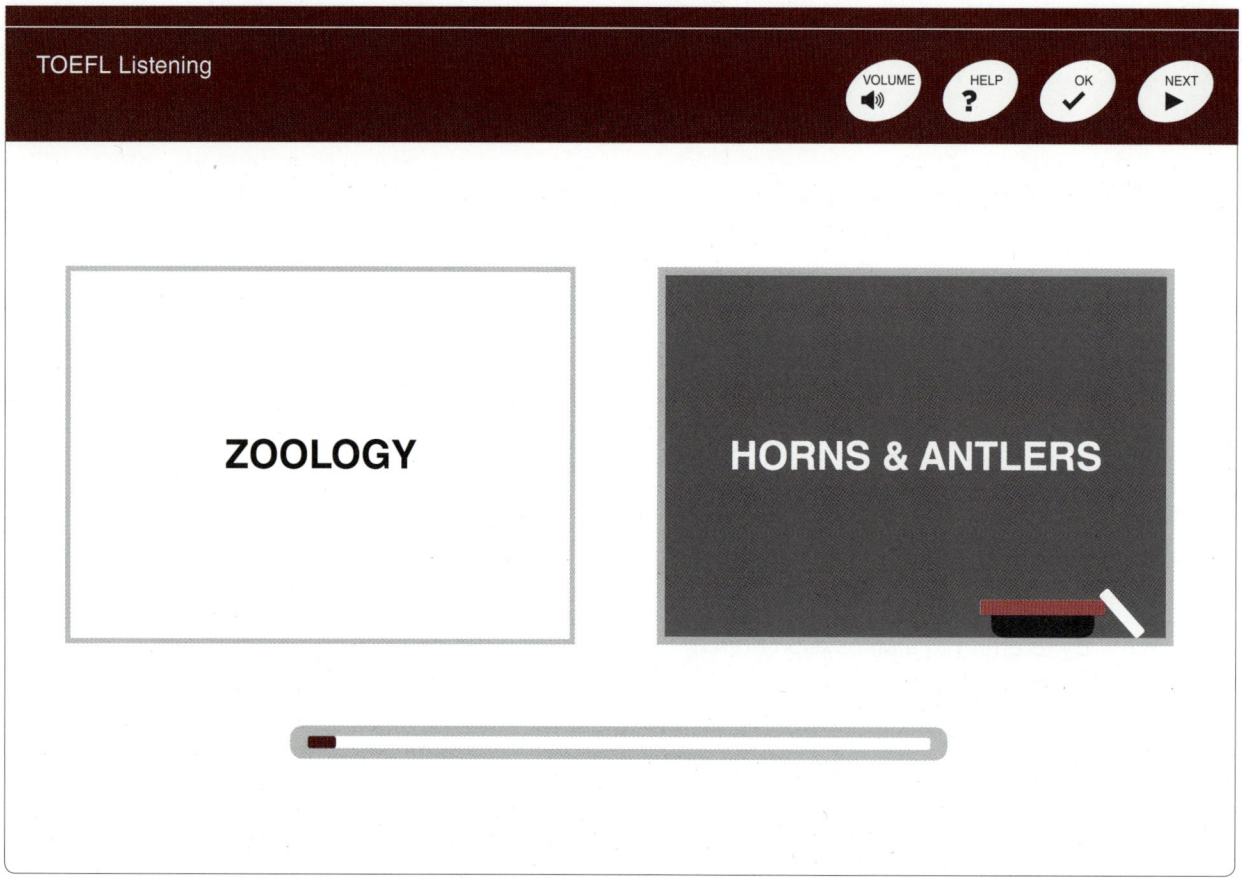

TOEFL Listening

12. What is the lecture mainly about?
    A The main functions of horns and antlers
    B The different lifestyles of animals with horns and antlers
    C A comparison of horns with antlers
    D The advantages of horns over antlers

13. How does the professor introduce horns and antlers?
    A By giving a general definition of them
    B By mentioning an anecdote about them
    C By comparing their distinct appearances
    D By correcting a mistaken notion about them

14. According to the professor, why does the growth rate of horns and antlers differ?
    A Because of their life cycles
    B Because of their functions
    C Because of their sizes
    D Because of their shapes

15. In the lecture, the professor discusses both horns and antlers. Indicate whether each of the following is a characteristic of horns or antlers.
    Click in the correct box for each phrase.

	Horns	Antlers
A Are hollow		
B Have many points		
C Are shed each year		
D Are covered in keratin		

16. Which of the following is NOT mentioned as a function of horns and antlers?
    A Fighting for dominance
    B Identifying a family group
    C Showing off to females
    D Defending against predators

Listen again to part of the lecture. Then answer the question.

17. Why does the professor say this:
    A To remind the students of what she said earlier in the lecture
    B To introduce a new discovery about horns and antlers
    C To explain another role of horns and antlers
    D To emphasize the point she is about to make

PART B

Pragmatic Understanding Questions

▶ **UNIT 03**   FUNCTION
UNIT 04   ATTITUDE

UNIT 03 Function

Introduction

- Function questions ask about the speaker's purpose for mentioning specific information.
- These questions are often assessed in Replay format, where they are accompanied by a relevant excerpt from the passage.
- 1 to 2 questions are given for each passage.

Question Types

- Why does the student say this: 🎧
- What does the professor mean when he/she says this: 🎧
- What does the professor imply when he/she says this: 🎧

Strategy

1. Determine the speaker's intent within the given situation.
   Keep in mind that a single expression can have different meanings depending on the situation. Therefore, instead of directly interpreting the speaker's statement, consider the context of the statement and what the speaker means given his/her particular situation. For example, the comment, "It sure is hot in here," could mean on the surface that the speaker is simply hot, but if an invited guest has said it while sweating profusely, the speaker could be implying that he/she would like to have the windows opened.

2. For questions that ask why the speaker has said something in particular, answer choices have such phrases as the following: to suggest, to recommend, to advise, to complain, to apologize, to accept, to question, to give directions, etc.

Sample Question

TOEFL Listening

Professor

Made without sound, silent films gave audiences tips to help them enjoy the film. First, subtitles were added to assist the audience's understanding. These were used to um... to inform the audience of important details such as the time, place, or date of a scene, and sometimes even to comment on the action. Secondly, silent films usually were not actually silent. Well, you wouldn't be surprised had you seen silent films before. Silent films were commonly accompanied by live music. Music was instantly recognized as essential: contributing to the atmosphere and giving the audience vital emotional cues. Movie theaters would typically employ either a pianist or an entire orchestra to create sound effects. Finally, emphasis on body language and facial expression was a pivotal tool for the actor. Modern-day audiences may um… feel uncomfortable watching films from the silent era as the actors in these films may seem to be overacting to an outrageous degree.

Listen again to part of the lecture. Then answer the question.

Secondly, silent films usually were not actually silent. Well, you wouldn't be surprised had you seen silent films before. Silent films were commonly accompanied by live music.

What does the professor mean when he says this:

Well, you wouldn't be surprised had you seen silent films before.

Ⓐ He hopes the students pay more attention to the lecture.
Ⓑ He expects the students to express their opinions about silent movies.
Ⓒ He thinks the students can understand what he said from past experience.
Ⓓ He doubts the students have ever watched silent films before.

Answer and Explanation

After the professor somewhat ironically states that silent films are not entirely silent, he says, "…you wouldn't be surprised had you seen silent films before." In other words, he assumes that if a student has seen a silent film, then s/he would already know about the sound element of silent films. The correct answer is Ⓒ.

Basic Drills

1

Listen again to part of the conversation. Then answer the question.
What does the man mean when he says this: 🎧

- Ⓐ He thinks it's no trouble to help the woman.
- Ⓑ He thinks it is a waste of time for the woman to wait in line.
- Ⓒ He wants to arrange for the woman to meet the professor.
- Ⓓ He wants to lend the woman the book she is seeking.

2

Listen again to part of the lecture. Then answer the question.
Why does the professor say this: 🎧

- Ⓐ To imply that there should be more research on penguins
- Ⓑ To explain why penguins eat so much
- Ⓒ To ask the students' opinions on a penguin's diet
- Ⓓ To emphasize the importance of fat to a penguin's survival

3

Listen again to part of the lecture. Then answer the question.
Why does the professor say this: 🎧

- Ⓐ To repeat what he said in the previous lecture
- Ⓑ To prevent the students from making mistakes
- Ⓒ To explain the meaning of a technical term
- Ⓓ To clarify a common misunderstanding

4 Listen again to part of the conversation. Then answer the question.
What does the librarian mean when he says this: 🎧

- Ⓐ He doesn't know the library's layout well.
- Ⓑ He didn't study engineering in school.
- Ⓒ He hasn't heard that terminology before.
- Ⓓ He couldn't hear what the student said.

5 Listen again to part of the lecture. Then answer the question.
Why does the professor say this: 🎧

- Ⓐ To explain a recently invented dating method
- Ⓑ To suggest there is evidence against the assumption
- Ⓒ To introduce the controversy over the Chauvet cave paintings
- Ⓓ To imply the ancient paintings are still a mystery

6 What does the professor mean when he says this: 🎧

- Ⓐ He thinks the students are confused about the new concept.
- Ⓑ He wants to encourage the students to give their opinions.
- Ⓒ He wants the students to recall what he previously explained.
- Ⓓ He thinks the students are aware of the relation between the two words.

Dictation

Listen and fill in the blanks.

1. In order to _____ _____ _____ _____ of the southern oceans, warm-blooded penguins _____ _____ feathers and fat for insulation.
2. A special gland at the base of the tail _____ _____ that the penguin can spread across its feathers _____ _____ _____.
3. Penguins _____ _____ _____ the cold by a thick layer of fat under their skin.
4. At the same time, _____ _____ also enables penguins to go without food while they molt or _____ _____ _____.
5. However, _____ _____ _____ _____ some risk in case of carelessness.
6. If the _____ _____ _____ _____ _____, serious injury or death can occur.
7. Therefore, MRI rooms must be _____ _____ _____ _____ _____... and of course, patients are prescreened for the presence of any metal objects to prevent potential risk.
8. Well, _____ _____ _____ many people to assume that the paintings must be relatively recent.
9. That's because, they thought... thousands of years of _____ _____ _____ _____ _____ was behind those paintings.
10. However, the result of analyzing the animal drawings and _____ _____ _____ in the cave was rather surprising.
11. You can probably guess that _____ _____ _____ _____ _____ _____ "remediate," which means to solve a problem.
12. But... if _____ _____ _____ such as oil contaminated this environment, a number of the microorganisms would be killed, um... while others would manage to survive as they are _____ _____ _____ such organic pollution.
13. They can _____ _____ _____ organic pollutants more quickly.

Listening Practice 01

SERVICE ENCOUNTER

1 What is the student's problem?
- Ⓐ He had a complaint about the lecture schedule.
- Ⓑ He didn't know how to use the school website.
- Ⓒ He forgot to sign up for a required course.
- Ⓓ He didn't know about the canceled lecture.

2 Why didn't the student receive notification?
- Ⓐ Because he didn't attend the first lecture
- Ⓑ Because his contact information was outdated
- Ⓒ Because there was an error on the college system
- Ⓓ Because his computer has been broken

Listen again to part of the conversation. Then answer the question.

3 Why does the registrar say this: 🎧
- Ⓐ To ask the student how to put personal information onto the college system
- Ⓑ To express doubt that the student has previously accessed the college system
- Ⓒ To find out whether she needs to tell the student how to input new data
- Ⓓ To remind the student that he should update his email address

Dictation 01

Listen and fill in the blanks.

Registrar: Hello. Can I help you?

Student: Well, I hope so... I just came from lecture hall 3B and it's empty. _____ _____ _____ which room the lecture on Modern Physics is in?

R: Hold on, let me check my computer, um... *[pause]* _____ _____ _____ the lecture by Professor Lee?

S: That's right... *[checking his schedule]* um, Professor Lee, 4 pm in Lecture Hall 3B. Is anything wrong?

R: I'm afraid so. The lecture was canceled, and the students _____ _____ _____ _____.

S: Canceled? You mean... _____ _____ _____ _____? Or...

R: Completely canceled. Hold on... *[pause]* Here's the problem. Not enough students _____ _____ _____ the lecture this semester, so it was automatically canceled.

S: That's... well, that's terrible. I was really _____ _____ _____ the lecture. By the way, _____ _____ _____ _____ _____ _____?

R: Hmm. Let me check... What's your name?

S: Wallace Colby.

R: *[pause]* Okay. And your email address is WallyC@freemail.com?

S: Yes, it... No! No, that's my old email address. Oh boy, that's why... *[pause]* Hmm, I guess _____ _____ _____ _____ _____.

R: Well, you probably need to update your email address on the college system. Do you know _____ _____ _____ _____?

S: Yeah. I'll take care of that tonight. Anyway, do you think this lecture _____ _____ _____ next semester?

R: Oh yes, I believe they offer it every semester. _____ _____ _____ enough students are interested, you'll be able to take it then.

S: Okay. Thank you very much for your help.

Listening Practice 02

ECONOMICS

1 What is the lecture mainly about?
- Ⓐ Strategies for finding substitutes for expensive products
- Ⓑ Elements that determine the price of a product
- Ⓒ Reasons why some products are more popular than others
- Ⓓ Factors that can have an effect on the sales of a product

2 According to the professor, what will happen if the price of a complementary product goes down?
- Ⓐ The price of substitute products will go up.
- Ⓑ Sales of your product will go up.
- Ⓒ It will have no effect on your product.
- Ⓓ Sales of both the complementary product and your product will go down.

Listen again to part of the lecture. Then answer the question.

3 Why does the professor say this: 🎧
- Ⓐ To emphasize an important point
- Ⓑ To correct a previous error
- Ⓒ To widen the discussion
- Ⓓ To summarize the lesson

Dictation 02

Listen and fill in the blanks.

Professor: So, I think the relationship between _____ _____ _____ is pretty clear. Imagine that you're a seller. If you _____ _____ _____ of your product, you can reasonably expect your sales to go up. Now, let's, um... let's make things a little more complex. For nearly every product you'll find in the marketplace, you'll also find _____ _____ _____ _____ _____. This is important because when the price of these related goods changes, it will affect the sales of your product.

Let me give you an example... we can start with substitutes. A substitute product is one that can _____ _____ _____ _____ _____ your product, _____ _____ _____. If you're selling chicken, for example, a substitute product might be pork. If the price of pork goes up, you can expect that some people will buy chicken instead. So when the price of a substitute product goes up, _____ _____ _____ _____.

As for complementary products... well, they're sort of _____ _____ _____ substitute products. A person who buys a complementary product _____ _____ _____ buy your product as well. For example, if you're selling CDs, a complementary product would be CD players. If the price of CD players goes down, we know the sales of CD players will go up... so will sales of your CDs, even if your prices _____ _____ _____.

Alright, so these two mean that the sales of your product _____ _____ _____ ... um increase or decrease by the price changes of other products, though the quality and price of your product _____ _____ _____.

Listening Practice 03

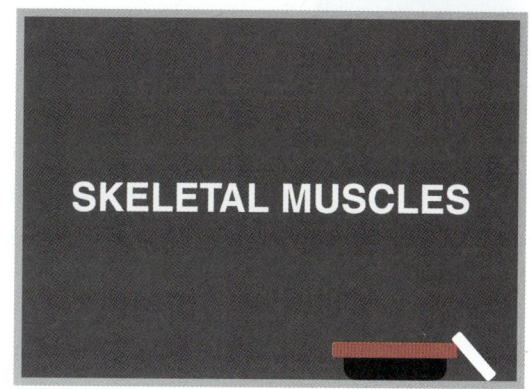

1 What is the lecture mainly about?
  Ⓐ How our muscles work when we run
  Ⓑ The structure of myoglobin in skeletal muscles
  Ⓒ Two types of skeletal muscle
  Ⓓ The relationship between muscles and bones

2 Which of the following is NOT true about red muscles?
  Ⓐ Their dark color comes from myoglobin.
  Ⓑ They are less frequently used than white muscles.
  Ⓒ They are found in chicken's legs.
  Ⓓ They need a constant supply of oxygen.

Listen again to part of the lecture. Then answer the question.

3 Why does the professor say this:
  Ⓐ To encourage the interest of the students
  Ⓑ To introduce a new idea into the lecture
  Ⓒ To apologize for providing the wrong information
  Ⓓ To clarify the main focus of the lecture

Dictation 03

Listen and fill in the blanks.

Professor: Today we're going to talk about skeletal muscles, which _____ _____ _____ _____ our skeleton. Well, there are three types of muscle: skeletal, smooth, and cardiac. But you needn't worry about the last two types right now, okay? Now, where was I? Ah, yes... skeletal muscles. These muscles create movement _____ _____ _____ _____ our bones and joints when they, um, contract. They can be _____ _____ _____ _____ _____: red muscle and white muscle. Red muscles are found in constantly-used muscles. And... as you know, muscles require oxygen during exercise. Therefore, red muscles _____ _____ _____ _____ of oxygen. _____ _____ _____ _____ _____ red muscles contain an oxygen-storing chemical known as myoglobin. The presence of myoglobin allows these muscles to work for long periods of time and gives them their _____ _____ _____ _____. White muscles, however, are only used occasionally and work best _____ _____ _____, so they don't need as much myoglobin to store oxygen and thus appear white in color. If you think of them _____ _____ _____ _____, white muscles are good for sprinting short distances, while red muscles are _____ _____ _____ _____ _____.

Student: Then, _____ _____ _____ _____, do turkeys or chickens have some white meat and dark meat?

P: Absolutely. They don't _____ _____ _____ _____ _____, so they have white muscles for short and quick flights in their breast and wings, and red muscles _____ _____ _____ _____ _____ _____. If you cut into a, um, chicken or turkey at the dinner table, you can find their breast and wings are white meat and the legs are dark meat.

iBT Practice 01

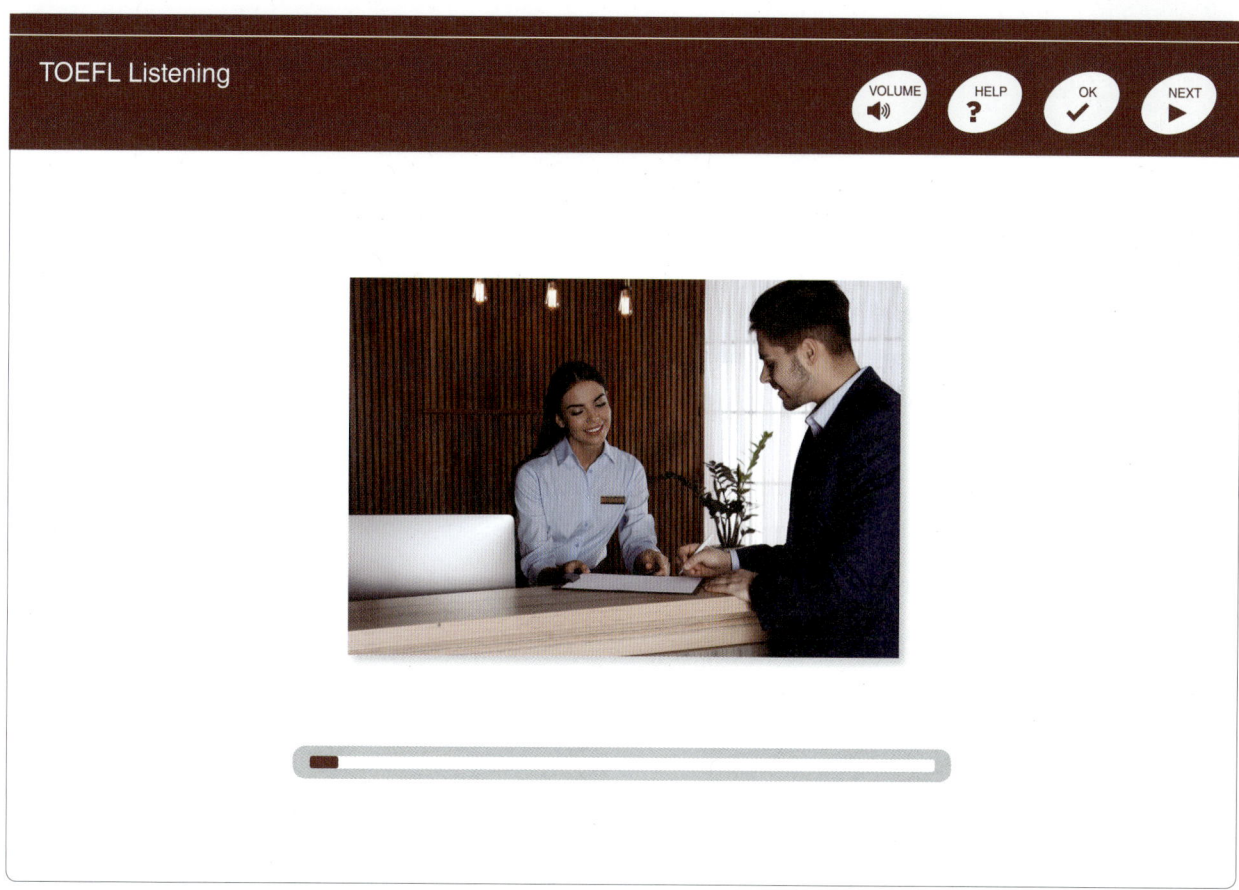

Note-Taking

TOEFL Listening

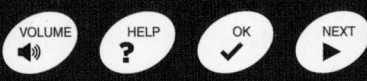

1. Why does the student go to the gymnasium office?
   - Ⓐ He wants to see the new swimming pool.
   - Ⓑ He wants to receive a free gym pass.
   - Ⓒ He wants to cancel his swimming lessons.
   - Ⓓ He wants to apply to be a gym instructor.

2. What did the student mistakenly think about the free pass card?
   - Ⓐ It includes free swimming lessons.
   - Ⓑ It includes free access to the gym.
   - Ⓒ It is only issued to full-time students.
   - Ⓓ It offers a student discount for lessons.

3. What will the student probably do next?
   - Ⓐ He will check out the number of credits required to graduate.
   - Ⓑ He will search for information on other free exercise programs.
   - Ⓒ He will talk about joining the swimming class with his parents.
   - Ⓓ He will have a conversation with the swimming instructor.

Listen again to part of the conversation. Then answer the question.
4. Why does the employee say this: 🎧
   - Ⓐ To apologize for a bad decision
   - Ⓑ To complain about her co-worker
   - Ⓒ To stress the instructor's qualifications
   - Ⓓ To explain how to become a volunteer

iBT Practice 02

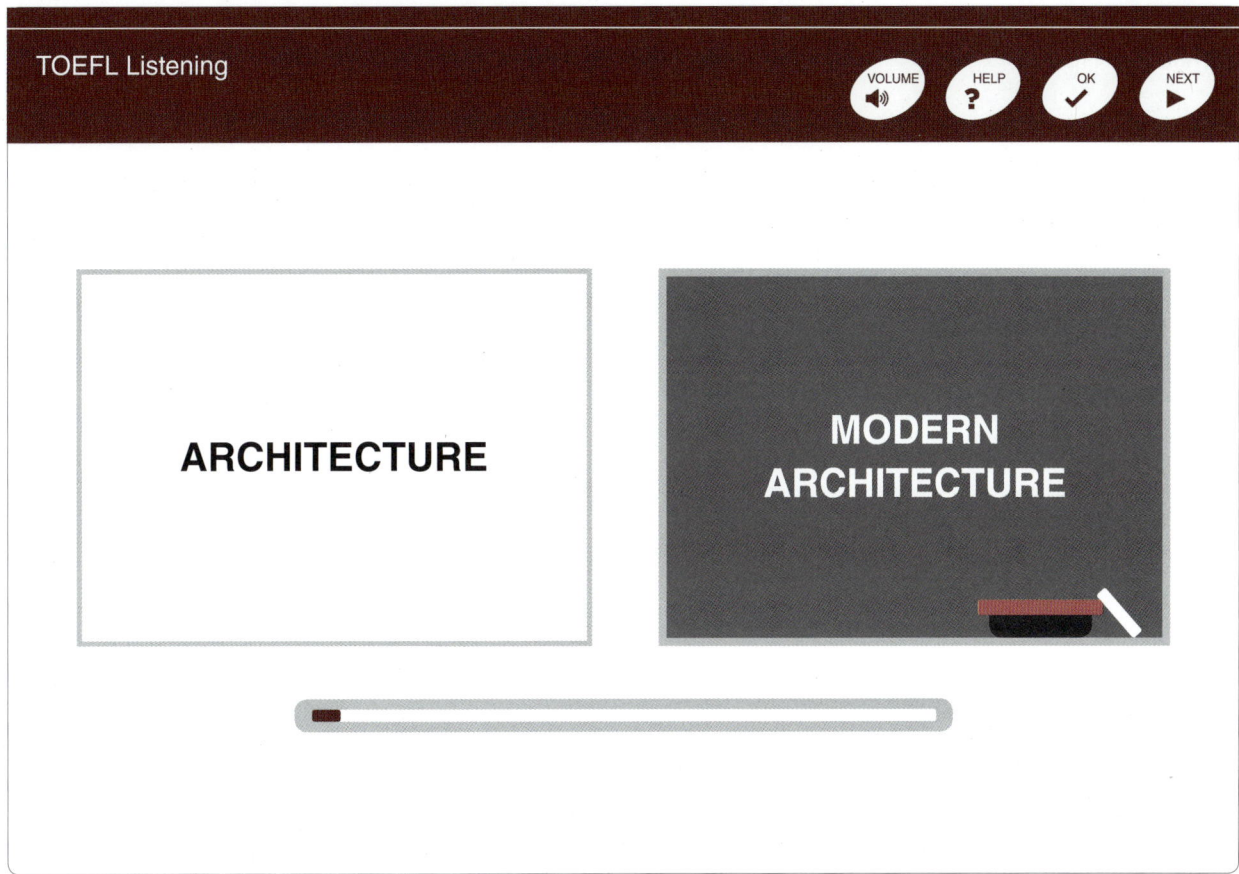

Note-Taking

TOEFL Listening

1. What is the lecture mainly about?
   - Ⓐ The historical origin of Modern architecture
   - Ⓑ The effect of new technologies on architectural styles
   - Ⓒ The emergence of Modern architecture and its characteristics
   - Ⓓ The differences between Modern architecture and present-day architecture

2. What are the features of Modern architecture mentioned in the lecture?
   Click on 2 answers.
   - Ⓐ It prized function over form.
   - Ⓑ It represented values borrowed from the past.
   - Ⓒ It was influenced by new materials and technology.
   - Ⓓ It imitated the ornamentation of 19th-century architecture.

3. According to the professor, which aspect of Modern architecture provoked criticism?
   - Ⓐ Its complicated design
   - Ⓑ Its excessive emphasis on aesthetic value
   - Ⓒ Its inappropriate use of building materials
   - Ⓓ Its lack of human quality

4. Why does the professor say this: 🎧
   - Ⓐ To emphasize the importance of the topic of the lecture
   - Ⓑ To express uncertainty about a definition
   - Ⓒ To discredit a commonly accepted theory
   - Ⓓ To differentiate between similar terms

Vocabulary Check

- [ ] subtitle
- [ ] cue
- [ ] pivotal
- [ ] overact
- [ ] outrageous

- [ ] current
- [ ] chilly
- [ ] insulation
- [ ] insulate
- [ ] overlap
- [ ] gland
- [ ] preen
- [ ] layer
- [ ] molt
- [ ] brood

- [ ] internal
- [ ] noninvasive
- [ ] penetrate
- [ ] incision
- [ ] injection
- [ ] gravitational
- [ ] field
- [ ] lethal
- [ ] metallic
- [ ] implant
- [ ] surgical
- [ ] pacemaker
- [ ] malfunction
- [ ] prescreen
- [ ] potential

- [ ] visualization
- [ ] dedicated

- [ ] fine
- [ ] engraving
- [ ] depict
- [ ] bison
- [ ] lifelike
- [ ] roam
- [ ] in packs
- [ ] sophistication
- [ ] charcoal
- [ ] radiocarbon
- [ ] dating
- [ ] precision

- [ ] bio-remediation
- [ ] microorganism
- [ ] break down
- [ ] pollutant
- [ ] contaminate
- [ ] contamination
- [ ] dissolve
- [ ] fertilizer
- [ ] subsequently
- [ ] sound
- [ ] biodegradation

- [ ] physics
- [ ] notify
- [ ] sign up for
- [ ] update

- [ ] substitute
- [ ] complementary
- [ ] vice versa

- [ ] skeletal
- [ ] skeleton

- [ ] cardiac
- [ ] joint
- [ ] contract
- [ ] fiber
- [ ] burst
- [ ] sprint

- [ ] pass
- [ ] access
- [ ] facility
- [ ] fabulous
- [ ] affordable
- [ ] instructor
- [ ] entail
- [ ] enroll
- [ ] advanced
- [ ] register

- [ ] contemporary
- [ ] height
- [ ] span
- [ ] column
- [ ] ornate
- [ ] ornamentation
- [ ] sleek
- [ ] aesthetic
- [ ] embrace
- [ ] rectangular
- [ ] bleak
- [ ] sterile
- [ ] dehumanize
- [ ] machinery
- [ ] critic
- [ ] accessible

PART B

UNIT 03 FUNCTION

Vocabulary Review

A Choose the correct word for each definition.

> brood   skeletal   layer   microorganism   sprint   fertilizer

1. to sit on eggs providing warmth and protection: _____
2. to run very fast for a short distance: _____
3. a substance applied to soil to increase the amount of crops it produces: _____
4. a living thing too small to be seen by the naked eye: _____
5. a piece that covers a surface or that is between two other things: _____

B Choose the best word or phrase to explain the underlined word.

1. If two items are complementary, they _____.
   - Ⓐ are attached
   - Ⓑ are the same color
   - Ⓒ go together
   - Ⓓ start fighting

2. If you embrace an idea, you _____.
   - Ⓐ challenge it passionately
   - Ⓑ think of it first
   - Ⓒ accept it enthusiastically
   - Ⓓ understand it well

3. If there are potential problems, it is _____ something might go wrong.
   - Ⓐ possible
   - Ⓑ difficult
   - Ⓒ common
   - Ⓓ inevitable

4. If something penetrates your skin, it _____ it.
   - Ⓐ goes around
   - Ⓑ comes across
   - Ⓒ passes through
   - Ⓓ turns toward

C Choose the best word or phrase to complete each sentence.

1. This desert island is _____ only by boat.
   - Ⓐ accessible
   - Ⓑ internal
   - Ⓒ noninvasive
   - Ⓓ gravitational

2. The house is cold because of the poor _____.
   - Ⓐ ornamentation
   - Ⓑ insulation
   - Ⓒ restriction
   - Ⓓ implant

3. I get a discount whenever I transfer from the bus to the subway and _____.
   - Ⓐ etcetera
   - Ⓑ as such
   - Ⓒ for short
   - Ⓓ vice versa

D Choose the correct word to complete each sentence.

1. He has to take his medicine via _____. (injection / incision)
2. I want a cozy hotel room with a(n) _____ view. (outrageous / fabulous)
3. She worked hard that semester and was _____ awarded a scholarship. (subsequently / previously)
4. Section A is an _____ language course for college students. (advanced / interior)
5. The sofa was uncomfortable but they liked it for its _____ value. (aesthetic / surgical)

E Choose the word that is closest in meaning to the underlined word.

1. We can't swim here. The water is contaminated.
   Ⓐ polluted　　Ⓑ consumed　　Ⓒ outdated　　Ⓓ reserved

2. It was a pivotal moment in her career.
   Ⓐ awful　　Ⓑ lethal　　Ⓒ crucial　　Ⓓ irrelevant

3. I'd like to volunteer, but first I'd like to hear about what that would entail.
   Ⓐ signify　　Ⓑ affect　　Ⓒ require　　Ⓓ involve

4. They lived in London at the height of the Industrial Revolution.
   Ⓐ onset　　Ⓑ peak　　Ⓒ state　　Ⓓ depth

5. I can't seem to make ends meet. I need to find more affordable housing.
   Ⓐ contemporary　　Ⓑ convenient　　Ⓒ elegant　　Ⓓ economical

6. The data was lost because of a computer malfunction.
   Ⓐ current　　Ⓑ operation　　Ⓒ failure　　Ⓓ cue

F Choose the word that is the opposite of the underlined word.

1. Under cold and dry conditions, it will cause the wood to contract.
   Ⓐ expand　　Ⓑ shrink　　Ⓒ break　　Ⓓ crack

2. The palace is famous for its dining room with ornate ceilings.
   Ⓐ high　　Ⓑ sleek　　Ⓒ plain　　Ⓓ sterile

PART B

Pragmatic Understanding Questions

UNIT 03   FUNCTION
▶ **UNIT 04**   ATTITUDE

UNIT 04 Attitude

Introduction

- Attitude questions ask about the speaker's attitude toward or opinion of the content of the conversation or lecture, or about the speaker's level of certainty regarding the information he/she is conveying.
- Sometimes, these questions appear in Replay format, asking you to infer the speaker's attitude based on an excerpt from the passage.
- 0 to 1 question is given for each passage.

Question Types

- What is the speaker's attitude toward X?
- What is the speaker's opinion of X?
- What can be inferred about the student?
- What does the professor mean when he/she says this:

Strategy

1. Recognize the speaker's attitude through his/her tone of voice.
   A speaker's tone of voice gives essential clues about his/her attitude. It may indicate emotion, preference, indifference, certainty, uncertainty, etc. Therefore, pay attention to the way a speaker talks, not only to what he/she says. Be careful not to let important clues such as hesitation, emphasis, change in speaking speed, etc. slip by without notice.

2. Infer the speaker's attitude from the overall content of the passage.
   A speaker's attitude is not revealed directly or in one or two sentences but in the passage's overall content. Understanding a passage's main idea and major points is crucial for answering Attitude questions. Follow the flow of the conversation or lecture and synthesize all the discernable clues to make an inference about the speaker's attitude.

3. The following expressions are commonly used in Attitude questions.
   (1) Attitude/opinion: like, dislike, loathe, understand, be keen on, be offended, be interested, be surprised, be astonished, be amused, be hopeful, be impressed, be upset, be annoyed, be confused, be apologetic
   (2) Degree of certainty: sure, certain, uncertain, doubtful, confident, possible, impossible, probable, plausible, apparently, potentially, relatively

Sample Question

TOEFL Listening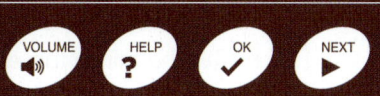

Professor

So... We've been talking a lot about environmental problems in this class, but today I want to talk about a, um, a solution. Or, at least, a proposed solution. It's called "rewilding," and it basically involves reintroducing flora and fauna into struggling ecosystems. We're talking about plants and animals that once lived in the area but are no longer present. The idea is that by essentially resetting the ecosystem to its original, um... condition, we can then step back and let it thrive without constant human intervention. It's an intriguing concept, and it has been attempted with some degree of success, such as the efforts to reintroduce beavers to Scotland, but it must be said that the economic benefits that it promises have largely failed to materialize in the case studies to date. Until that hurdle is cleared and it becomes both environmentally and financially beneficial, I'm afraid it's going to be justifiably passed over for more traditional methods of conservation.

What is the speaker's attitude toward rewilding?
- Ⓐ She wishes more funding would be invested in it.
- Ⓑ She worries that it could cause serious problems.
- Ⓒ She believes it is a promising but flawed idea.
- Ⓓ She thinks it will replace traditional conservation.

Answer and Explanation
The professor is talking about a conservation method called rewilding. Although she shows some optimism and points out that it has had some success, she clearly states that it is not currently financially viable. Therefore, the correct answer is Ⓒ.
- Ⓐ Money is mentioned as a problem, but there is nothing in the lecture about increasing monetary investments in rewilding.
- Ⓑ The professor worries that rewilding doesn't bring sufficient financial return, which could not be considered "serious problems."
- Ⓓ The professor actually states the opposite opinion, that rewilding is not yet ready to replace traditional conservation methods.

Basic Drills

1 What can be inferred about the student?

Ⓐ She prefers to live alone than to live with a stranger.
Ⓑ She is angry with the employee for not listening to her.
Ⓒ She thinks the office is responsible for the situation.
Ⓓ She thinks the employee is unaware of the dormitory rules.

2 What is the professor's opinion about Roman sculpture?

Ⓐ It developed its own realistic style.
Ⓑ It was no more than an imitation of Greek sculpture.
Ⓒ It contributed to the development of Greek art.
Ⓓ It was superior to Greek sculpture.

Listen again to part of the lecture. Then answer the question.

3 What can be inferred about the student?

Ⓐ She is certain that the professor made a mistake.
Ⓑ She is surprised by the information in the lecture.
Ⓒ She is interested in a concept mentioned in the lecture.
Ⓓ She is doubtful about the evidence presented by the professor.

4 What can be inferred about the student?

- Ⓐ She does not think she is qualified as a captain.
- Ⓑ She fully expected to be the captain of the team.
- Ⓒ She does not want the heavy responsibility.
- Ⓓ She is surprised and proud to be elected team leader.

5 What is the professor's opinion about method acting?

- Ⓐ She thinks it is effective in performing tragic roles.
- Ⓑ She thinks it is appropriate in expressing mixed emotions.
- Ⓒ She thinks actors with little experience are unable to use it.
- Ⓓ She thinks it revolutionized acting in a realistic way.

6 What does the professor mean when he says this: 🎧

- Ⓐ He thinks the old saying has been scientifically proven.
- Ⓑ He thinks laughter is important in social relationships.
- Ⓒ He thinks the students are doubtful of the old saying.
- Ⓓ He thinks it is quite difficult to struggle not to laugh.

Dictation

Listen and fill in the blanks.

1. _____ _____ _____ _____ Roman art and Greek art can be seen in their concentration on sculptures.
2. Actually, a lot of famous Roman sculptors _____ _____ _____ _____ their Greek predecessors.
3. Roman artists tried to recreate what the person really looked like _____ _____ _____ _____ _____ _____.
4. Glacial movement, known as basal sliding, occurs when the growing ice mass _____ _____ _____ _____ _____ its rigid shape and begins to flow.
5. It is _____ _____ _____ _____ in which immense pressure of the overlying glacial mass causes the ice making contact with the ground to melt.
6. The melting ice then forms a layer of water _____ _____ _____ _____ between the glacial ice and the uh… the ground surface.
7. Okay, method acting, or simply the Method as it's known… is an acting technique in which actors draw on their own emotions and experiences to _____ _____ _____ _____ of their characters.
8. When depicting love, he would _____ _____ _____ _____ on the chest.
9. So when actors began to _____ _____ _____ _____ _____ of an incident, their performances became much more realistic.
10. According to scientists, positive sounds, such as laughter, _____ _____ _____ _____ in the listener's brain.
11. The response occurs in the same area _____ _____ when we smile, just like when we prepare our _____ _____ _____ _____.
12. But positive sounds provoke a much more powerful reaction, which um… er, suggests that _____ _____ _____ _____.
13. Now, _____ _____ _____ _____ _____ _____ "Laugh and the whole world laughs with you."

Listening Practice 01

OFFICE HOURS

1 Why does the student visit the professor?
- Ⓐ To have his essay topic approved
- Ⓑ To get advice on how to write an essay
- Ⓒ To find out the difference between outlines and road maps
- Ⓓ To discuss the Evolution vs. Creationism debate

2 What is the professor's opinion of outlines?
- Ⓐ She thinks that they make writing more interesting.
- Ⓑ She thinks that they are effective in writing a longer paper.
- Ⓒ She thinks that they help the writer stay focused.
- Ⓓ She thinks that they are more common than road maps.

Listen again to part of the conversation. Then answer the question.

3 Why does the professor say this: 🎧
- Ⓐ To complain about the frequency of printer problems
- Ⓑ To express indifference to the student's situation
- Ⓒ To imply she doesn't believe the student's excuse
- Ⓓ To show she isn't annoyed by the student's being late

Dictation 01

Listen and fill in the blanks.

Student: *[apologetic]* Sorry I'm late. I had a printer problem.

Professor: Don't worry about it. I know _____ _____ _____ _____ _____. So, you wanted to talk to me about your paper?

S: Right. I've decided on a topic, but I don't know where to begin. I want to write about Evolution vs. Creationism. I've done a lot of _____ _____ _____ _____ and I have a lot to say... but, I'm just having trouble _____ _____ how to start.

P: Okay, what you need to do before you try to write the paper _____ _____ _____ _____. Organization is so important when writing a paper. If you write an outline first, it will _____ _____ _____ _____. That way you _____ _____ _____ _____.

S: An outline? Is that the same thing as a road map?

P: No, they're similar, but the difference is that a road map _____ _____ _____ you could take. It could be useful when you _____ _____ _____ _____ or guideline for a goal, but _____ _____ _____ _____ _____ writing the paper, you really need an outline.

S: I see.

P: And there's one more thing I want to emphasize. When writing papers for any class, try to be creative. We professors _____ _____ _____ _____ virtually the same paper over and over again. If your paper stands out from the rest, it makes it more enjoyable to read and, _____ _____ _____ _____ _____, you'll probably get a better grade. So, be creative by... um, by approaching your topic _____ _____ _____.

S: I'll keep that in mind. Thanks.

Listening Practice 02

BIOLOGY

1 What is the lecture mainly about?
- Ⓐ Hormone treatment for sleeping problems
- Ⓑ The function and application of melatonin
- Ⓒ The difference between natural and synthetic melatonin
- Ⓓ The efficacy of a new dietary supplement

2 According to the professor, what influences the production of melatonin?
- Ⓐ The duration of sleep
- Ⓑ Dietary habits
- Ⓒ Changes in body temperature
- Ⓓ The amount of exposure to light

3 What is the professor's attitude toward melatonin supplements?
- Ⓐ He is excited about the possible medical applications.
- Ⓑ He is suspicious of some of the benefits that are claimed.
- Ⓒ He is concerned that people ignore their effects.
- Ⓓ He is convinced that science has proved their safety.

Dictation 02

Listen and fill in the blanks.

Professor: Most of you have probably heard of melatonin. Well, melatonin is the hormone that our body uses _____ _____ _____ _____ _____. It is produced by the pineal gland, a small organ located in our brain, and its production _____ _____ _____ _____ _____... well, to be precise, changes in light. At night, our body increases melatonin production, which _____ _____. When the sun comes back up, the light _____ _____ _____ _____, helping us to, um... to awaken. So it maintains our circadian rhythm, which is um... an internal 24-hour timekeeping system.

However, when we're _____ _____ _____ _____ in the evening or too little light during the day, our normal melatonin cycle can _____ _____ and we can experience a temporary sleep problem. For example, night shifts or jet-lag. In these cases, people can take synthetic melatonin _____ _____ _____ _____ to help them regain natural sleep cycles. And this has become common. It's also taken by people with _____ _____ _____ _____, such as insomnia.

But now... it's important to note that there are questions about whether taking melatonin is _____ _____ _____. Studies show that it _____ _____ _____ _____ _____ in fighting minor disruptions of sleep patterns in the short term, but we're still not sure what the long term effects might be. Furthermore, taken at the wrong time or _____ _____ _____ _____, it can further disrupt sleep patterns rather than correct them. Definitely more research is needed on the use of melatonin _____ _____ _____ _____.

Listening Practice 03

ART   FRESCO

1 What does the professor mainly discuss?
- Ⓐ The differences between buon and secco fresco
- Ⓑ The history of fresco painting
- Ⓒ The main characteristics of buon fresco
- Ⓓ The artistic value of buon fresco

2 According to the professor, why is creating buon fresco art difficult?
Click on 2 answers.
- Ⓐ Because of the time constraints
- Ⓑ Because of the size of the projects
- Ⓒ Because of the lack of painting materials
- Ⓓ Because of the problem of correction

Listen again to part of the lecture. Then answer the question.

3 What can be inferred about the professor?
- Ⓐ She thinks it is important to define a new term.
- Ⓑ She thinks she is giving the students a clear hint.
- Ⓒ She is sure the students have knowledge of Italian.
- Ⓓ She hopes she doesn't have to explain more.

Dictation 03

Listen and fill in the blanks.

Professor: Fresco is _____ _____ _____ _____ _____ of painting. In painting a fresco, wet plaster is used as the base and the artist _____ _____ _____ _____ to paint directly onto this wet surface. As it dries, _____ _____ _____ _____ _____, and the painting literally becomes a part of the surface. This is what we call buon fresco, or true fresco. Buon means "good" in Italian, but we _____ _____ _____ _____ _____ "pure" or "true." Besides this, there is also secco fresco. Now, can anybody tell me the difference between the two? _____ _____ _____ _____ if you know that secco is Italian for "dry."

Student: Um, you mean… secco fresco uses dry plaster instead of wet plaster?

P: Exactly. But, secco fresco is not _____ _____ _____ _____ because dry plaster does not absorb and integrate with the paint. Now, let's talk about the process and the difficulties _____ _____ buon fresco. Buon fresco is difficult to create because of the _____ _____ _____ _____ _____ of plaster. An artist needs to _____ _____ what he or she wishes to accomplish before the plaster dries, dividing the piece into sections that can be expediently completed. _____ _____ _____ _____ _____ feature is the fact that mistakes are very difficult to cover up. Normally, a painter _____ _____ _____ by simply painting over them, but this is not the case with buon fresco where the pigment is absorbed. Once dried, no more buon fresco can be _____ _____ _____ the dried plaster from the wall.

090

iBT Practice 01

Note-Taking

TOEFL Listening

1. What is the student's problem?
   - Ⓐ She doesn't have enough money to buy her textbook.
   - Ⓑ She is not familiar with using the school message board.
   - Ⓒ She found out that the textbook she bought is an old edition.
   - Ⓓ She finds it difficult to get a new copy of her textbook.

2. What is NOT one of the ways suggested by the store clerk for obtaining a textbook?
   - Ⓐ Looking for a used copy
   - Ⓑ Visiting downtown bookstores
   - Ⓒ Borrowing a copy from the professor
   - Ⓓ Placing a special order

Listen again to part of the conversation. Then answer the question.

3. Why does the clerk say this: 🎧
   - Ⓐ To apologize for providing incorrect information
   - Ⓑ To imply that the student came too late in the semester
   - Ⓒ To recommend another recently published book
   - Ⓓ To explain why he can't remember the price of the book

Listen again to part of the conversation. Then answer the question.

4. What can be inferred about the student?
   - Ⓐ She is reluctant to ask the professor to make a special order.
   - Ⓑ She wants to end the conversation with the clerk.
   - Ⓒ She thinks the policy of the bookstore is unreasonable.
   - Ⓓ She is disappointed she can't buy the book immediately.

iBT Practice 02

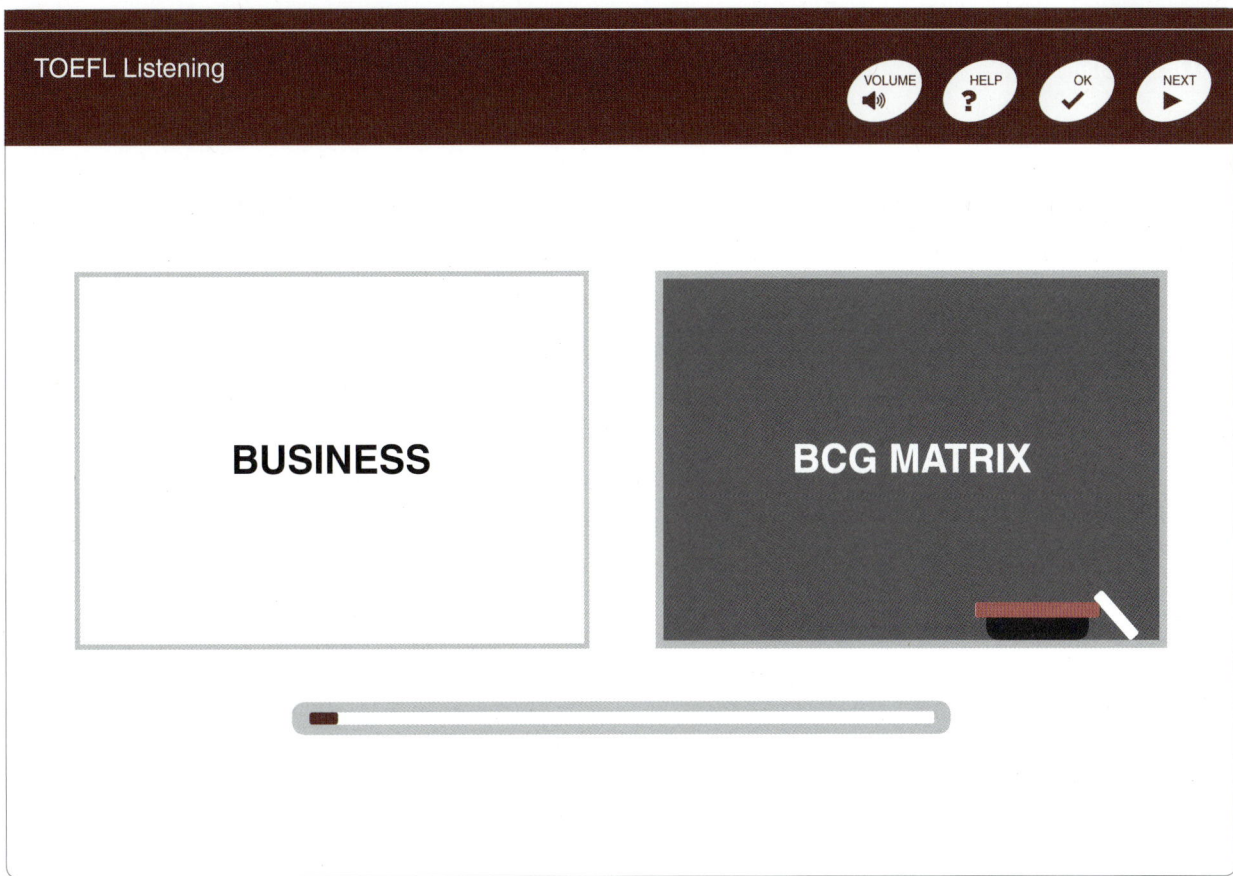

Note-Taking

TOEFL Listening

1. What is the lecture mainly about?
   - Ⓐ An explanation of a business planning model
   - Ⓑ The importance of business management strategies
   - Ⓒ An overview of recent investment trends
   - Ⓓ An analysis of common business mistakes

2. According to the professor, what are the factors that determine BCG Matrix categories?
   - Ⓐ Profit and loss
   - Ⓑ Consumer targets and cash distribution
   - Ⓒ Market growth and market share
   - Ⓓ Market size and cash allocation

3. What does the professor say about the weaknesses of the BCG Matrix?
   Click on 2 answers.
   - Ⓐ It is only applicable to big companies that invest large amounts of cash.
   - Ⓑ It narrowly defines the factors comprising a market.
   - Ⓒ The definition of its factors is controversial among analysts.
   - Ⓓ It treats each business unit as an independent body.

4. What is the professor's attitude toward the BCG Matrix?
   - Ⓐ He is interested in researching alternatives to it.
   - Ⓑ He doubts whether it can be applied to every company.
   - Ⓒ He is curious as to why its importance has decreased.
   - Ⓓ He recognizes its benefits in spite of its weaknesses.

Vocabulary Check

- [ ] rewild
- [ ] flora and fauna
- [ ] struggling
- [ ] ecosystem
- [ ] thrive
- [ ] intervention
- [ ] intriguing
- [ ] materialize
- [ ] hurdle
- [ ] justifiably

- [ ] assign
- [ ] dormitory
- [ ] make an exception

- [ ] resemblance
- [ ] sculptor
- [ ] predecessor
- [ ] commission
- [ ] embellish
- [ ] distinguishable
- [ ] portrayal
- [ ] as opposed to
- [ ] blemish
- [ ] wart
- [ ] portraiture

- [ ] glacial
- [ ] glacier
- [ ] basal
- [ ] rigid
- [ ] enhance
- [ ] immense
- [ ] overlie
- [ ] friction
- [ ] lubricant

- [ ] sophomore
- [ ] draw on
- [ ] conventional
- [ ] swing
- [ ] fist
- [ ] stamp
- [ ] clasp
- [ ] demonstration
- [ ] immerse

- [ ] mirror
- [ ] mimic
- [ ] activate
- [ ] provoke
- [ ] contagious

- [ ] troublesome
- [ ] evolution
- [ ] creationism
- [ ] organization
- [ ] organized
- [ ] get off
- [ ] road map
- [ ] when it comes down to
- [ ] virtually
- [ ] providing
- [ ] perspective

- [ ] regulate
- [ ] pineal gland
- [ ] induce
- [ ] circadian
- [ ] disrupt
- [ ] disruption
- [ ] shift
- [ ] jet-lag
- [ ] synthetic

- [ ] dietary
- [ ] supplement
- [ ] regain
- [ ] insomnia
- [ ] dosage

- [ ] fresco
- [ ] plaster
- [ ] pigment
- [ ] secco
- [ ] authentic
- [ ] integrate with
- [ ] meticulously
- [ ] expediently
- [ ] disguise

- [ ] intro
- [ ] out of stock
- [ ] bulletin board

- [ ] corporation
- [ ] market share
- [ ] assumption
- [ ] generation
- [ ] consumption
- [ ] elaboration
- [ ] signify
- [ ] unprofitable
- [ ] profitability
- [ ] attractiveness
- [ ] competitive advantage
- [ ] overlook
- [ ] impact
- [ ] interrelatedness
- [ ] diminish
- [ ] snapshot
- [ ] allocation

Vocabulary Review

A Choose the correct word for each definition.

> distinguishable   swing   dietary   portrayal   mimic   perspective

1. point of view: _____
2. able to be told apart: _____
3. to imitate the behavior of another: _____
4. the manner in which a thing is shown or described: _____
5. to move back and forth: _____

B Choose the best word or phrase to explain the underlined word.

1. If you overlook something, you _____ its importance.
   - A neglect
   - B criticize
   - C enhance
   - D confront

2. To induce a change means to _____ it.
   - A undergo
   - B realize
   - C prevent
   - D cause

3. If you immerse yourself in something, you become _____ it.
   - A able to do
   - B less interested in
   - C completely involved in
   - D increasingly aware of

4. You can embellish your cake by _____ it.
   - A immediately eating
   - B taking a picture of
   - C making comments about
   - D adding decorations to

C Choose the best word or phrase to complete each sentence.

1. If your ring is stuck on your finger, you can use cooking oil as a _____.
   - A supplement
   - B lubricant
   - C barrier
   - D preservative

2. She put on some makeup to cover her _____.
   - A blemish
   - B portraiture
   - C fist
   - D pigment

3. The professor didn't go into detail. I'm going to ask for some _____.
   - A assumption
   - B elaboration
   - C allocation
   - D attractiveness

4. The promised recovery failed to _____ and unemployment kept on rising.
   - A decline
   - B remain
   - C materialize
   - D associate

D Choose the correct word to complete each sentence.

1. I will be able to _____ on my work experience as a human resource manager. (apply / draw)
2. The professor tends to _____ off topic, but it's always an interesting digression. (get / turn)
3. The device is made of a(n) _____ steel frame for durability. (rigid / applicable)
4. The product you are looking for is out of _____, but we can order it. (step / stock)
5. Name recognition gives a company a(n) _____ advantage. (alternative / competitive)

E Choose the word that is closest in meaning to the underlined word.

1. This is an authentic two dollar bill.
   - Ⓐ fake
   - Ⓑ exchangeable
   - Ⓒ initial
   - Ⓓ genuine

2. You two must be brothers. I can see the resemblance.
   - Ⓐ similarity
   - Ⓑ familiarity
   - Ⓒ inheritance
   - Ⓓ relationship

3. The impact of the decision was immense.
   - Ⓐ unusual
   - Ⓑ tiny
   - Ⓒ huge
   - Ⓓ notable

4. This kind of behavior could provoke violence.
   - Ⓐ call upon
   - Ⓑ make up
   - Ⓒ bring about
   - Ⓓ hold back

5. This disease is highly contagious, so don't share your towel with others.
   - Ⓐ uncommon
   - Ⓑ infectious
   - Ⓒ undesirable
   - Ⓓ synthetic

F Choose the word that is the opposite of the underlined word.

1. He always cleans his house meticulously before his parents visit.
   - Ⓐ basically
   - Ⓑ carelessly
   - Ⓒ expediently
   - Ⓓ nervously

2. She refused to listen to new ideas and preferred conventional practices.
   - Ⓐ efficient
   - Ⓑ radical
   - Ⓒ traditional
   - Ⓓ predominant

3. When I give you the signal, activate the robot with this remote control.
   - Ⓐ strike
   - Ⓑ regain
   - Ⓒ disguise
   - Ⓓ stop

Actual Practice Test 2

Listening Section Directions

This section measures your ability to understand conversations and lectures in English. You will listen to 1 conversation and 2 lectures. You will hear each conversation or lecture only one time. After each conversation or lecture, you will answer some questions about it. The questions typically ask about the main idea and supporting details. Some questions ask about a speaker's purpose or attitude. Answer the questions based on what is stated or implied by the speakers.

You may take notes while you listen. You may use your notes to help you answer the questions. Your notes will not be scored. If you need to change the volume while you listen, click on the Volume icon at the top of the screen.

In some questions, you will see this icon: 🎧 This means that you will hear, but not see part of the question. Some of the questions have special directions. These directions appear in a gray box on the screen.

Most questions are worth one point. If a question is worth more than one point, it will have special directions that indicate how many points you can receive.

You must answer each question. After you answer, click on **Next**. Then click on **OK** to confirm your answer and go on to the next question. After you click on **OK**, you cannot return to previous questions.

Actual Practice Test 01

TOEFL Listening

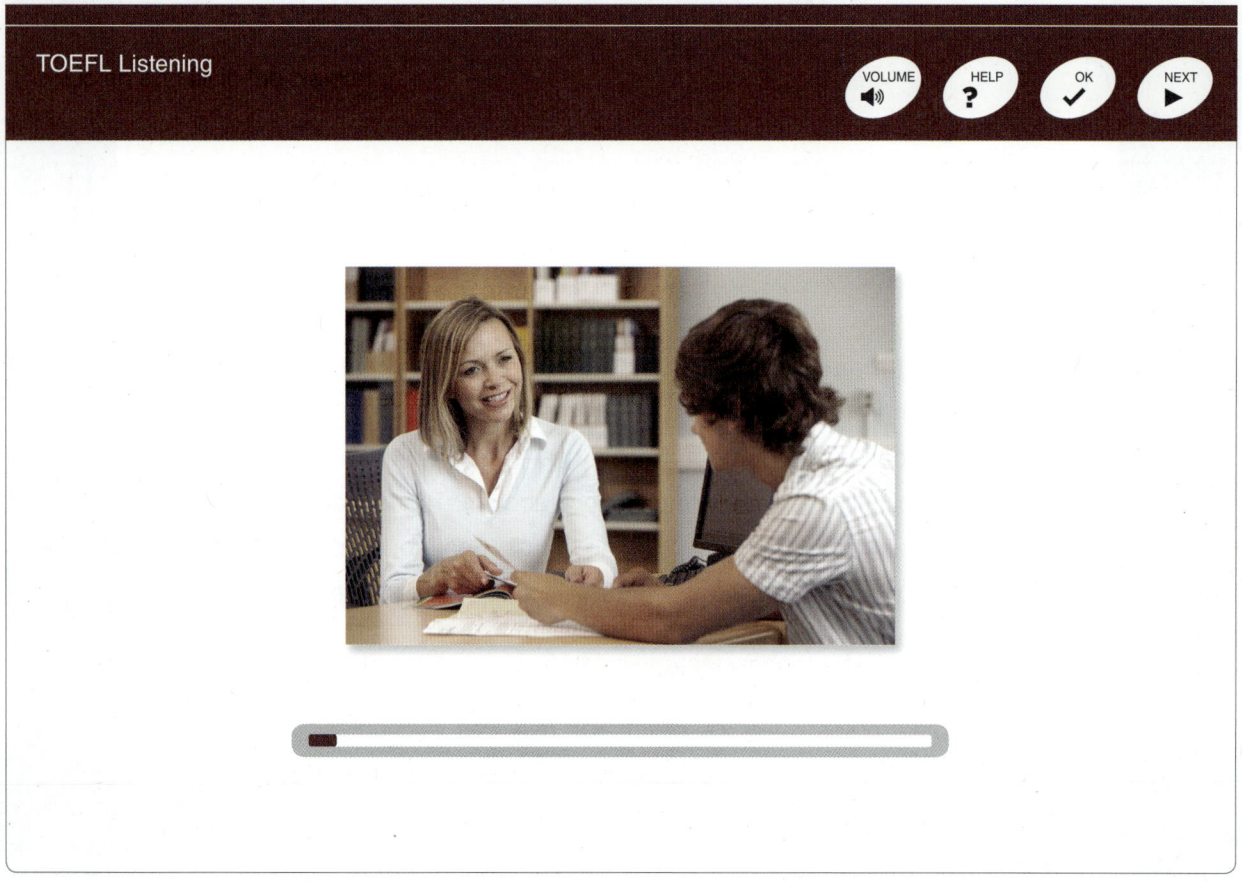

Note-Taking

TOEFL Listening

1. Why did the professor want to talk to the student?
   A To ask him to help her with a presentation
   B To give advice about his project for the seminar
   C To suggest that he take part in the seminar
   D To persuade him to go to graduate school

2. What is the student's first response to the professor's request?
   A He agrees with surprise.
   B He puts off making a decision.
   C He agrees with some reluctance.
   D He politely turns it down.

3. Why does the professor give the student the website address of the conference?
   A To help him have a better understanding of the seminar
   B To convince him to contact the person in charge of the seminar
   C To suggest that he should upload his paper onto the website
   D To request that he make a presentation about the conference

4. How does the professor feel about the student?
   A She worries about his future career.
   B She is disappointed with his paper.
   C She thinks he is a very competent student.
   D She is impressed with his enthusiasm about teaching.

Listen again to part of the conversation. Then answer the question.

5. Why does the professor say this:
   A To inform the student of other potential chances
   B To convince the student to accept her request
   C To indicate that the student did a tremendous job with his report
   D To express that she is uncomfortable with the student's decision

Actual Practice Test 02

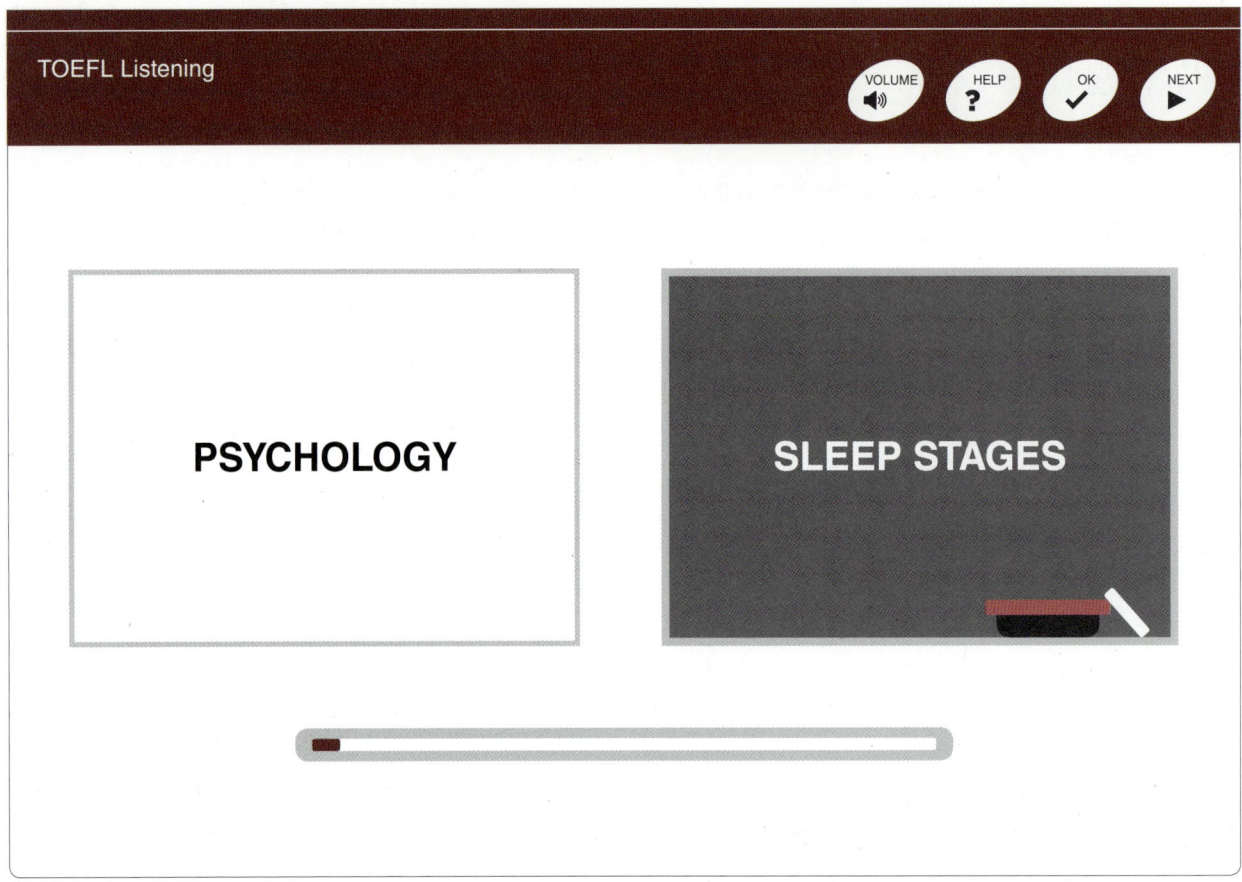

TOEFL Listening

6. What is the lecture mainly about?
   - A) An overview of typical sleep patterns
   - B) How dreaming affects brain activity
   - C) The difference between REM and non-REM sleep
   - D) The factors determining quality sleep

7. How does the professor introduce the sleep stages?
   - A) By emphasizing the importance of getting enough sleep
   - B) By mentioning a similarity in how most people sleep
   - C) By providing recent statistics on how long people sleep on average
   - D) By explaining how previous research on sleep was carried out

8. What does the professor say about non-REM sleep?
   - A) People are no longer aware of their environment.
   - B) It only happens during the deepest sleep.
   - C) There is a rise in the amount of brain activity.
   - D) It occurs in the first three stages of sleep.

9. Which of the following does NOT occur during REM sleep?
   - A) The body is unable to move.
   - B) Dreaming occurs.
   - C) Heart rate increases.
   - D) The brain produces delta waves.

Listen again to part of the lecture. Then answer the question.

10. What does the professor mean when he says this:
    - A) He thinks non-REM sleep has more to discuss.
    - B) He wants to maintain the focus of the lecture on REM sleep.
    - C) He believes the name "non-REM sleep" is clear.
    - D) He thinks the students are already familiar with the sleep cycles.

11. What does the professor imply when he says this:
    - A) A relaxed body falls asleep faster.
    - B) Continuous sleep cycles are the key to quality sleep.
    - C) People should get enough sleep to feel rested and refreshed.
    - D) Healthy people don't easily awaken while sleeping.

Actual Practice Test 03

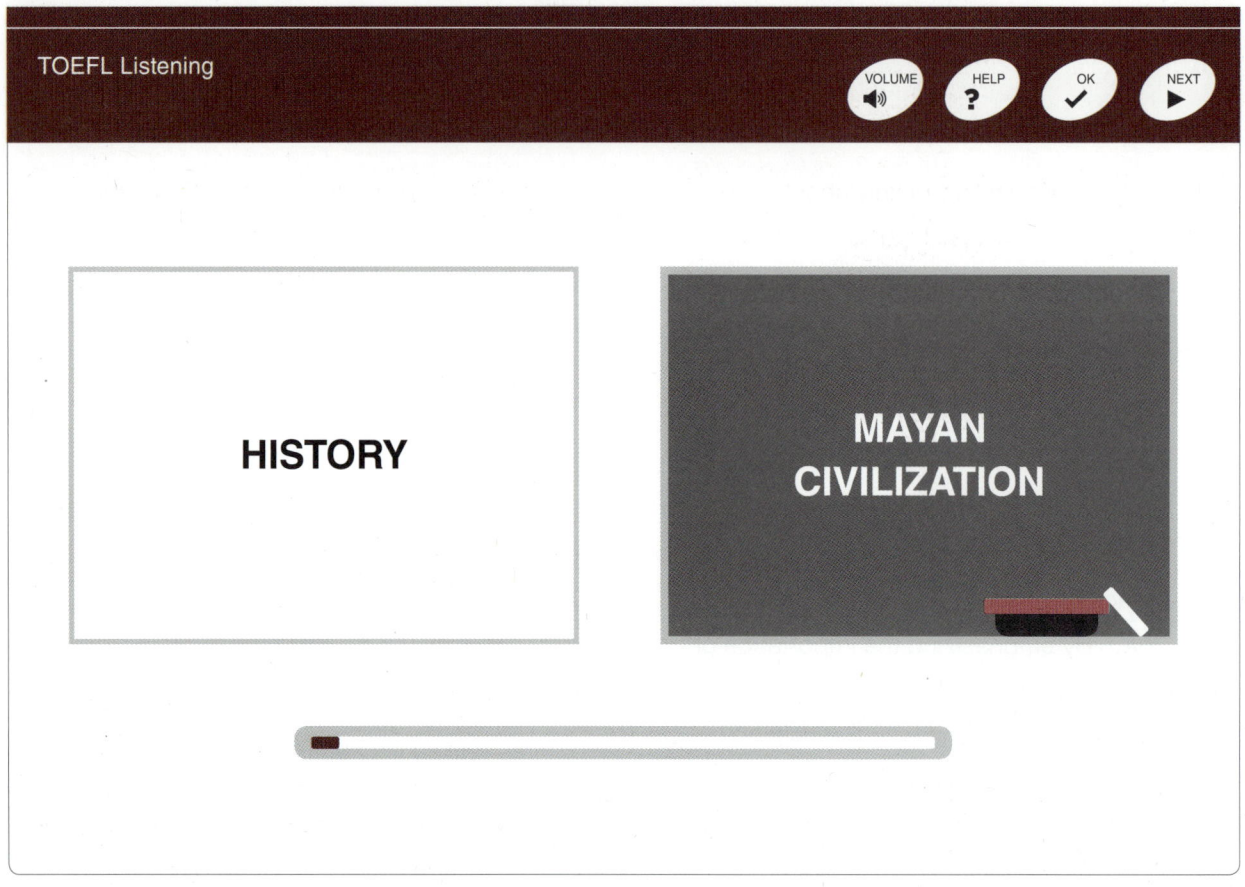

TOEFL Listening

12. What aspect of Mayan civilization does the professor mainly discuss?
    A) Its advanced techniques and practices
    B) Its superior astronomical technology
    C) Its reliance on a hunter-gatherer lifestyle
    D) Its relations with other North American tribes

13. How does the professor introduce the Mayan civilization?
    A) By describing how Mayans became interested in astronomy
    B) By outlining its technological advancements over time
    C) By showing a map of Mayans' migratory patterns in the Americas
    D) By contrasting Mayans with an image of nomadic Native Americans

14. According to the professor, what was the mathematical advancement of the Mayan civilization?
    Click on 2 answers.
    A) It was based on a base ten numeral system.
    B) It dealt with fairly large numbers.
    C) It understood and used zero.
    D) It had twenty symbols to represent numbers.

15. Which of the following is mentioned as a special function of Mayan constructions?
    A) They provided shelter from outside enemies.
    B) They displayed the passage of time during the year.
    C) They offered protection from natural disasters.
    D) They gathered public opinions about political issues.

16. What does the professor say about the Mayan writing system?
    A) It was borrowed from neighboring nations and elaborated.
    B) It was based on graphic symbols of animals and plants.
    C) It consisted of pictorial representations of the spoken language.
    D) It laid the foundation for the development of various literary genres.

Listen again to part of the lecture.
Then answer the question.

17. Why does the professor say this:
    A) To point out how creative the Mayans were in building structures
    B) To give a detailed explanation of the Mayan architecture principle
    C) To emphasize how the calendar system influenced Mayan architecture
    D) To indicate how structures were built to get maximum sunlight

PART C

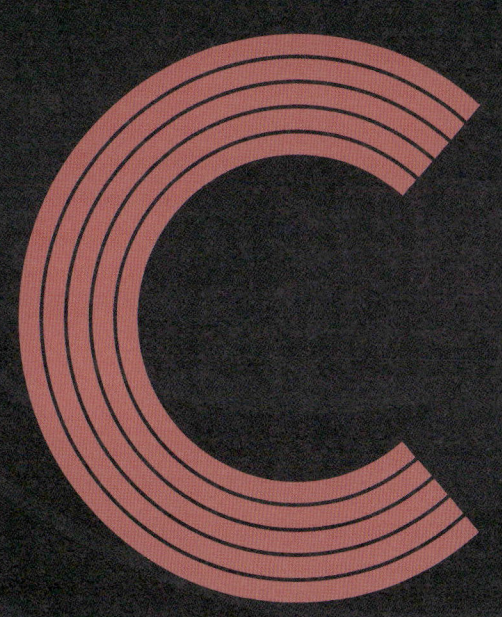

Connecting Information Questions

- **UNIT 05** ORGANIZATION
- **UNIT 06** CONNECTING CONTENT
- **UNIT 07** INFERENCE

UNIT 05 Organization

Introduction

- Organization questions ask about the relationship between a specific piece of information and the organization of the lecture as a whole. Essentially, the purpose is to identify how the main idea and its supporting explanation are organized and why the speaker has chosen this method of organization.
- These questions require a thorough understanding of the passage. Partial understanding of the passage is simply not sufficient to answer Organization questions.
- 0 to 1 question is given for each passage – generally lectures, not conversations.

Question Types

1. Question forms that ask about the overall organization of the lecture:
   - How is the lecture organized?
   - In what order does the professor explain the topic?

2. Question forms that ask about the relationship between a specific piece of information and the lecture as a whole:
   - Why does the professor mention X?

Strategy

1. Identify the point of the lecture and how the speaker supports the main idea. Take notes on the general flow of the lecture while paying attention to the following signal words.
   (1) Compare/contrast: in contrast, on the other hand, however, similarly, likewise
   (2) Cause/effect: because of, X is caused by Y, Y results from X, consequently
   (3) Exemplification: for example, for instance, such as, to illustrate
   (4) Chronology: first, second, next, then, later, previously, finally

2. Consider why the speaker has chosen to include specific pieces of information. When you are aware of the relationship between a specific detail and the lecture as a whole, it is much easier to recognize the speaker's motive for including certain details. Potential motives that commonly appear as answer choices are as follows: to emphasize, to introduce, to conclude, to describe, to suggest, to explain, to give an example.

Sample Question

TOEFL Listening

Professor

All right, let's talk about something called "anchoring." In terms of psychology, anchoring is a kind of cognitive bias that occurs in the brain during the decision-making process. What happens is that we are heavily influenced by the initial information we receive. As a result, we undervalue or even ignore any subsequent information that is conveyed. Retailers have recognized this behavior in their customers, and they definitely take advantage of it. We, um, we call this type of strategy "price anchoring." It works like this: Suppose a store plans to sell a shirt for $30. The shirt is marked at $50, but then this price is crossed out and $30 is written below it. This establishes $50 as the anchor price. Customers see this number first and accept that this is the true value of the shirt. As a result, the shirt's $30 price appears to be a real bargain.

How is the lecture organized?

Ⓐ A psychological strategy is discussed, followed by tips on how to resist it.
Ⓑ Two contrasting but related concepts are described in detail side by side.
Ⓒ A concept is introduced generally and then a specific use of it is explained.
Ⓓ The original meaning of a term is presented and compared to its modern usage.

Answer and Explanation
The lecture begins with the definition of a psychological concept. The professor then specifically explains how this concept is utilized by retailers. Therefore, the best answer choice to the question is Ⓒ.

Basic Drills

1 How is the lecture organized?

- Ⓐ The features of glaciers are explained.
- Ⓑ Various types of glacier are classified.
- Ⓒ The process of glacier formation is outlined.
- Ⓓ The effects of glaciers on land are described.

2 How does the professor introduce his explanation of tasting?

- Ⓐ By explaining the structure of a taste organ
- Ⓑ By emphasizing the importance of the tongue
- Ⓒ By showing the connection between taste buds and the brain
- Ⓓ By illustrating different kinds of taste

3 How does the professor organize the topic of stress and trauma?

- Ⓐ She classifies their various types.
- Ⓑ She analyzes their main causes.
- Ⓒ She outlines their development processes.
- Ⓓ She compares the differences between them.

4 Why does the professor mention a fruitcake?

- Ⓐ To emphasize the size of the initial universe
- Ⓑ To illustrate the concept of cosmic expansion
- Ⓒ To give an example of particles in the early universe
- Ⓓ To introduce a different theory of the cosmic beginning

5 How does the professor compare autobiographies and memoirs?

- Ⓐ By discussing their differences from fictional novels
- Ⓑ By contrasting their popularity among readers
- Ⓒ By giving examples of famous works of each
- Ⓓ By making statements about the time and focus of each

6 Why does the professor mention radiation sickness?

- Ⓐ To contrast the use of gamma rays and X-rays
- Ⓑ To explain how gamma radiation was discovered
- Ⓒ To support the point that gamma rays are highly dangerous
- Ⓓ To suggest that gamma rays have medical uses

Dictation

Listen and fill in the blanks.

1. Okay, so we know that glaciers begin to form when snow remains in the same area year-round, and where enough snow _____ _____ _____ _____ _____.

2. Gradually the grains grow and _____ _____ _____ _____ between them, causing the snow to slowly compact and increase in density.

3. At this point, it is about _____ _____ _____ _____ _____, but the process isn't complete.

4. Basically a receptor can respond to all tastes, but it _____ _____ _____ _____ _____ _____ ... sweet, sour, salty, or bitter.

5. So, when recognizing taste, the flavor dissolved in your saliva _____ _____ _____ _____ at the bottom of all the taste buds.

6. However, people who go through... erm... a traumatic experience are _____ _____ _____ _____ _____ because of the severity of the event.

7. The traumatic event _____ _____ _____ in their minds and impedes their ability to live their lives.

8. According to the theory, initially all of the matter and energy of space was contained, erm... _____ _____ _____ _____, like a fireball.

9. I mean... while an autobiography tends to _____ _____ _____ through a person's life, a memoir usually doesn't _____ _____ a chronological timeline.

10. So memoirs are more subjective and _____ _____ _____.

11. This penetrating property is what makes gamma rays _____ _____ _____.

12. Once they penetrate human tissue, they can cause DNA to change _____ _____ _____ _____ the genetic material of the cell.

13. Also, the... uhm... the gamma rays _____ _____ _____ _____ on human skin.

Listening Practice 01

ZOOLOGY

1 How is the lecture organized?
- Ⓐ It shows the change in attitudes from past to present and then lists benefits.
- Ⓑ It weighs the pros and cons of attitudes from both the past and present.
- Ⓒ It charts the historical step-by-step progression of human-animal relationships.
- Ⓓ It explains the benefits of pets in detail and presents an opposing view.

2 What is NOT mentioned as a benefit of owning a pet?
- Ⓐ Children can learn to be responsible.
- Ⓑ Parents become closer to their children.
- Ⓒ People can increase their social interactions.
- Ⓓ Homes are protected from unwanted visitors.

3 Why does the professor mention Gandhi?
- Ⓐ to present an opposing view from a respected figure
- Ⓑ to give a historical example of a famous animal lover
- Ⓒ to emphasize his point about human-animal relationships
- Ⓓ to show how attitudes have changed from the past to today

Dictation 01

Listen and fill in the blanks.

Professor: In the past, people had a very different attitude toward household pets than most of us do today. In essence, they were viewed _____ _____ _____ _____ possessions. It's not that people didn't form emotional attachments to them, but they _____ _____ _____ more for, um, practical purposes.

Student 1: Do you mean like the fact that dogs could protect your house?

Professor: Yes, exactly like that. Dogs had value because they _____ _____ _____ intruders or help control livestock. And cats would keep the household _____ _____ _____ and other vermin. Today, however, pets primarily _____ _____ _____ _____ _____. What do you think that is?

Student 1: Um... companionship? I mean, it seems like people _____ _____ _____ _____ their pets. You know, just taking them for walks or playing with them.

Professor: Correct. Almost _____ _____ _____ _____ members of the family, right? Which is exactly the way many modern people view their pets. They treat them like children, and _____ _____ they receive friendship and loyalty. Also, as any parent can tell you, pets are great with kids. They _____ _____ _____ and happy, and taking care of them can teach a child important lessons about responsibility. What's more, pets can _____ _____ _____ _____ other people in their community.

Student 2: I'm sorry, but I don't understand. How can pets do that?

Professor: Well, for example, dogs love going to the park, but their owners also _____ _____ _____ _____ _____ to meet and chat with other dog owners. So, ultimately, welcoming a pet into your home is _____ _____ _____. Interestingly, Gandhi once commented about that. He wrote that the relationship between man and beast should involve "_____ _____" rather than one taking advantage of the other. Like many great thinkers, he recognized the importance of _____ _____ _____ between humans and animals.

114

Listening Practice 02

1 What is the lecture mainly about?
- Ⓐ The characteristics of classical ballet
- Ⓑ Isadora Duncan's contributions to modern dance
- Ⓒ Popular music used in traditional ballet
- Ⓓ Various dance types developed by Isadora Duncan

2 Why does the professor mention the master composers?
- Ⓐ To explain how they reflected their feelings in the music
- Ⓑ To indicate what instrument they preferred to use for composing music
- Ⓒ To show how Duncan was different in her musical choices
- Ⓓ To emphasize their contribution to the development of modern dance

3 How did Isadora Duncan express natural movement?
Click on 2 answers.
- Ⓐ By wearing a loose costume with bare feet
- Ⓑ By imitating the motions of traditional ballet
- Ⓒ By using common human movements
- Ⓓ By creating dances to waltzes and polkas

Dictation 02

Listen and fill in the blanks.

Professor: Isadora Duncan was perhaps one of the most important dancers in the early twentieth century in America. People called her the mother of modern dance because she revolutionized dance _____ _____.

In the 1920s, ballet lacked the grace it has today – it was, umm... all acrobatics and gymnastics. Ballet dancers also _____ _____ _____ to their bodies such as corseted costumes and shoes that were too small. Duncan criticized these conventions for _____ _____ _____ and unnatural. So _____ _____ _____ _____ her toe shoes and wore a long, flowing Grecian gown to enhance the expressiveness of the human body.

Duncan also _____ _____ _____ _____ _____ the use of music. Traditionally, ballet scores like waltzes and polkas were the means of creating dances which _____ _____ _____ _____. However, Duncan believed dancers shouldn't think about music but should _____ _____ _____ _____ _____. For her, music was an inspirational element that brought excitement and emotional energy. So she _____ _____ _____ _____ _____ of the master composers – Beethoven, Chopin, Bach, and Schumann. Her unique approach certainly _____ _____ _____ _____ future dancers and opened up the world of _____ _____.

Isadora Duncan also emphasized moving dance away from _____ _____ _____ and toward more free-flowing forms of personal expression. She _____ _____ _____ _____ such as skipping and running, in her dance. With such motions she _____ _____ in her dancing. For example, she and her fellow dancers would move together _____ _____ _____ _____ _____ to imitate a person or animal breathing, making the whole stage seem alive. That's what made her dancing truly unique.

Listening Practice 03

1 What is the lecture mainly about?
- Ⓐ The composition of the food chain
- Ⓑ The importance of food chains in ecosystems
- Ⓒ The difference between herbivores and carnivores
- Ⓓ The factors affecting the shape of the food chain

2 How is the lecture organized?
- Ⓐ How the food chain is shaped is described.
- Ⓑ Different components in the food chain are listed with examples.
- Ⓒ The importance of each level in the food chain is compared.
- Ⓓ How environmental factors affect the food chain is explained.

3 What does the professor say about the decomposers?
- Ⓐ They use light to get energy.
- Ⓑ They live on the organisms that eat plants.
- Ⓒ They are placed in the middle of the food pyramid.
- Ⓓ They consume dead plants and animals.

Dictation 03

Listen and fill in the blanks.

Professor: The food chain is _____ _____ _____ of the feeding relationships between species in an ecological community. Today we'll examine some of the features that _____ _____ _____ _____ _____. Okay, let's start with the producers, which are at the bottom of the food chain. They... uhm... they can make their own food and include such organisms as plants and vegetables. The producers obtain energy _____ _____ _____ _____ sugars and starches through photosynthesis.

The... uhm... next link in the chain are the consumers. They cannot make food for themselves so instead survive by _____ _____ _____ _____. Scientists have classified three sublevels of consumer, the first of which, the primary consumers, are the herbivores. _____ _____ _____ _____ _____ _____, herbivores eat only plants. Secondary consumers eat the primary consumers. They are also called carnivores, which means "_____ _____." Lastly, the third consumers are called omnivores. Omnivores are organisms such as humans that _____ _____ _____ _____ _____.

_____ _____ _____ are the decomposers. These are mainly... uhm... bacteria and fungi that convert... uh... dead matter into gases such as carbon dioxide and nitrogen _____ _____ _____ _____ _____ the air, soil, or water. In other words, they play an important role _____ _____ _____ to be used again by producers.

Now, as you _____ _____ _____, the food chain is depicted as a pyramid. There are _____ _____ _____ _____ consumers, and far more herbivores than omnivores. This pattern is _____ _____ _____ _____.

iBT Practice 01

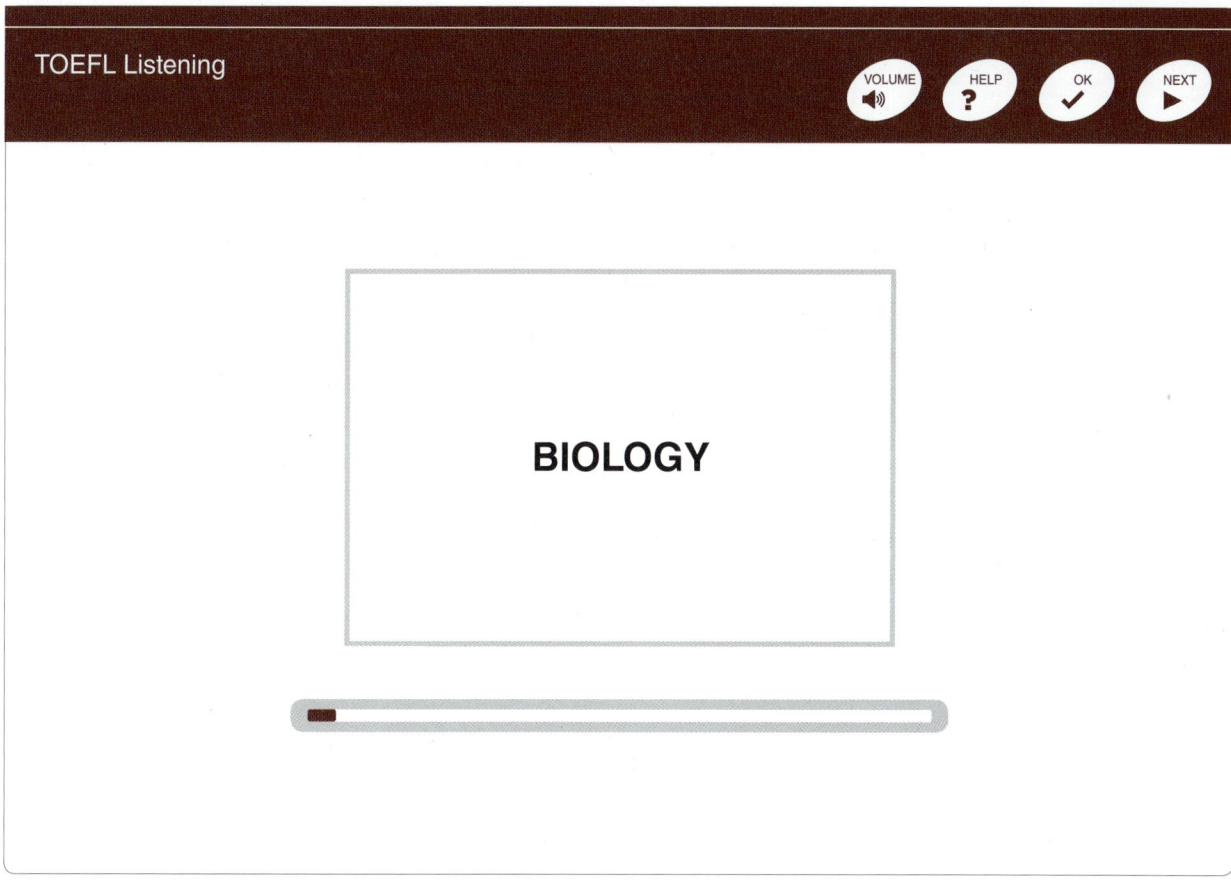

Note-Taking

TOEFL Listening

1. What is the lecture mainly about?
   - Ⓐ The relationship between heredity and allergies
   - Ⓑ The causes and symptoms of allergies
   - Ⓒ How our immune system works against allergens
   - Ⓓ Allergens causing fatal reactions in humans

2. How does the professor introduce the topic of allergies?
   - Ⓐ By giving an example of the most common allergy
   - Ⓑ By listing the symptoms of an allergic reaction
   - Ⓒ By comparing the body's normal response to an allergic reaction
   - Ⓓ By emphasizing the risk of an allergic reaction

3. Which of the following is NOT mentioned as a symptom of an allergy?
   - Ⓐ Runny nose
   - Ⓑ Itchy eyes
   - Ⓒ Rash on the skin
   - Ⓓ Interruption of blood flow

4. What does the professor mean when she says this: 🎧
   - Ⓐ Heredity only suggests the probability of allergy occurrence.
   - Ⓑ An allergic person is more likely to develop hereditary diseases.
   - Ⓒ Our immune system gets damaged while fighting allergens.
   - Ⓓ The same symptoms of allergy appear in both parents and their children.

iBT Practice 02

TOEFL Listening

CLIMATOLOGY

Note-Taking

TOEFL Listening

1. What is the lecture mainly about?
    - Ⓐ How the inclination of the Earth's axis changes
    - Ⓑ External causes of the Earth's climate change
    - Ⓒ What affects the rotation of the Earth
    - Ⓓ The relationship between the Sun and climate

2. How does the professor organize the lecture?
    - Ⓐ By comparing external factors with human activities
    - Ⓑ By providing an example of climate change
    - Ⓒ By explaining why the Earth's axis changes over time
    - Ⓓ By introducing various phenomena in outer space

3. According to the professor, what causes the difference between the same seasons?
Click on 2 answers.
    - Ⓐ Getting more sunlight in northern areas
    - Ⓑ The Earth's axis moving in a circle
    - Ⓒ Changes in the tilt of the Earth's axis
    - Ⓓ Different shapes of the Earth's orbit

4. What does the professor say about a result of the precession?
    - Ⓐ Winter will be much colder than before.
    - Ⓑ Winter and summer will be reversed.
    - Ⓒ Winter will appear only in the southern hemisphere.
    - Ⓓ Winter will be much shorter than summer.

Vocabulary Check

- in terms of
- psychology
- cognitive
- bias
- undervalue
- subsequent
- convey
- cross out
- a real bargain

- accumulate
- transform
- compress
- compression
- squeeze out
- compact
- density
- firn
- intermediate

- palate
- detector
- taste bud
- bump
- papilla
- receptor
- dissolve
- saliva
- stimulus

- trauma
- traumatic
- overwhelm
- cope
- vulnerable
- severity
- relive

- impede
- cosmic
- explosion
- initially
- condense
- particle
- embryonic

- autobiography
- memoir
- representation
- as a rule
- chronological
- adhere to
- objective
- viewpoint
- intimate
- subjective
- fictional
- general

- gamma ray
- penetrate
- hazard
- mess around with
- genetic
- alteration
- correlate with
- leukemia
- thermal
- radiation

- attachment
- scare away
- intruder
- livestock

- vermin
- companionship
- loyalty
- engaged
- win-win
- ultimately
- mutual

- revolutionize
- acrobatics
- gymnastics
- endure
- torturous
- restriction
- corseted
- convention
- literally
- Grecian
- score
- inspirational
- pave the way for
- interpretive

- ecological
- comprise
- organism
- convert
- starch
- photosynthesis
- classify
- herbivore
- carnivore
- omnivore
- decomposer
- fungus
- nitrogen

- release
- sustain
- substance
- immune system
- mobilize
- have to do with
- exaggerated
- allergen
- mite
- pollen
- symptom
- itchy
- ingest
- rash
- inject
- sting
- fatal
- heredity
- inherit
- tendency

- external
- tilt
- hemisphere
- latitude
- phase
- inclination
- inclined
- axis
- calculate
- elliptical
- complication
- spinning top
- wind
- precession
- reversed

PART C

UNIT 05 ORGANIZATION

Vocabulary Review

A Choose the correct word for each definition.

> elliptical   inherit   embryonic   subsequent   chronological   comprise

1. happening or coming after something else: _____
2. having an oval shape: _____
3. ordered in accordance with time: _____
4. in an early stage of development: _____
5. to receive a character or appearance from one's ancestors: _____

B Choose the best word or phrase to explain the underlined word.

1. If you adhere to the rules, you _____ them.
   - Ⓐ violate
   - Ⓑ establish
   - Ⓒ disagree with
   - Ⓓ stick to

2. If you make an alteration, you _____ something.
   - Ⓐ raise
   - Ⓑ adopt
   - Ⓒ change
   - Ⓓ achieve

3. A fatal illness can _____.
   - Ⓐ disappear suddenly
   - Ⓑ be passed to others
   - Ⓒ be treated without surgery
   - Ⓓ cause death

4. A herbivore eats _____.
   - Ⓐ only meat
   - Ⓑ only plants
   - Ⓒ meat and plants
   - Ⓓ no meat nor plants

C Choose the best word or phrase to complete each sentence.

1. His experiences as a soldier were a(n) _____. He still has nightmares.
   - Ⓐ endeavor
   - Ⓑ adventure
   - Ⓒ trauma
   - Ⓓ scheme

2. _____ I was interested, but now I think it's a bad idea.
   - Ⓐ Literally
   - Ⓑ Initially
   - Ⓒ Internally
   - Ⓓ Conclusively

3. Children are particularly _____ to violence on television.
   - Ⓐ intimate
   - Ⓑ appropriate
   - Ⓒ crucial
   - Ⓓ vulnerable

4. There is a machine that _____ old cars into small steel boxes.
   - Ⓐ compresses
   - Ⓑ overwhelms
   - Ⓒ sustains
   - Ⓓ revolutionizes

D Choose the correct word to complete each sentence.

1. They managed to scare the bears _____. (away / into)
2. Stop messing _____ with the lights. Leave them on. (against / around)
3. What does this mean in _____ of cost? (need / terms)
4. You should get lots of rest so your immune _____ can fight the virus. (action / system)
5. As the first female doctor, Blackwell _____ the way for many young women. (craved / paved)

E Choose the word that is closest in meaning to the underlined word.

1. Dust has been accumulating since the family moved out.
   - (A) piling up
   - (B) settling in
   - (C) falling down
   - (D) going away

2. He ignored conventions and did things his own way.
   - (A) phases
   - (B) standards
   - (C) advice
   - (D) agreements

3. This process converts the wind energy to heat energy.
   - (A) disrupts
   - (B) condenses
   - (C) triggers
   - (D) transforms

4. The pilot noticed the slight tilt of the aircraft.
   - (A) complication
   - (B) inclination
   - (C) disposition
   - (D) latitude

5. Parking on the sidewalk is a hazard to pedestrians.
   - (A) criterion
   - (B) density
   - (C) manner
   - (D) danger

6. Some houseplants can be poisonous if ingested by children or pets.
   - (A) eaten
   - (B) endured
   - (C) touched
   - (D) discovered

F Choose the word that is the opposite of the underlined word.

1. You should dissolve the pills in warm water before taking them.
   - (A) solidify
   - (B) release
   - (C) absorb
   - (D) melt

2. The new passport laws impeded our travel plans.
   - (A) ruined
   - (B) altered
   - (C) facilitated
   - (D) reversed

PART C

Connecting Information Questions

UNIT 05   ORGANIZATION
▶ UNIT 06   CONNECTING CONTENT
UNIT 07   INFERENCE

UNIT 06 Connecting Content

Introduction

- Connecting Content questions ask about the relationship between pieces of information in the passage.
- These questions require you to do one of the following three things:
  - Classify information
  - List information in order
  - Synthesize information in different parts of the passage and draw a conclusion
- Tables and charts may be included in questions that require you to classify or list information.
- 0 to 1 question is given for each passage – generally lectures, not conversations.

Question Types

1. Question forms that require you to classify or list:
   - In the lecture, the professor describes X and Y. Put the following events in order. Drag each sentence to the space where it belongs.
   - Indicate whether each of the following is X or Y. Click in the correct box for each sentence.

2. Question forms that require you to synthesize information and draw a conclusion:
   - What is the likely outcome of doing procedure X before procedure Y?

Strategy

1. Quickly note the lecture's main idea and flow.
   (1) When the lecture is a compare-and-contrast description of more than two ideas, Connecting Content questions might ask you to classify ideas from the lecture. In this case, find out the criteria based on which you can categorize the given information and sort the content.
   (2) When the lecture is historical or chronological, Connecting Content questions might ask you to list information in order. Pay attention to words that signal time and sequence.

2. Like Organization questions, Connecting Content questions cannot be answered with only a partial understanding of the lecture. Therefore, it is important to synthesize information scattered throughout the lecture and understand the overall flow.

Sample Question

TOEFL Listening

Professor

The term "traditional media" is used to refer to newspapers, magazines and television, as opposed to the newer forms of media known as "social media." Today I want to talk about some of the more meaningful differences between the two. We can start with content. With traditional media, content decisions are made by editorial teams, based on rather inflexible criteria. In the case of social media, such decisions are almost purely audience-driven. Basically, consumers of social media are given whatever they demand. This leads us to purpose. Educating the public is the primary goal of traditional media, which creates a one-way flow of information. This is in contrast to the interactive nature of social media, in which there is a significant amount of audience feedback and response. So which is better? I really don't know. But due to its ability to reach more people more quickly than traditional media ever could, social media appears to be the wave of the future.

Indicate whether each of the following is a characteristic of traditional media or social media. Click the correct box for each.

	Traditional media	Social media
Ⓐ It can spread both widely and quickly.		
Ⓑ Its information moves in a multi-directional flow.		
Ⓒ Its content is chosen by a fixed process.		
Ⓓ It seeks simply to deliver information to the masses.		

Answer and Explanation

The professor mentions three differences between traditional media and social media. First, he says traditional media content is based on *inflexible criteria*, while social media content is controlled by its audience. This tells us Ⓒ is a trait of traditional media. Next, he says traditional media information flows *from creator to audience*, while social media is *interactive*. This tells us Ⓑ is a trait of social media, while Ⓓ is a trait of traditional media. Finally, he says social media "*reach(es) more people more quickly than traditional media.*" This tells us that Ⓐ is a trait of social media.

Basic Drills

1 What has changed since last semester that would indicate that the woman has health insurance?

    Ⓐ She purchased an insurance policy.
    Ⓑ She paid her tuition.
    Ⓒ She is studying full time.
    Ⓓ She received a bursary.

2 In the lecture, the professor describes the two conditions of the tropical Pacific. Decide which of the following process is related to which condition.
Click in the correct box for each phrase.

	Non-El Niño condition	El Niño condition
Ⓐ Weakened westerly trade winds		
Ⓑ Higher surface level in the western Pacific		
Ⓒ Inactive upwelling in the eastern Pacific		
Ⓓ Enough nutrients in eastern waters		

3 In the lecture, the professor talks about the process of art appreciation. Put the following steps in order.
Drag each phrase to the space where it belongs.

    Ⓐ To identify the artist's objective or meaning of expression
    Ⓑ To evaluate the value of the artwork
    Ⓒ To analyze how the artwork is composed
    Ⓓ To examine visual aspects such as colors and shapes

1	
2	
3	
4	

4 Why does the professor say that the test won't be a problem?

(A) Because he understands the student's dilemma and will let her take it another time
(B) Because he had been planning to change the test date to the following Monday
(C) Because the test is relatively easy so the student will be able to study for it on the plane
(D) Because the test can be completed at home, so the student doesn't have to attend class to do it

5 In the lecture, the professor explains the neuroticism personality trait. Indicate whether each of the following is related to a high N score, a low N score, or neither.
Click in the correct box for each phrase.

	High N score	Low N score	Neither
(A) Easily irritated			
(B) Feeling calm and at ease			
(C) Generally feeling satisfied			
(D) Being anxious about many things			

6 In the lecture, the professor describes complete metamorphosis. Indicate whether each of the following is related to the larva, the pupa, or the adult stage.
Drag each sentence to the space where it belongs.

(A) Its structure transforms into adult form.
(B) Most of its life is spent eating.
(C) It emerges from its case fully developed.

Larva	Pupa	Adult

Dictation

Listen and fill in the blanks.

1. These winds _____ _____ _____ _____ _____ in the western Pacific, so that the surface level in the west is a half meter higher than in the east.

2. This cold water is nutrient-rich and _____ _____ _____ _____.

3. What I mean is, we should _____ _____ _____ _____ _____, including specific shapes, colors, and textures.

4. Now we include our emotions and thoughts, based upon what we observe... so our judgment shouldn't _____ _____ _____ _____, you know?

5. For example, questioning whether a work is an extraordinary example of a particular artistic style _____ _____ _____ _____ other works of the same style.

6. Now, the test... it won't be a problem because I was planning to _____ _____ _____ _____.

7. This uh... this trait is about the tendency to experience _____ _____ _____.

8. In other words, such people are _____ _____ _____ _____ ordinary situations as threatening, and minor frustrations as _____ _____.

9. Instead, those people show a relatively stable and _____ _____ _____ _____.

10. All these insects go through _____ _____ _____.

11. First, an adult female _____ _____ _____ _____ from which a small worm-like creature called a larva _____.

12. Most insects with complete metamorphosis spend _____ _____ _____ their lives in this humble larval form, _____ _____ _____ _____ eating and growing.

13. Once the change is complete, the pupa cover _____ _____ and the adult insect _____ _____.

Listening Practice 01

SERVICE ENCOUNTER

1 Why does the student visit the adviser?
- Ⓐ To get information about their sister school abroad
- Ⓑ To sign up for Spanish language courses
- Ⓒ To ask information about student exchange programs
- Ⓓ To schedule a meeting with the head of the language department

2 What is compared between structured and unstructured exchange programs?
- Ⓐ Admission requirements
- Ⓑ Features included in the package
- Ⓒ Potential countries for exchange
- Ⓓ Availability of a host family

3 What will the student probably do next?
- Ⓐ She will schedule an appointment with Dr. Sullivan.
- Ⓑ She will save up money for the unstructured program.
- Ⓒ She will speak with her Spanish teacher about the program.
- Ⓓ She will fill out the application form.

Dictation 01

Listen and fill in the blanks.

Academic adviser: What can I help you with?

Student: _____ _____ _____ _____ you knew of any student exchange programs... for Spain I mean. I'm doing pretty well in my Spanish class and I want to become fluent.

A: Yes, _____ _____ _____ _____, but you'll need to see Dr. Sullivan about that. _____ _____ _____ _____ the language department and he'd be the one with the application forms. Let me ask you... _____ _____ _____ _____ _____?

S: I'm a sophomore.

A: Good. It's best to _____ _____ _____ _____ _____ _____ rather than when you're getting close to graduation.

S: That makes sense.

A: Well, as far as I know, there are two options. One is _____ _____ _____. This is where you go to study at a sister school and you are provided with _____ _____ _____ _____ _____.

S: What's the other option?

A: With the other option _____ _____ _____ _____ _____ the sister school, but you have to find your own place to live and pay for your own meals. Of course, this is _____ _____ _____.

S: I see. I think it would _____ _____ _____ _____ _____ the extra money for the structured program. After all, I've never been to Spain before. It might be hard to find housing and stuff, especially before _____ _____ _____ _____ _____. What is the difference in price, anyway?

A: Unfortunately, I don't know _____ _____. You'll have to talk to Dr. Sullivan for more information because he has a lot _____ _____ _____ _____ _____ with the exchange programs.

S: Okay, well, I really _____ _____ _____.

134

Listening Practice 02

BIOLOGY

CAMOUFLAGE

1 What does the professor mainly discuss?
- Ⓐ Ways predators approach their prey
- Ⓑ Methods that animals use to avoid being seen
- Ⓒ How an animal's environment affects its survival
- Ⓓ How animals change their appearance to attract mates

2 How is the lecture organized?
- Ⓐ A few reasons why animals use camouflage are explained.
- Ⓑ Different types of animal camouflage are classified with examples.
- Ⓒ The environmental conditions for animal survival are compared.
- Ⓓ Various color patterns of animals are described.

3 Indicate whether each of the following is related to coloration, countershading, or disguise.
Drag each sentence to the space where it belongs.

- Ⓐ Animals have lightly colored lower bodies.
- Ⓑ Animals take on the appearance of another object.
- Ⓒ Animals change color to match their habitat.

Coloration	Countershading	Disguise

Dictation 02

Listen and fill in the blanks.

Professor: Another _____ _____ _____ is camouflage. Some animals use it _____ _____ _____ _____ _____, while others use it to avoid predators. Generally, camouflage works by, um... by allowing an animal to _____ _____ _____ _____ _____. So... who can give me an example of an animal that uses camouflage?

Student: How about leopards? The _____ _____ _____ _____ _____ sort of blend in with the light and shadows of the grass. It makes them really hard to see.

P: Right. _____ _____ _____ and many animals rely on their coloration for camouflage. You know, animals that live in the snow are often white, while ones that live in the desert _____ _____ _____ _____ _____. Other animals, like leopards, rely on multi-colored patterns... sometimes spots, sometimes stripes... to make their bodies resemble _____ _____ _____ _____ _____ around them.

Another type of color-based camouflage is _____ _____ _____ countershading. Many fish, for example, are darkly colored on top and lighter underneath. By _____ _____ _____ _____ – with sunshine above and dark shadows below – this type of coloration makes fish difficult _____ _____ _____ _____ _____.

And some animals _____ _____ as camouflage, a technique we call mimicry. This means they appear to _____ _____ _____ _____ _____, either an object or another kind of animal. In trees, for example, you'll find some insects that resemble leaves and others that resemble twigs. _____ _____ _____ when predators approach, they seem to be part of the tree.

Listening Practice 03

1 What is the lecture mainly about?
- Ⓐ The effects of knights on French literature
- Ⓑ Differences between medieval and modern literature
- Ⓒ The origins of chivalric literature
- Ⓓ Popular styles of literature in medieval France

2 According to the professor, what caused a change of themes between the two styles of chivalric literature?
- Ⓐ The beginning of the medieval period
- Ⓑ The end of a series of epic wars
- Ⓒ The demand for more fantasy stories
- Ⓓ The lack of interest in valiant knights

3 Indicate whether each of the following refers to chansons de geste or chivalric romances.
Click in the correct box for each sentence.

	Chansons de geste	Chivalric romances
Ⓐ They were generally sung by performers.		
Ⓑ They focused on emotions like love.		
Ⓒ They were usually written by famous figures.		
Ⓓ They were about epic battles.		

Dictation 03

Listen and fill in the blanks.

Professor: During the medieval period, French literature _____ _____ _____ _____ _____ that we refer to as chivalric literature. Now, can anybody tell me what the two, um, predominant forms of French chivalric literature were?

Student: Um, I'm not sure but... romance?

P: Yes, chivalric romance. That's one... but do you know _____ _____ _____ chivalric romances? Anybody? [pause] Before chivalric romances, there were the chansons de geste, which means "_____ _____ _____ _____" in old French. These epic poems _____ _____ _____ the late eleventh century, with chivalric romance coming along about... well, about one hundred years later. Now, the, um, line between these two styles is _____ _____ _____ _____ _____, but we can identify some basic contrasting characteristics.

For example, the chansons de geste _____ _____ _____ _____ _____ by performers known as troubadours, but chivalric romances were designed to be read in private _____ _____ _____ _____. And while the writers of these chivalric romances were mostly well-known figures, most early chansons de geste were _____ _____.

And as for theme... well, chansons de geste usually _____ _____ _____ _____ _____ and their courage, perhaps because there were major wars in French military history, such as the Crusades. The intent was _____ _____ _____ among their listeners, but as the Crusades ended, romance _____ _____ _____ _____ _____ _____. While the, um... the chivalric romances also revolved around valiant knights, the genre focused more on themes of courtly love and _____ _____ _____ _____.

iBT Practice 01

Note-Taking

TOEFL Listening

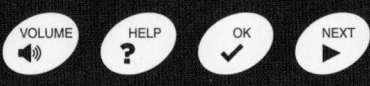

1. Why does the student try to enter the building?
   - (A) She is trying to find her stolen wallet.
   - (B) She needs to get her ID card reissued.
   - (C) She requires permission to use her ID card.
   - (D) She wants to replace her cafeteria card.

2. Why did the student think it's possible to enter the building without an ID card?
   - (A) Because she's a new student
   - (B) Because she read it was possible on a notice
   - (C) Because many students were allowed to do so before
   - (D) Because she is a university employee

3. Indicate whether each of the following helped the student get into the building.
   Click in the correct box for each item.

	Yes	No
(A) Passport		
(B) Cafeteria card		
(C) Class schedule		
(D) Driver's license		
(E) Student ID number		

Listen again to part of the conversation. Then answer the question.

4. What can be inferred about the student?
   - (A) She is annoyed with the guard because he took so much time.
   - (B) She is wondering about the guard's attitude toward her.
   - (C) She doesn't think the guard is glad.
   - (D) She is relieved because the problem is solved.

iBT Practice 02

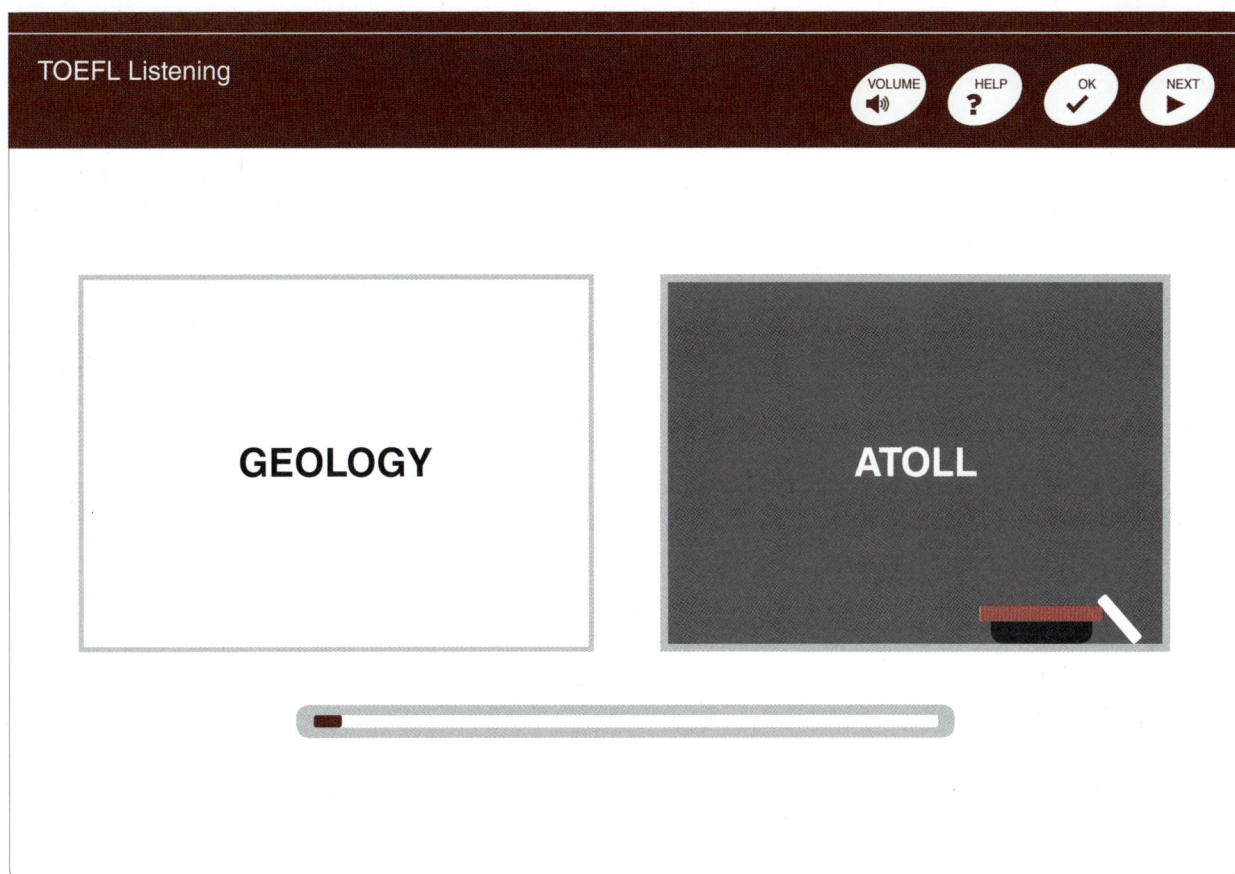

Note-Taking

TOEFL Listening

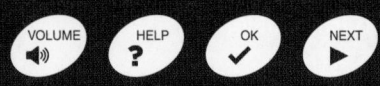

1. What does the professor mainly discuss?
   - A The difference between atolls and islands
   - B The formation of South Pacific islands
   - C The composition of different types of reefs
   - D The process by which atolls are created

2. What does the professor say about the explanation of atoll formation?
   - A It has been scientifically proven since Darwin suggested the idea.
   - B Darwin organized the voyage through the South Pacific to prove it.
   - C It is a widely accepted theory based on the observations of Darwin.
   - D There was a heated argument about it between Darwin and other geologists.

3. Put the following steps in order.
   Drag each sentence to the space where it belongs.
   - A Volcanic activity occurs under the sea.
   - B Corals continue to grow upward as an island sinks.
   - C A fringing reef surrounds a volcanic island.
   - D An island sinks leaving the reef and lagoon above sea level.

1	
2	
3	
4	

Listen again to part of the lecture. Then answer the question.
4. Why does the professor say this: 🎧
   - A To explain the main idea of a theory
   - B To correct a mistaken statement she made
   - C To offer a definition for a difficult word
   - D To make a transition to a new subject

Vocabulary Check

- [ ] as opposed to
- [ ] inflexible
- [ ] criteria
- [ ] in contrast to
- [ ] interactive

- [ ] bug
- [ ] insurance
- [ ] policy
- [ ] credit
- [ ] relief

- [ ] tropical
- [ ] trade wind
- [ ] pile up
- [ ] westerly
- [ ] upwelling
- [ ] drift

- [ ] appreciate
- [ ] texture
- [ ] analyze
- [ ] symmetrical
- [ ] asymmetrical
- [ ] prevailing
- [ ] cloud
- [ ] apparent
- [ ] evaluate
- [ ] extraordinary
- [ ] acquaintance

- [ ] take-home

- [ ] trait
- [ ] neuroticism
- [ ] emotionality
- [ ] frustration

- [ ] get stressed out
- [ ] relatively
- [ ] stable

- [ ] metamorphosis
- [ ] developmental
- [ ] larva
- [ ] larval
- [ ] hatch
- [ ] humble
- [ ] pupa
- [ ] cocoon
- [ ] crack
- [ ] crawl

- [ ] structured
- [ ] sister school
- [ ] hook sb up with sth
- [ ] get sth down

- [ ] camouflage
- [ ] sneak up
- [ ] prey
- [ ] predator
- [ ] blend in with
- [ ] coloration
- [ ] countershading
- [ ] offset
- [ ] detect
- [ ] disguise
- [ ] mimicry
- [ ] twig

- [ ] medieval
- [ ] dominate
- [ ] chivalric
- [ ] predominant

- [ ] deed
- [ ] epic
- [ ] blurred
- [ ] troubadour
- [ ] anonymously
- [ ] the Crusades
- [ ] intent
- [ ] revolve around
- [ ] valiant
- [ ] courtly love

- [ ] temporary
- [ ] exceptional
- [ ] identification
- [ ] identity
- [ ] get through
- [ ] mess
- [ ] by any chance
- [ ] punch
- [ ] verify
- [ ] reissue

- [ ] atoll
- [ ] enclose
- [ ] lagoon
- [ ] put forth
- [ ] reef
- [ ] barrier reef
- [ ] fringing reef
- [ ] coral
- [ ] subsidence
- [ ] crust
- [ ] atop
- [ ] skeleton
- [ ] encircle
- [ ] placid

Vocabulary Review

A Choose the correct word for each definition.

> interactive   verify   skeleton   extraordinary   subsidence   offset

1. a condition whereby something sinks to a lower level: _____
2. exceptional; beyond the norm: _____
3. to counterbalance: _____
4. requiring people to talk with each other or do things together: _____
5. the frame of bones that provides support for an animal body: _____

B Choose the best word or phrase to explain the underlined word.

1. If one thing is in contrast to another, it is very _____ it.
    - Ⓐ different from
    - Ⓑ similar to
    - Ⓒ matching with
    - Ⓓ superior to

2. If something is symmetrical, it is _____.
    - Ⓐ upside down
    - Ⓑ the same on both sides
    - Ⓒ perfectly round
    - Ⓓ one of a kind

3. We tend to get stressed out when we are _____.
    - Ⓐ on vacation
    - Ⓑ under pressure
    - Ⓒ not feeling well
    - Ⓓ getting enough exercise

4. If you do something anonymously, you _____.
    - Ⓐ do it by accident
    - Ⓑ consider others first
    - Ⓒ don't give your name
    - Ⓓ don't get paid

C Choose the best word or phrase to complete each sentence.

1. I _____ a faint smell of perfume when she entered the room.
    - Ⓐ detected
    - Ⓑ expressed
    - Ⓒ encountered
    - Ⓓ delivered

2. Charles was a man of settled habits and _____ routine.
    - Ⓐ demanding
    - Ⓑ training
    - Ⓒ workout
    - Ⓓ inflexible

3. You have to be twenty-one to get in. Do you have any _____?
    - Ⓐ insurance
    - Ⓑ identification
    - Ⓒ credits
    - Ⓓ textures

4. He was severely injured, but now he is in a _____ condition in hospital.
    - Ⓐ humble
    - Ⓑ harsh
    - Ⓒ central
    - Ⓓ stable

D Choose the correct word to complete each sentence.

1. Some animals preserve food to ensure that they can get _____ the winter. (around / through)
2. This book _____ around three friends who live together in a dormitory. (revolves / stands)
3. The chameleon _____ in perfectly with its background. (combines / blends)
4. In most parts of the world, mammals sit _____ the food chain. (atop / beside)
5. Are you from Britain by any _____? (accident / chance)

E Choose the word that is closest in meaning to the underlined word.

1. The swimmer suddenly realized that he had been encircled by sharks.
   - Ⓐ attracted
   - Ⓑ surrounded
   - Ⓒ noticed
   - Ⓓ bitten

2. What criteria are used for assessing a student's ability?
   - Ⓐ principles
   - Ⓑ methods
   - Ⓒ medications
   - Ⓓ data

3. The woman put forth an interesting theory.
   - Ⓐ dismissed
   - Ⓑ suggested
   - Ⓒ concluded
   - Ⓓ discovered

4. In the Middle Ages, it was the predominant opinion that the Earth was flat.
   - Ⓐ spectacular
   - Ⓑ suspicious
   - Ⓒ medieval
   - Ⓓ prevailing

5. My intent was not to cause any harm.
   - Ⓐ deed
   - Ⓑ disguise
   - Ⓒ purpose
   - Ⓓ relief

F Choose the word that is the opposite of the underlined word.

1. He received a medal to reward him for his valiant deed.
   - Ⓐ immoral
   - Ⓑ frivolous
   - Ⓒ selfish
   - Ⓓ cowardly

2. The change in class time is temporary. Normal hours will resume next week.
   - Ⓐ permanent
   - Ⓑ optional
   - Ⓒ optimal
   - Ⓓ inconvenient

3. The sea is placid today.
   - Ⓐ calm
   - Ⓑ rough
   - Ⓒ shallow
   - Ⓓ blurred

PART C

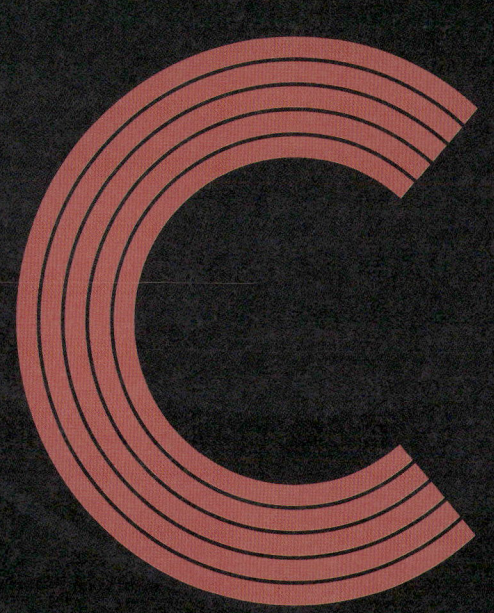

Connecting Information Questions

UNIT 05   ORGANIZATION
UNIT 06   CONNECTING CONTENT
▶ UNIT 07   INFERENCE

UNIT 07 Inference

Introduction

- Inference questions ask you either to make inferences or draw conclusions based on information in the passage.
- Occasionally, the given question will appear in Replay format, requiring you to listen to a certain section of the passage again.
- 0 to 1 question is given for each passage.

Question Types

- What will the student probably do next?
- What does the professor imply about X?
- What can be inferred about X?
- What does the professor imply when he/she says this: 🎧

Strategy

1. Make logical inferences based on the overall context.
   This type of question usually asks about suggestions or implications related to the main idea or theme of the conversation or lecture. Therefore, you need to consider what might be logically inferred based on the passage's main idea.

2. Draw conclusions based on information mentioned in the conversation or lecture.
   Such conclusions must be logical and based only on the information in the passage, not on outside information.

3. In many cases, incorrect answer choices include words and phrases mentioned in the conversation or lecture. Select the correct answer choice that contains information indirectly stated in the passage.

Sample Question

TOEFL Listening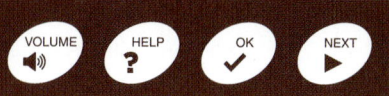

Professor

But there is a more essential factor influencing metabolic rate. Warm-blooded animals generate heat from inside their bodies, but they… well, they unfortunately lose it through their skin. This means that the amount they lose is related to its… to the animal's uhm… surface area, although the amount of heat they require is related to the volume of the animal. Think about small mammals. Their surface area per unit is much greater than large mammals, you must realize. This means that they lose heat at a faster rate. Therefore, the smallest mammals have to continuously eat so as to generate enough energy to maintain their body heat. To do this, they have to eat high-energy food, like meat or insects. Their bodies process this food quickly, and this means that they have to uhm… breathe very fast and have a very fast heart beat.

What can be inferred about small mammals?

- Ⓐ They have to eat food very fast to make their heart beat fast.
- Ⓑ They have greater surface areas from which they generate necessary heat.
- Ⓒ They lose little amounts of heat because of the small size of their bodies.
- Ⓓ They have fast metabolism rates to regulate their body temperatures.

Answer and Explanation

The professor mentions how small mammals lose heat faster than large ones because the former have greater surface areas per unit; they must intake more energy in order to maintain their body heat. Based on this information, we can infer that compared to large mammals, small mammals have a higher metabolism for maintaining their body heat. The best answer choice to the question is choice Ⓓ.

- Ⓐ is incorrect because the fact that small mammals having higher metabolisms was mentioned but it does not mean that they eat faster.
- Ⓑ Body heat is lost through the skin but we don't know whether it generates heat.
- Ⓒ The information in this choice is the opposite of what the professor said: small mammals lose body heat faster from having greater surface areas per unit.

Basic Drills

1 What does the professor offer to do to solve the problem?

- A She will have Matt moved to a different group.
- B She will grade the entire group on the final results.
- C She will speak to the student who is not contributing.
- D She will change the grading process for future projects.

2 What can be inferred about the number of fossil plant stomata?

- A It reflects the evolution of trees in the high mountains.
- B It shows that CO2 concentration was a lot higher in the past.
- C It indicates the amount of CO2 in the air when the fossilized leaf was alive.
- D It proves that fossils have nothing to do with the elevation of land surfaces.

3 What does the professor imply when he says this: 🎧

- A Farmed salmon isn't edible because of the waste and farm chemicals.
- B Salmon fisheries aren't contributing to a healthy and balanced diet.
- C Waste and chemicals produced by salmon contaminate seafood.
- D Salmon farming is not environmentally sustainable.

4 What can be inferred about the student?

- A She sent the email to sign up for the three-meal plan.
- B She sent the email after the 5th of the month.
- C She will have three meals per day next month.
- D She can't afford the three-meal plan bill.

5 What can be inferred about tragic heroes according to Aristotle?

- A Due to their greed, they commit crimes and meet with disaster.
- B They are genuinely admirable, but misfortune strikes them.
- C Despite their noble nature, their own decisions lead to their downfall.
- D They facilitate emotional cleansing through blind accidents.

6 What can be inferred about early feudalism in France?

- A Feudal government reduced royal authority.
- B Feudal order was against liberalism.
- C A king was not needed in feudalism.
- D The government existed based on military power.

Dictation

Listen and fill in the blanks.

1. Okay, so uhm... Dr. McElwain, a field museum scientist, has developed a new method of understanding the _____ _____ _____ _____ _____ by observing the stomata of plants.

2. Stomata, which as we know are _____ _____ on the surface of leaves, _____ _____ _____ necessary gases, including uhm, carbon dioxide for photosynthesis.

3. With historical and modern collections of uhm, let me see... oh yes... California black oak leaves, which grow _____ _____ _____ _____ _____ altitudes, she proved her new method is effective with a much _____ _____ _____ than existing methods.

4. First, salmon in fish farms are _____ _____ containing large amounts of fish _____ _____ _____ _____.

5. When these new kinds of salmon escape from the farm, they have harmful effects on the ocean's ecosystem _____ _____ _____ or attacking original species.

6. Aristotle suggested tragic heroes must be essentially admirable to _____ _____ _____ _____ _____ or emotional cleansing, like a catharsis.

7. After all, a genuinely tragic downfall can't ever really be purely a matter of _____ _____ _____ _____ _____.

8. In feudal systems, a ruler offered fighters control of a unit of land _____ _____ _____ _____ _____.

9. The individual or individuals who accepted this land became a vassal, and the man _____ _____ _____ became his lord.

10. This means that while individual barons, dukes, earls, and so forth _____ _____ _____ _____ _____ to the king or a centralized noble family, there was no strong _____ _____ to prevent them from having more power than the king.

Listening Practice 01

OFFICE HOURS

1 What is the student's problem?
  A She is struggling to understand some marketing terms.
  B She is thinking about changing her career plans.
  C She is unhappy with the company she is working for.
  D She is having difficulty choosing a company to work for.

2 Why does the student hesitate to make up her mind?
  A Because the car company is appealing in terms of its reputation
  B Because the advertising firm pays a small salary
  C Because the car company provides a better position
  D Because the advertising firm offers a more promising future

3 What will the student probably do next?
  A Write a new version of her resume
  B Accept the offer of the advertising firm
  C Quit her part-time job at the car company
  D Request permission to change her major

Dictation 01

Listen and fill in the blanks.

Student: Can I come in, Professor Ryan?

Professor: Of course, Rachel. Have a seat.

S: Thank you. I, um, I wanted to talk to you about my internship this summer. I have _____ _____ _____ _____, but I'm not sure which way to go.

P: What are your options?

S: Well, they're _____ _____ _____, but one is with an advertising firm and the other is with a car company. Right now _____ _____ _____ the advertising firm.

P: Why's that?

S: Because I'm really interested in advertising. It's such an exciting field, and there're so many _____ _____ _____ _____... It's really something I'd like to _____ _____ _____.

P: That sounds reasonable to me. So, er... why are you _____ _____ _____ _____ _____?

S: Well... because the car company is National Motors. They're one of the biggest companies in the country. And it _____ _____ _____ _____ _____ _____ my resume after I graduate.

P: I see. But... well, I'd advise you to _____ _____ _____. Just talking to you for a few minutes, I can see that you're really _____ _____ _____.

S: I am. But it's a... small firm and not very well-known.

P: I understand, Rachel, but you shouldn't be so, um, so concerned about _____ _____ _____ _____ impressive names. This might be your last chance to _____ _____ _____ _____ advertising. What if you _____ _____ _____ _____?

S: You're right. I've _____ _____ _____ _____. Thanks for your advice, Professor.

P: I'm glad I could help.

154

Listening Practice 02

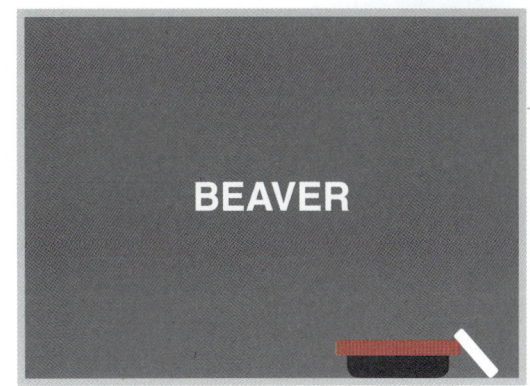

1 What is the lecture mainly about?
- Ⓐ Recent efforts to protect European beavers
- Ⓑ The important ecological role of beavers
- Ⓒ Ecological concerns caused by beavers
- Ⓓ The life cycle of the North American beaver

2 What does the professor say about beaver dams?
- Ⓐ They help reduce the number of foreign species.
- Ⓑ They supply enough water during drought periods.
- Ⓒ They reduce soil erosion of the surrounding area.
- Ⓓ They improve water quality by creating wetlands.

Listen again to part of the lecture. Then answer the question.

3 What can be inferred about beavers?
- Ⓐ They have recently been threatened by human activities.
- Ⓑ They don't affect human home construction any longer.
- Ⓒ They are not always favored by local residents.
- Ⓓ They are often included in transportation planning.

Dictation 02

Listen and fill in the blanks.

Professor: Another animal _____ _____ _____ _____ and plays an important ecological role is the beaver. Beavers, of course, are large rodents that spend _____ _____ _____ _____ _____ _____ in the water. They are best known as ecosystem engineers because of their _____ _____ _____ _____ _____ in rivers. These dams create ponds, which give beavers a place to live that is _____ _____ _____ and near food sources. Because of their dam making, beaver populations have a heavy impact on their environments. _____ _____ _____ _____ _____, they could potentially cause great harm. But in their natural habitats of North America and Europe, beaver dams and ponds _____ _____ _____ _____ in the health of our rivers and streams. For instance, when heavy rains occur, beaver ponds impound water, and then the dams gradually _____ _____ _____ _____. In this way, beaver dams _____ _____ _____ _____ _____ just like human dams. Additionally, they slow down the flow of water, _____ _____ _____ erosion of the land surrounding rivers. And most importantly, beaver dams play a role in forming wetlands. These wetlands develop in and around abandoned beaver ponds, _____ _____ _____ _____ _____ for many rare as well as common species. And that is _____ _____ biodiversity and the well-being of the entire ecosystem.

Well, of course, the beaver dams _____ _____ _____ _____ _____ the plans of humans; they occasionally affect property and disrupt transportation. But because of their importance to our ecosystem, it is necessary we, er... we should _____ _____ _____.

Listening Practice 03

1. What is the lecture mainly about?
   - Ⓐ Literature of the colonial period
   - Ⓑ A popular author from India
   - Ⓒ An influential detective novel
   - Ⓓ Popular modern mystery novels

2. According to the professor, what does the moonstone's curse represent?
   - Ⓐ The hostility toward British colonialism
   - Ⓑ The beginning of the mystery genre
   - Ⓒ The treasure that Britain took from India
   - Ⓓ The attitude of writers during the colonial period

Listen again to part of the lecture. Then answer the question.

3. What does the professor imply when he says this: 🎧
   - Ⓐ He doesn't believe the idea has become common.
   - Ⓑ The idea was copied from another book.
   - Ⓒ He hadn't heard about the idea before he read the book.
   - Ⓓ The idea was new when the book was written.

Dictation 03

Listen and fill in the blanks.

Professor: The novel we'll be looking at today is _____ _____ _____ _____ the forerunner of the modern detective story. It is of course *Wilkie Collins' The Moonstone*, written in 1868. It _____ _____ a young English woman _____ _____ _____ a large valuable diamond for her eighteenth birthday. During her birthday party the diamond is stolen. _____ _____ _____ _____ _____ it was originally taken from India and that... um, _____ _____ _____ _____ and disaster will strike anyone who possesses it.

The significance of the novel is that it introduced a number of aspects that are now considered _____ _____ of modern mystery novels. For example um... heroes and villains that are now _____ _____ _____ _____ _____.

It also featured so-called common plot settings and situations... you know, like _____ _____ and a large number of suspects.

Student: I'm sorry, Professor Irving, but a book about a cursed jewel? I've read that kind of story a million times.

P: Well... cursed jewels weren't a cliché until Collins wrote this novel, and really... he _____ _____ _____ _____ _____ many ideas that have become common. And The Moonstone is far more than just a story about a cursed jewel. We _____ _____ _____ _____ when this book was written and what was going on in the world. The age of colonialism had reached India, where the British were taking _____ _____ _____ _____. The moonstone symbolizes one of those Indian assets taken by the British, so its curse can be thought of as _____ _____ the imperialist invaders.

iBT Practice 01

TOEFL Listening

Note-Taking

TOEFL Listening

1. Why does the student go to see the professor?
   - Ⓐ To discuss the first draft of her report
   - Ⓑ To ask for tips on conducting her project
   - Ⓒ To share data on people's walking habits
   - Ⓓ To get advice about her grant application

2. What is the research subject of the student?
   - Ⓐ What makes Chicago a pedestrian-friendly city
   - Ⓑ The considerations involved in urban planning
   - Ⓒ How to control the volume of traffic in Chicago
   - Ⓓ The environmental changes caused by expanding urban areas

3. What does the professor advise the student to do?
   - Ⓐ Rewrite the whole proposal
   - Ⓑ Change the arrangement of the contents
   - Ⓒ Add more explanation about the topic
   - Ⓓ Get rid of the private information part

4. What does the professor imply about the grants committee?
   - Ⓐ They often lack knowledge of the project details.
   - Ⓑ They don't want to read personal information.
   - Ⓒ They are mainly influenced by the project details.
   - Ⓓ They remember most of the applications they receive.

iBT Practice 02

TOEFL Listening

ZOOLOGY

Note-Taking

TOEFL Listening

1. What aspect of crocodiles does the professor mainly discuss?
   - Ⓐ Interesting behavior patterns
   - Ⓑ Unique organs and their function
   - Ⓒ Camouflage in wetlands
   - Ⓓ Underwater hunting ability

2. According to the professor, what can the alligator's skin detect?
   - Ⓐ Smell
   - Ⓑ Light
   - Ⓒ Pressure
   - Ⓓ Electricity

3. What can be inferred about the ISOs?
   - Ⓐ They sense water vibration such as a splash on the surface.
   - Ⓑ They help crocodiles and alligators to see more clearly with their eyes.
   - Ⓒ They pick up changes in light and help crocodiles and alligators to respond.
   - Ⓓ They can detect saltiness of water in which crocodiles and alligators live.

Listen again to part of the lecture. Then answer the question.

4. Why does the professor say this: 🎧
   - Ⓐ To introduce the intended purpose of the experiment
   - Ⓑ To remind the students of differences between crocodiles and alligators
   - Ⓒ To make the students do experiments in the laboratory
   - Ⓓ To keep focusing on the main subject of the lecture

Vocabulary Check

- ☐ metabolic
- ☐ generate
- ☐ volume
- ☐ mammal

- ☐ assign
- ☐ motivate

- ☐ elevation
- ☐ stoma
- ☐ altitude
- ☐ come up with
- ☐ fossil
- ☐ estimate

- ☐ fishery
- ☐ transmit
- ☐ genetically modified
- ☐ settle
- ☐ sediment
- ☐ underlying

- ☐ regulation

- ☐ influential
- ☐ admirable
- ☐ genuine
- ☐ compassion
- ☐ cleansing
- ☐ catharsis
- ☐ downfall
- ☐ causation
- ☐ authentic
- ☐ fatal
- ☐ blind accident

- ☐ feudalism
- ☐ feudal
- ☐ in exchange for
- ☐ vassal
- ☐ grant
- ☐ swear
- ☐ arrangement
- ☐ baron
- ☐ duke
- ☐ earl

- ☐ internship
- ☐ lean
- ☐ component
- ☐ resume
- ☐ passionate
- ☐ blow

- ☐ inhabit
- ☐ ecological
- ☐ rodent
- ☐ habitat
- ☐ vital
- ☐ impound
- ☐ erosion
- ☐ wetland
- ☐ abandon
- ☐ crucial
- ☐ biodiversity

- ☐ forerunner
- ☐ detective
- ☐ curse
- ☐ villain
- ☐ stereotypical
- ☐ suspect

- ☐ cliché
- ☐ colonialism
- ☐ asset
- ☐ revenge
- ☐ imperialist
- ☐ invader

- ☐ insight
- ☐ pedestrian
- ☐ invaluable
- ☐ reorganize
- ☐ on the right track
- ☐ adjust

- ☐ coloration
- ☐ dimple
- ☐ integumentary
- ☐ sensory
- ☐ saltiness
- ☐ desperately
- ☐ illuminate
- ☐ perceive
- ☐ stimulate
- ☐ ground-up
- ☐ odor
- ☐ lap
- ☐ swamp
- ☐ blurry

Vocabulary Review

A Choose the correct word for each definition.

> blurry   catharsis   stereotypical   stimulate   abandon   volume

1. the amount of space a thing takes up: _____
2. to leave behind; to give up claim on: _____
3. the process of letting out strong feelings: _____
4. to cause a thing to activate: _____
5. conforming to a fixed image or idea: _____

B Choose the best word or phrase to explain the underlined word.

1. If you inhabit a place, you _____.
   - Ⓐ flee it
   - Ⓑ surround it
   - Ⓒ live there
   - Ⓓ work there

2. If something is vital, it is _____.
   - Ⓐ essential
   - Ⓑ worthwhile
   - Ⓒ advantageous
   - Ⓓ conventional

3. If you are a pedestrian, you are _____.
   - Ⓐ driving
   - Ⓑ cycling
   - Ⓒ walking
   - Ⓓ pedaling

4. If you illuminate a room, you _____.
   - Ⓐ paint it brightly
   - Ⓑ clean it up
   - Ⓒ close the blinds
   - Ⓓ turn the lights on

C Choose the best word or phrase to complete each sentence.

1. I love the sound of waves _____ at the seashore.
   - Ⓐ lapping
   - Ⓑ diminishing
   - Ⓒ settling
   - Ⓓ expanding

2. Streamside plants hold soil and help prevent _____.
   - Ⓐ sediment
   - Ⓑ erosion
   - Ⓒ coloration
   - Ⓓ regulation

3. I need to update my _____ because I'm going to start looking for a new job.
   - Ⓐ internship
   - Ⓑ resume
   - Ⓒ grant
   - Ⓓ assets

4. The story was about an angry man who sought _____ on the man who killed his wife.
   - Ⓐ reliance
   - Ⓑ explanation
   - Ⓒ justice
   - Ⓓ revenge

D Choose the correct word to complete each sentence.

1. I was confused but she helped me get on the right _____. (track / board)
2. I'll leave my car with you in _____ for your truck. (exchange / trade)
3. These tomatoes are really big because they are _____ modified. (genetically / artificially)
4. She _____ her chance of making it to the finals with that mistake. (blew / got)
5. She tried to come up _____ another excuse for breaking the appointment. (to / with)

E Choose the word that is closest in meaning to the underlined word.

1. I estimated the distance to be about a hundred kilometers.
   - Ⓐ guessed   Ⓑ measured   Ⓒ doubted   Ⓓ confirmed
2. The disease is transmitted through the air.
   - Ⓐ cured   Ⓑ tested   Ⓒ spread   Ⓓ strengthened
3. He was self-centered and didn't feel any compassion for other people.
   - Ⓐ affection   Ⓑ sympathy   Ⓒ cleansing   Ⓓ discontent
4. This model was a forerunner to the more popular model we use today.
   - Ⓐ imitation   Ⓑ predecessor   Ⓒ descendant   Ⓓ original
5. I didn't perceive any change in his condition.
   - Ⓐ notice   Ⓑ believe   Ⓒ invoke   Ⓓ impound

F Choose the word that is the opposite of the underlined word.

1. She's very passionate about her work because she wants to make a difference.
   - Ⓐ defensive   Ⓑ competent   Ⓒ illogical   Ⓓ indifferent
2. The Internet is an invaluable educational tool if managed properly.
   - Ⓐ intellectual   Ⓑ expensive   Ⓒ worthless   Ⓓ portable
3. He will be remembered as an admirable man.
   - Ⓐ influential   Ⓑ unimportant   Ⓒ wealthy   Ⓓ despicable

Actual Practice Test

Listening Section Directions

This section measures your ability to understand conversations and lectures in English. You will listen to 1 conversation and 2 lectures. You will hear each conversation or lecture only one time. After each conversation or lecture, you will answer some questions about it. The questions typically ask about the main idea and supporting details. Some questions ask about a speaker's purpose or attitude. Answer the questions based on what is stated or implied by the speakers.

You may take notes while you listen. You may use your notes to help you answer the questions. Your notes will not be scored. If you need to change the volume while you listen, click on the Volume icon at the top of the screen.

In some questions, you will see this icon: 🎧 This means that you will hear, but not see part of the question. Some of the questions have special directions. These directions appear in a gray box on the screen.

Most questions are worth one point. If a question is worth more than one point, it will have special directions that indicate how many points you can receive.

You must answer each question. After you answer, click on **Next**. Then click on **OK** to confirm your answer and go on to the next question. After you click on **OK**, you cannot return to previous questions.

Actual **Practice Test 01**

Note-Taking

TOEFL Listening

1. Why does the student visit his professor?
   - Ⓐ He wants to discuss his grades.
   - Ⓑ He wants to ask for assistance with his assignment.
   - Ⓒ He wants advice about his business career.
   - Ⓓ He wants feedback on the interview project.

2. Why does the student mention his high school newspaper?
   - Ⓐ To explain why he's going to be a reporter after graduation
   - Ⓑ To make sure his professor will purchase a subscription
   - Ⓒ To ask if he can be excused from his assignment
   - Ⓓ To indicate his confidence in conducting an interview

3. What is the student's research project?
   - Ⓐ Conducting an interview with a businessperson
   - Ⓑ Contributing an article to a local newspaper
   - Ⓒ Writing an essay about his career aspirations
   - Ⓓ Reading articles in the weekly business paper

4. How is the student's attitude toward searching through a newspaper changed?
   - Ⓐ Doubtful → Positive
   - Ⓑ Hopeful → Disappointed
   - Ⓒ Bored → Interested
   - Ⓓ Reluctant → Depressed

Listen again to part of the conversation. Then answer the question.

5. What can be inferred about the professor?
   - Ⓐ She wants the student to learn a little bit more about interview skills.
   - Ⓑ She doubts the student will be a successful businessperson.
   - Ⓒ She is ready to help the student with the research assignment.
   - Ⓓ She thinks the student will be motivated by being reminded of his future.

Actual Practice Test 02

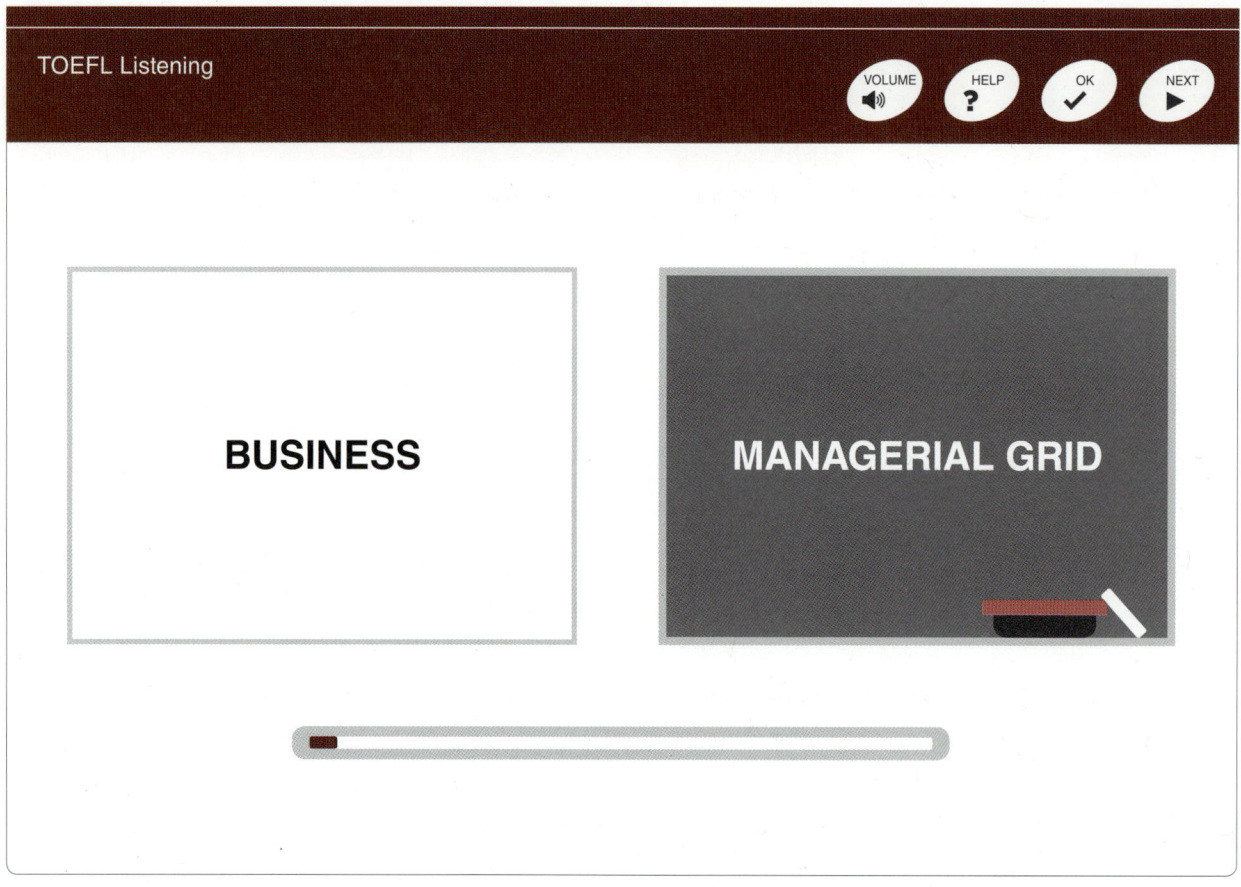

Note-Taking

TOEFL Listening

6. What is the lecture mainly about?
   - Ⓐ The most effective way to accomplish goals in the business world
   - Ⓑ How to keep a balance between people and production
   - Ⓒ General decision making patterns of leading companies
   - Ⓓ Types of leadership style and their characteristics

7. What are the two dimensions to identify leader styles in the managerial grid?
   Click on 2 answers.
   - Ⓐ Effort for self-development
   - Ⓑ Concern for relationships
   - Ⓒ Orientation to achieving goals
   - Ⓓ Ability to deal with risks

8. Which of the following is NOT mentioned as a characteristic of authoritarian leaders?
   - Ⓐ They are also called the "produce or perish" type.
   - Ⓑ They sometimes fail to employ a coercive attitude.
   - Ⓒ They focus highly on production needs.
   - Ⓓ They usually blame other people when facing problems.

9. What can be inferred about middle-of-the-road leaders?
   - Ⓐ They create a friendly atmosphere but don't allow cooperation.
   - Ⓑ They are task-oriented people, focusing on overall achievement.
   - Ⓒ They achieve good results in their tasks despite their lack of courage.
   - Ⓓ They seem ideal at first and then prove somewhat disappointing.

10. According to the professor, which leadership styles are the least and most successful?

	Least successful	Most successful
Ⓐ	Country club leaders	Team leaders
Ⓑ	Country club leaders	Authoritarian leaders
Ⓒ	Impoverished leaders	Team leaders
Ⓓ	Impoverished leaders	Authoritarian leaders

Listen again to part of the lecture.
Then answer the question.

11. What can be inferred about the professor?
    - Ⓐ He is sure this leadership type is the perfect one.
    - Ⓑ He thinks the title reflects the leadership style quite well.
    - Ⓒ He believes country clubs are very popular with leaders.
    - Ⓓ He thinks leaders should pay more attention to security and comfort.

Actual Practice Test 03

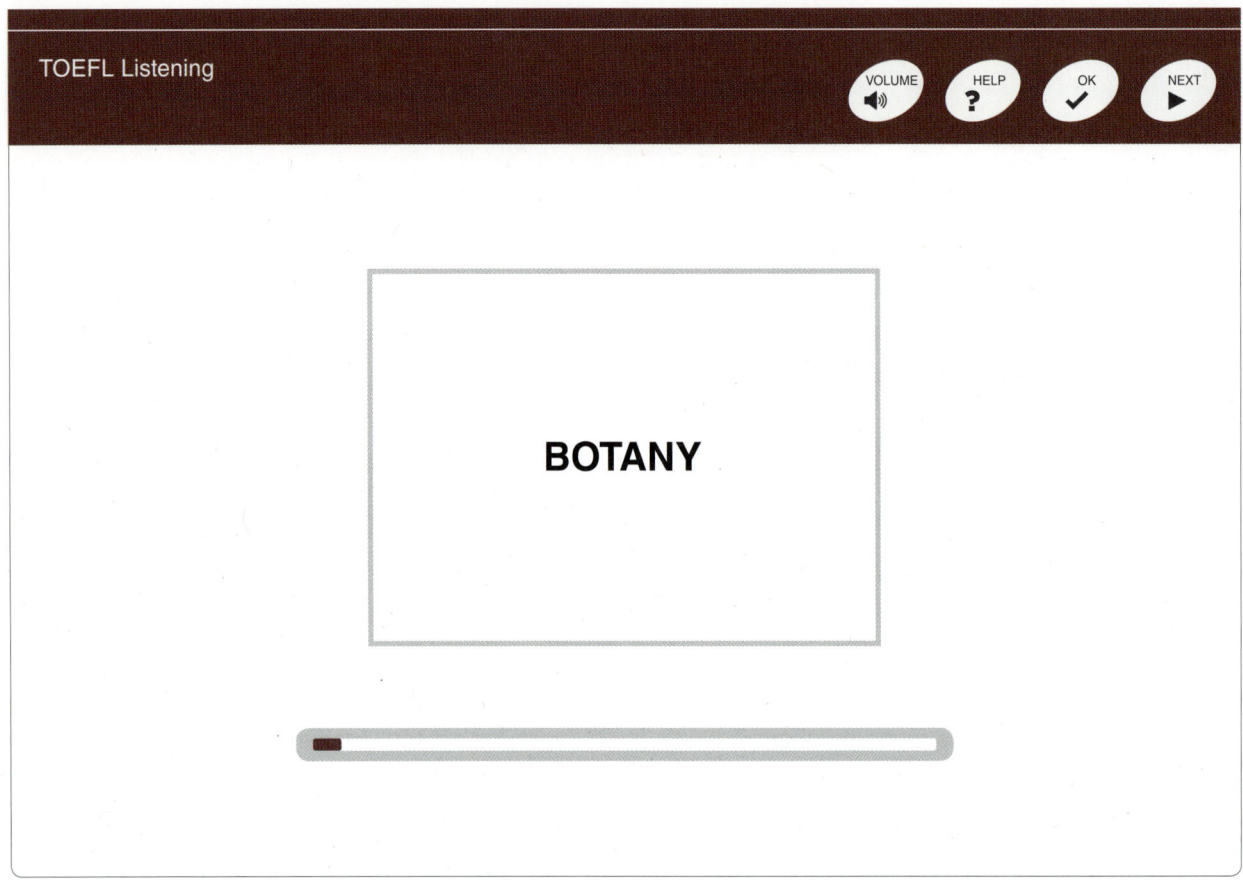

TOEFL Listening

12. What is the lecture mainly about?
    A) The condition and process of flower fossilization
    B) The finding of flower fossils and its significance
    C) An overview of how flowers evolved over millions of years
    D) A look at the methods botanists use to find fossils

13. According to the professor, why are fossilized flowers so rare?
    Click on 2 answers.
    A) Because flower fossils are extremely small
    B) Because flower fossils have been charcoalified
    C) Because scientists don't look for flower fossils
    D) Because scientists focus only on pollinators

14. What does the professor say about the charcoalified process?
    A) It started with intense heat and ended with rain.
    B) It hardened flowers and protected them from water.
    C) It made flowers sink to the bottom of wetlands.
    D) It prevented flowers from being washed into the marsh.

15. According to the professor, what are the possible explanations for the small size of flower fossils?
    Click on 2 answers.
    A) Big flowers were swept away by heavy rains.
    B) Ancient flowers were originally small and evolved into larger ones later.
    C) Flowers dried up and became small during fossilization.
    D) In forest fires, small flowers were able to survive better than big flowers.

16. Why does the professor mention insects inside flower fossils?
    A) To explain how insects worked in the fossilized flowers
    B) To describe various types of plant reproduction in detail
    C) To provide a new approach to research into the evolution of insects
    D) To introduce the significance of flower fossils found in New Jersey

Listen again to part of the lecture.
Then answer the question.

17. What can be inferred about the professor?
    A) She is surprised by the unexpected question.
    B) She is confused about the student's opinion.
    C) She disagrees with the student's assumption.
    D) She thinks the student misunderstands the lecture.

Practice TOEFL iBT

Listening Section

Listening Section Directions

This section measures your ability to understand conversations and lectures in English. You will listen to 1 conversation and 2 lectures. You will hear each conversation or lecture only one time. After each conversation or lecture, you will answer some questions about it. The questions typically ask about the main idea and supporting details. Some questions ask about a speaker's purpose or attitude. Answer the questions based on what is stated or implied by the speakers.

You may take notes while you listen. You may use your notes to help you answer the questions. Your notes will not be scored. If you need to change the volume while you listen, click on the Volume icon at the top of the screen.

In some questions, you will see this icon: 🎧 This means that you will hear, but not see part of the question. Some of the questions have special directions. These directions appear in a gray box on the screen.

Most questions are worth one point. If a question is worth more than one point, it will have special directions that indicate how many points you can receive.

You must answer each question. After you answer, click on **Next**. Then click on **OK** to confirm your answer and go on to the next question. After you click on **OK**, you cannot return to previous questions.

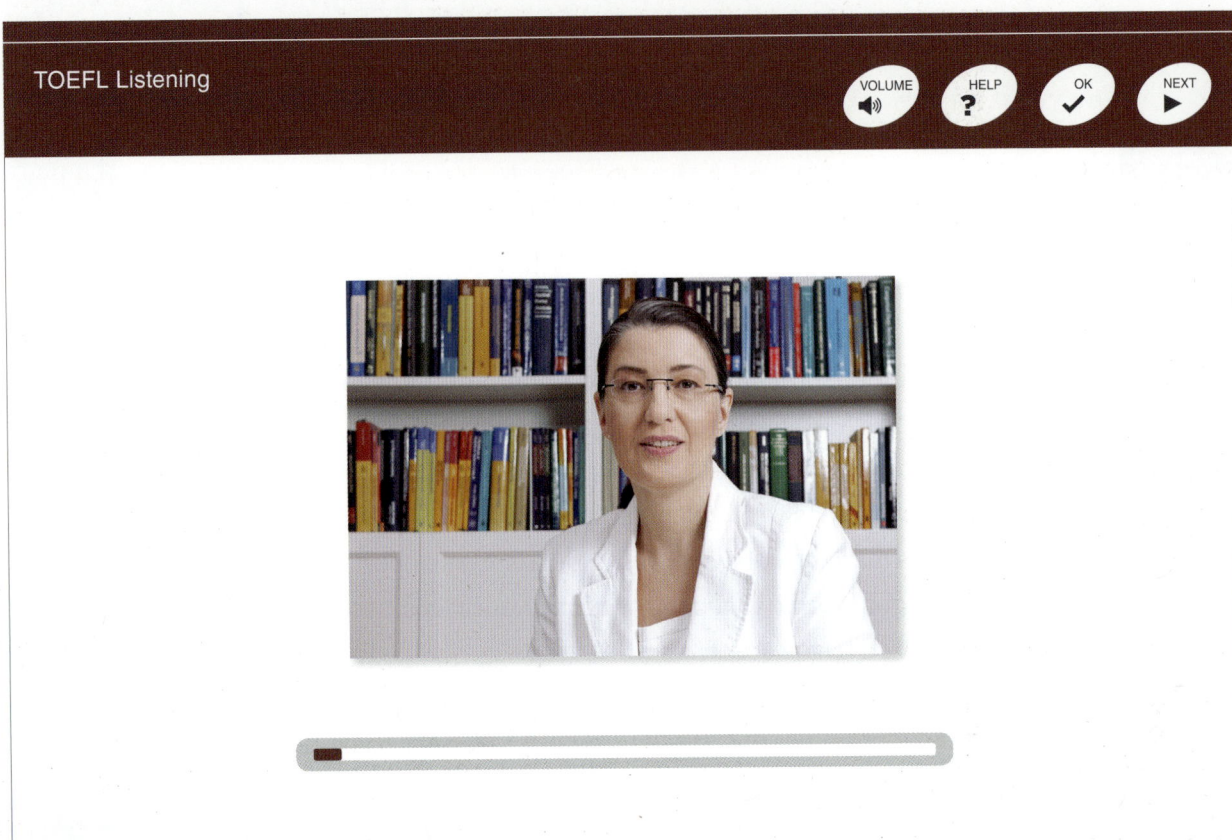

Note-Taking

1. Why does the student want to talk to the professor?
   - Ⓐ He wants advice about a presentation.
   - Ⓑ He wants to share his experiences.
   - Ⓒ He wants to discuss his final grade.
   - Ⓓ He wants a letter of recommendation.

2. What is Mr. Sullivan's class currently studying?
   - Ⓐ Class organization and curriculum
   - Ⓑ Roman mythology and its origin
   - Ⓒ Stars and the solar system
   - Ⓓ Presentation skills and surveys

3. Which of the following does the student mention as the methods that Mr. Sullivan uses?
   Click on 2 answers.
   - Ⓐ He asks many questions.
   - Ⓑ He lets the students choose the topic for each class.
   - Ⓒ He often gives a pop quiz to his class.
   - Ⓓ He makes the students research subjects.

4. What can be inferred about Mr. Sullivan's class?
   - Ⓐ It is organized in a systemic and integrated way.
   - Ⓑ It is a specialized class in Astronomy.
   - Ⓒ It is made up of mostly group discussion.
   - Ⓓ It is arranged according to the scientific method.

Listen again to part of the conversation. Then answer the question.

5. Why does the student say this:
   - Ⓐ To suggest that he will be Mr. Sullivan's student next semester
   - Ⓑ To emphasize that he was impressed by Mr. Sullivan's teaching style
   - Ⓒ To explain that he was once a student of Mr. Sullivan
   - Ⓓ To indicate that he doesn't want to work as an assistant teacher anymore

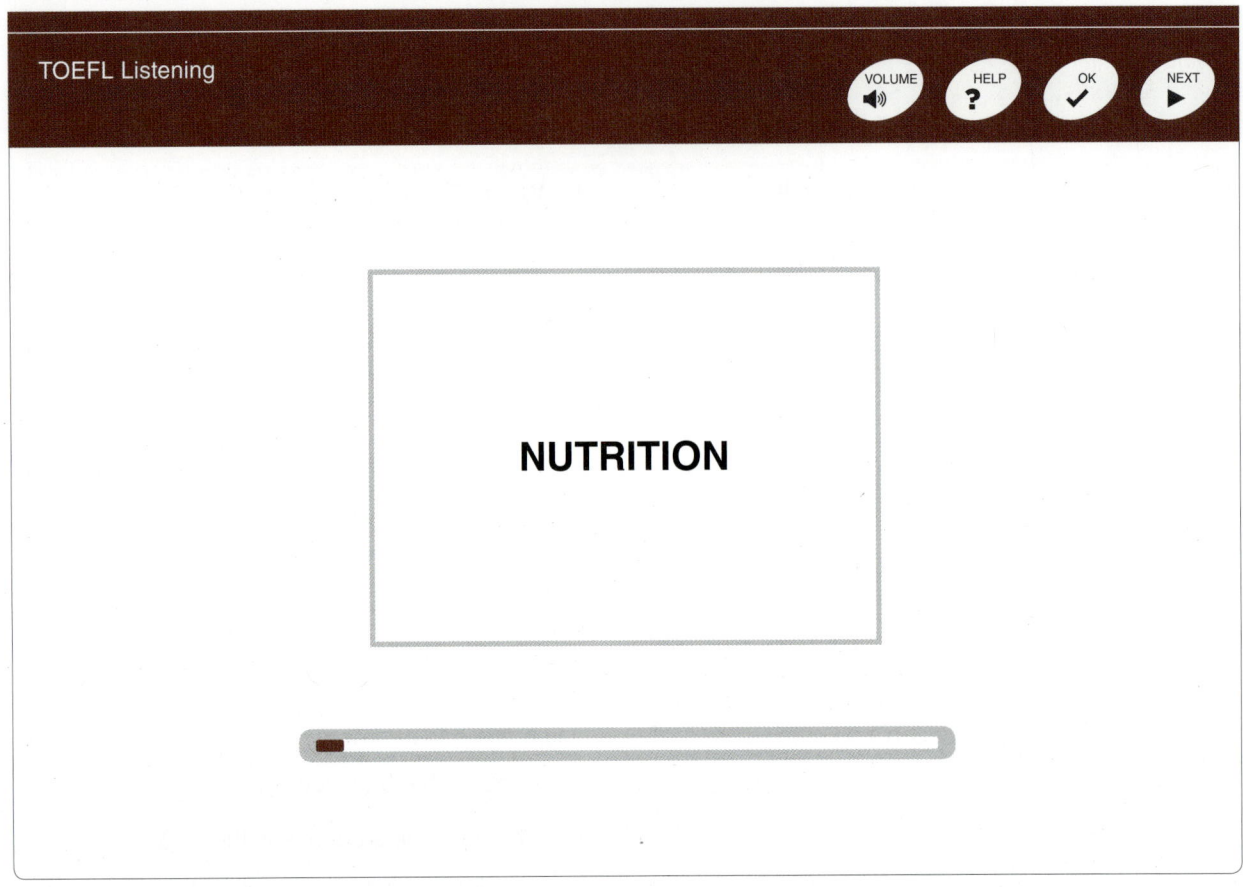

Note-Taking

TOEFL Listening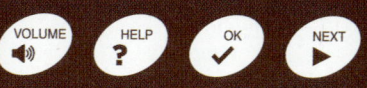

6. What is the lecture mainly about?
   A) Plants that have been historically considered medicinal
   B) The health benefits derived from a compound in garlic
   C) The various historical uses of garlic
   D) Chemicals present in garlic plants

7. Why does the professor mention Sanskrit records and Chinese medicine?
   A) To classify garlic as a medicinal plant with Asian origins
   B) To indicate garlic has been used medicinally from ancient times
   C) To give instructions about how garlic should be used
   D) To show the diverse uses of garlic

8. According to the professor, what are some of the medical effects attributed to garlic?
   Click on 3 answers.
   A) Reducing blood pressure
   B) Increasing longevity
   C) Reducing cholesterol levels
   D) Lowering the risk of certain kinds of cancer
   E) Preventing enzyme and tissue damage

9. What does the professor say about allicin?
   A) It is changed into another compound by the enzyme alliinase.
   B) It is commonly used in medicines that treat upset stomachs.
   C) It is not present in garlic that has not been crushed or damaged.
   D) It is a common compound that is found in many foods.

Listen again to part of the lecture.
Then answer the question.

10. Why does the professor say this:
    A) To stress that garlic has a positive effect on health
    B) To repeat an important point from earlier in the lecture
    C) To give an example of a common medical problem
    D) To define a term that the students may not know

Listen again to part of the lecture.
Then answer the question.

11. What can be inferred about the professor?
    A) He wants to give the essential point of allicin production.
    B) He is concerned that the explanation of allicin would be complex.
    C) He asks the students to move to the chemistry lab for an experiment.
    D) He wants the students to memorize the names of compounds in garlic.

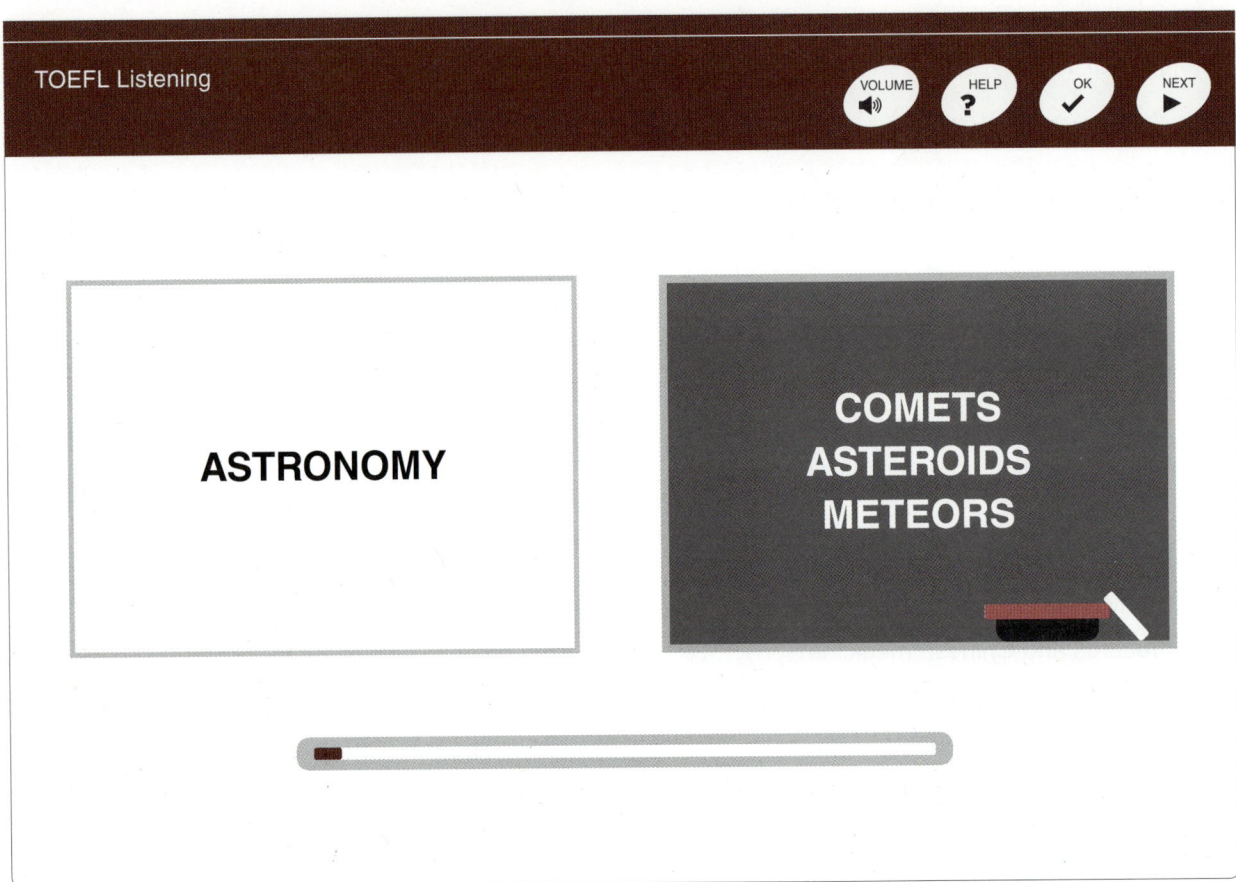

Note-Taking

TOEFL Listening

12. What is the lecture mainly about?
    - (A) The composition of comets, asteroids, and meteorites
    - (B) A formula for distinguishing meteoroids from asteroids
    - (C) Various phenomena generated in the solar system
    - (D) An overview of several kinds of small solar bodies

13. In the lecture, the professor describes some features of comets and asteroids. Indicate whether each of the following is related to comets or asteroids.
    Click in the correct box for each word.

	comets	asteroids
(A) comas and tails		
(B) metals or rock		
(C) ice and dust		
(D) planet-like		
(E) usually found between Mars and Jupiter		

14. According to the professor, what is true about meteoroids and meteorites?
    - (A) Meteoroids are much bigger than meteorites.
    - (B) Their visibilities change depending on their compositions.
    - (C) They orbit around the sun for the same orbital period.
    - (D) They are the same objects in different positions.

15. How does the professor introduce the preciousness of meteorites?
    - (A) By mentioning their market price
    - (B) By contrasting them with comets
    - (C) By explaining their composition
    - (D) By emphasizing their origins

Listen again to part of the lecture.
Then answer the question.

16. What can be inferred about the Oort cloud?
    - (A) It is a mass of condensed water droplets.
    - (B) It is the place where the Hale-Bobb comet was heading.
    - (C) It originates from parts of comets that turned into vapor.
    - (D) It is a hypothetical cloud where some comets originate.

Listen again to part of the lecture.
Then answer the question.

17. What does the professor mean when she says this: 🎧
    - (A) She believes the Greek scientists didn't know much about asteroids.
    - (B) She thinks the origin of the name doesn't provide correct information.
    - (C) She doubts asteroids accurately orbit the sun like other planets.
    - (D) She agrees the terminology goes back to ancient mythology.

181

Answer Keys & Audio Scripts

UNIT 01 Main Idea

NOTE

Highlighting and bold types respectively indicate the first and second repeated part in Replay Questions.

Underlined phrases show the answers of Dictation in Listening Practice.

Basic Drills   pp. 14~15

1. ⓓ 2. ⓒ 3. ⓐ 4. ⓑ 5. ⓓ 6. ⓒ

1.

Listen to a conversation between a student and a professor.

Student: Can I speak with you for a moment?
Professor: Sure, come on in.
S: Thanks.
P: What can I do for you?
S: Actually I'm here to ask you if I could change the assignment you gave us last class. I mean… to design a name card.
P: Hmm… I wonder why you want to change…
S: Well, I have this great idea to design a cover for an issue of a magazine that has a feature on classic car models.
P: That sounds like it would be a lot more fun than designing a name card. But, the thing is, when I give you an assignment, I give it to you for a reason. Sure, I want you to have fun and get creative, but I'm also preparing you for a career in design. Designing a name card is the basic skill for designing other works. So you should try to make it first.
S: Okay. I got it.

2.

Listen to part of a lecture in a film studies class.

Professor: So, as I'm sure you all know, superhero movies are quite popular these days. But these movies and similar, um… television shows have been an integral part of pop culture for decades. Throughout the years, however, one thing has been lacking from these films and TV series. Do you know what it is? That's right, diversity. Today, though, the, um… the movies that are being made have undergone a dramatic increase in diversity. And it is not simply in the main characters. The 2017 film *Wonder Woman*, for example, didn't just feature a strong female hero. It also had a female director and a strong female cast. Similarly, 2018's *Black Panther* was considered groundbreaking for introducing an African-American protagonist, something that had been lacking in the genre. However, its supporting cast and crew were also predominantly African American. These movies and others are bringing a, um, much needed new dimension to traditional superhero tales.

3.

Listen to part of a lecture in a music class.

Professor: The piano's secure status as the favorite form of domestic recreation began to change with the development of technology. First of all, technology made possible the enjoyment of music in a passive form. I mean, people were given options other than music performed on the spot.
Student: Are you talking about the appearance of electronic appliances?
P: Exactly. In the decade before World War I, the home phonograph became common among ordinary people. By the 1920s, the popularity of radio was huge. Every home either had one or wanted one, and as a result, the role of the piano as the domestic centerpiece quickly ebbed away. Another blow to the piano was the appearance of the electronic keyboard in the late 20th century. As this instrument was not only cheap but also much more flexible, its popularity spread quickly.

4.

Listen to a conversation between a student and a secretary.

Student: Excuse me.
Secretary: Yes, what's the problem?
Student: Well, I've just transferred here, and I got a notice that I should take part in orientation next weekend. The trouble is, I was going to go camping with my family that weekend. So I wonder if I can skip the orientation program.
Secretary: Umm… It's not mandatory, but I think you'd better attend it. It's the best way to get settled in. You can make friends, get used to the school system, and find out where everything is.
Student: Oh, I already know the area. I grew up in this city and my brother went to school here. I already know a lot of people here because I went to high school with some of them.
Secretary: But it's important to meet your professors and learn about the requirements for your major and all that kind of stuff.
Student: I guess I should try not to miss it, then.

5.

Listen to part of a lecture in a zoology class.

Professor: Hummingbirds, you may be surprised to learn, include more than 300 species of a family of small birds native only to the Americas. They are known for their ability to hover in mid-air by... by uhm... rapidly flapping their wings 15 to 80 times per second. Because of this rapid flapping, these birds... hummingbirds that is... have the highest metabolic rates and energy needs relative to their weights of any birds. During daytime activity, hummingbirds' hearts beat 600~1,000 times per minute, which as you can imagine requires frequent feeding. So they visit hundreds of flowers daily. At night, or any other time food is not readily available, they are capable of slowing down their metabolism. They enter a... er... a hibernation-like state known as "torpor" to prevent them from starving to death. During torpor, the heart rate and rate of breathing are both slowed dramatically... the heart rate to roughly 50~180 beats per minute, reducing their need for food.

6.

Listen to part of a lecture in a botany class.

Professor: Alright, when leaves appear green, it is because they contain plenty of chlorophyll, which is green. Chlorophyll is the compound most responsible for the manufacture of foods, and it so... it increases during summer when more sunlight and water are available for uhm... for food-making through photosynthesis. But as autumn approaches and the hours of daylight and humidity diminish, a layer of cells develops between the uhm... the leaf stalk and the woody part of the tree. This layer interferes with the transport of water and foods, so the production of chlorophyll slows down. In a relatively short time period, the chlorophyll disappears completely and the green color in fact... does fade from the leaves. Now the yellow, brown, orange, and red pigments which chlorophyll masked during summer become... become visible when the green chlorophyll is gone. And thus, the autumn colors are revealed.

Dictation p. 16

1. an integral part of 2. lacking from these films
3. have undergone a dramatic increase 4. much needed new dimension 5. domestic recreation
6. on the spot 7. much more flexible 8. have the highest metabolic rates 9. is not readily available
10. both slowed dramatically 11. most responsible for / are available for 12. a layer of cells develops

Listening Practice 01 p. 17

1. D 2. D 3. B

Listen to a conversation between a student and a cafeteria manager.

Student: Ms. Davidson, can I talk to you about changing my hours?
Manager: Changing your hours? Peter, we've already set the cafeteria work schedule for this month.
S: I know... but I just joined the school jazz band a few days ago and they practice at night.
M: Well, what kind of change are you proposing?
S: Well, I'm scheduled to wait tables from five to nine in the evenings, Monday through Thursday. I was hoping to keep the days but switch my hours to the afternoon.
M: Sorry, we have enough lunchtime waiters already. How about coming in for the breakfast shift instead?
S: Oh, I can't. I've got my Music Appreciation class at 9 am.
M: Hmmph. Tell you what... I can move you to, um, afternoons if you switch from waiting tables to kitchen prep. The pay's the same and we've got an opening from one to five.
S: Q3 Kitchen prep? You mean chopping vegetables and stuff? Hmm... I've never thought about it. Actually I took this job because it lets me, um, interact with the professors... I figured it could be helpful if I, you know, got to know them better. I don't want to be trapped in the kitchen.
M: Hmm... Peter, **I don't think kitchen prep is that bad, and you wouldn't be taking a pay cut. And if you can't work evenings anymore, you don't have any other options.**
S: All right, all right. Count me in. I'll switch to kitchen prep.
M: Good choice. When can you start?
S: I'm available from tomorrow.

Listening Practice 02 p. 19

1. C 2. B 3. C

Listen to part of a lecture in a marine biology class.

Professor: Seahorses are among the most unique creatures in the animal kingdom. You've all seen pictures, if not the real thing, right? They look like... well... their heads and necks are kind of like a horse's... hence the name. Their mouths are at the end of their snout, which they use to suck in prey. And they've got prehensile tails... meaning that they can use their tails to grab onto things... you know... like a monkey.

Besides this unique appearance, perhaps the most

fascinating thing about seahorses is the way they breed. In this species, it is actually the males who carry and give birth to the young. Interesting, huh? Okay, let me tell you about their mating process. They have a courtship period of a few days. When they meet, they change colors to sort of let each other know that they are interested. Then they grab each other's tail... kind of like holding hands... and basically float around together for a few days. Finally, when the female is ready to mate she raises her snout and the male responds by doing the same. Then he opens up his pouch and the female deposits her eggs in it so that the fertilization can occur. Then the male carries the fertilized eggs around for two to three weeks... the length of time depends on the species... but when the young are ready, the father delivers them.

Student: Wait... but which parent looks after the young once they're born?

P: Neither. The young seahorses are independent of their parents. They simply swim off and are able to care for themselves.

Listening Practice 03   p. 21

1. B   2. C   3. C

Listen to part of a lecture in a physics class.

Professor: Last time we discussed two forms of heat transfer... conduction and radiation. Now we're going to cover a third kind: convection. Convection occurs only in fluids, which are generally liquids or gases, and transfers heat via movement. This, um... this movement is due to unequal density in different parts of the fluid, which is generally caused by heating.

Let me explain a bit further. First, imagine a fluid. If we heat a section of the fluid, the molecules in that area will expand, reducing density. So... because it is less dense, these heated molecules will begin to rise. As they rise, cool molecules descend toward the bottom, setting up a circulatory motion. The process repeats as the fluid is heated up again and once again begins to rise, causing heat transfer. Can you picture the movement in your heads? We call this a convection current, and you can easily observe it in the swirling action of any liquid that is heated to a boil.

Now, convection can either be forced or natural. In forced convection, the movement occurs when artificial means such as a pump or a fan move heated fluid. Ovens and refrigerators are examples of this. As for natural convection, a good example occurs in our everyday weather. Sunlight heats the land, warming the air directly above it, which rises up into the atmosphere. The convection current created when cool air sinks, is,

umm... is what we feel as a wind.

iBT Practice 01   pp. 23~24

1. B   2. B   3. D   4. A

Note-Taking

Purpose: extend report due?
- No. Tight deadlines for time management skills & taking responsibility

Why?
- find own apartment & part-time job → not sufficient time (Next semester, cut down classes)
- already researched and made an outline → So, just need to put it all together

OK. How much time?
- by Mon. morning

Listen to a conversation between a student and a professor.

Student: Excuse me, Professor Ingersoll? Can I talk to you for a minute?

Professor: Hello, Caroline. I've got a few free minutes, but then I need to get to my next class. If you need more time than that, you could come back during my posted office hours.

S: I'm sorry to bother you... I'll make this brief.

P: Okay. Go ahead.

S: I'm afraid to say this... but... I'm wondering if you can extend my report, which is due on Friday.

P: An extension? I'm sorry, Caroline, but I have a strict policy against extending deadlines.

S: But...

P: I know the end of the term is a busy time. You might think I'm too demanding. But I set tight deadlines for a reason. One of the things you should learn in my class is time management skills. When you've graduated and have a real job, you'll understand the importance of effectively managing your schedule and taking responsibility for your work.

S: I understand, and I do appreciate the importance of meeting deadlines. But... this is the first time I've ever asked for an extension.

P: Well, if you've never needed an extension before, why ask for one now?

S: Well, last month my family moved to a new house that's far from the school. So I had to find my own apartment and a part-time job... you know, to pay for food and rent.

P: Umm... Okay...

S: Q3 🎧 I'm sorry, Professor. I thought I could manage work and school, but I just haven't had sufficient time to do every thing. Next semester, I'm going to cut down my classes from five to four. Anyway, I'm working on a topic... how migrating birds sense direction. I've already researched the information I need and made an outline for the report. I just have to put it all together with my thoughts. If you give me some more time, I'll definitely do a good job.

P: All right.... how much time would you need?

S: Just until Monday. I'm not working this weekend, so I'll have plenty of time to get it done. I promise to have it on your desk first thing in the morning next Monday.

P: Q4 🎧 Hmm... well, against my better judgment, I'm going to grant you an extension. But just this once. And I want it before my 10 am class on Monday. I'm going to have high expectations for this report, Caroline. Don't let me down.

S: I won't, Professor Ingersoll. Thank you so much.

P: No need to thank me. Now, I really must be going.

S: Okay. See you in class.

iBT Practice 02
pp. 25~26

1. Ⓑ 2. Ⓓ 3. Ⓓ 4. Ⓐ

Note-Taking

Intro_ Great Depression & Bank crisis

Bank goes bankrupt, what to do? Withdraw all money
⇒ bank panic

Weak banks went broke during GD
→ People took out savings & didn't deposit
→ Bank: no money to lend, couldn't collect loan
   (companies broke)
→ 80% of banks broke: National crisis!

Solution?
1. President closed all banks - (student) really solution?
2. Passed new legislation during banking holiday
3. Banking act - guarantee policy
→ relieved people deposited money
∴ economy started to expand

Listen to part of a lecture in an American history class.

Professor: Are you ready to get started? Good. In the last class, we discussed the Great Depression of 1929, and today we're going to study about the bank crisis at that time. Before we start, I'd like to ask you a question. What would you likely do if your main bank were to go bankrupt?

Student 1: I think I'd rush to withdraw all my money from the bank. It's because I'd be worried about... umm, the situation, you know, it's possible I couldn't get my money back.

P: Yes. That's the so-called bank panic. And the same thing happened during the Great Depression. Some weak banks went broke in the middle of the economic crisis, and many people watching the situation took out their savings. Well, why did this situation bring about the national economic crisis? Anybody? [pause] Banks make money by giving loans to companies, and this money comes from the customers' deposits. However, when they thought the banks would become insecure, people didn't deposit their money, which means the banks didn't have money to lend. In addition, lots of businesses went broke; banks didn't have any company clients to give loans to, and they couldn't collect their loans, either.

More than 80% of banks went broke during the Great Depression. That's almost 9,000 banks that declared insolvency from 1930 to 1933. Now, the bank panic became the national crisis. So, do you have any idea how... umm, what's the best solution for this situation?

Student 2: Are you talking about the New Deal policy? If so, it was a series of programs President Roosevelt introduced to overcome the Great Depression.

P: Q4 🎧 Exactly. The first thing the president did was to close all banks. As all banks in the country were...

S1: Sorry, sir. But was it really a solution to close the banks?

P: Actually, yes, it was because almost every bank was about to collapse, so there was nothing else the president could have done. Roosevelt kept them all closed until he could pass new legislation. During this "Banking Holiday," Roosevelt sent to Congress the Emergency Banking Act, which included the new guarantee policy, or "Government Guarantee." In other words, Government promised that... even if one bank goes bust, the clients could still get their money back. People were relieved by this policy and deposited money in their savings accounts. Finally, as we know, the economy, which had hit bottom, started to expand.

Vocabulary Review
pp. 28~29

A 1. loan   2. fade   3. hover   4. compound
   5. humidity
B 1. Ⓑ   2. Ⓑ   3. Ⓓ   4. Ⓓ
C 1. Ⓒ   2. Ⓑ   3. Ⓐ   4. Ⓒ
D 1. extension   2. for   3. broke   4. crisis
   5. judgment
E 1. Ⓓ   2. Ⓑ   3. Ⓒ   4. Ⓐ   5. Ⓓ
F 1. Ⓐ   2. Ⓒ   3. Ⓑ

UNIT 02 Detail

Basic Drills   pp. 34~35

1. Ⓓ   2. Ⓐ, Ⓒ   3. Ⓐ   4. Ⓐ   5. Ⓒ   6. Ⓑ

1.

Listen to a conversation between two students.

Student 1: What's wrong?
Student 2: I got a parking ticket. It's so unfair. I have to pay an extra forty-five bucks.
S1: Where did you park?
S2: In front of the library.
S1: Don't you live in the dorms?
S2: Yeah, why?
S1: The parking spots in front of the library are reserved for students who live off-campus. The sign is clearly posted. I'm surprised you didn't see it.
S2: I know, but I was just parking there for a minute while I returned a book.
S1: Well. That's a shame, but you have to follow the rules. I was late for a lecture this morning because I couldn't find a parking place. It kind of upsets me when people who live on campus and already have a parking spot use up the other ones. This is a small campus. You can walk from place to place.
S2: I guess you have a point.

2.

Listen to part of a lecture in an art class.

Professor: Pop art. Is that a familiar term? I would, um, I would suppose it is. The name Keith Haring, on the other hand, might not be so familiar. But trust me, you would immediately recognize his, um... his work. Like other artists from the movement, Haring's primary goal was to blur the line between high art and low art. That is... How should I put this? Basically, Haring wanted to make art accessible to everyone. His style was extremely simple. He used images that were cartoonish and colorful, but at the same time, he... he addressed important contemporary issues, such as drug addiction. Haring also opened up his own retail store, called, er... the Pop Shop, I believe. There, he sold products, such as T-shirts and posters, that featured his designs. It was another way of making sure his work was enjoyed by and available to the general public, not just wealthy art lovers.

3.

Listen to part of a lecture in a biology class.

Professor: All right. So, whale sharks are not whales and they are not mammals. Actually, they are the largest fish species. On average, whale sharks are around 25 feet long, but they can reach up to 40 feet long. The mouth can open up to four feet wide and has 310 rows of teeth, or about 3,000 teeth in all. Now what image can you come up with of this big fish?
Student: I guess it sounds like a fierce predator of the seas.
P: That's a decent guess. But this giant fish is quite gentle and mild-mannered. It likes its privacy. And the interesting thing is... it's a filter feeder, so it eats by filtering tiny organisms from water. The truth is, it doesn't even really use its teeth. When feeding, it opens its mouth, draws in tons of water containing krill and shrimp, and passes this sort of fish soup through spongy tissue between its gill arches. After closing its mouth, the shark uses gills to filter the nourishment from the water.

4.

Listen to a conversation between a student and an employee in a Student Help Center.

Student: Excuse me. My phone hasn't worked since yesterday. I wonder what's wrong with the phone service.
Employee: What's your room number?
S: Room 456.
E: Ah, Ellen McCully?
S: Yes, that's me.
E: You didn't pay your phone bill for the past three months. Your service has been disconnected.
S: Really? I guess it slipped my mind. Why didn't I get any prior notice about the bill? I would have paid it if I'd known.
E: We sent four or five notices to your email.
S: Oh! I haven't been checking my email. I've been so busy with mid-terms I didn't think of it. Okay, what do I need to do to get my phone back on?
E: You have to pay all of the bills. And there's a late penalty of forty dollars.
S: Forty dollars? Okay then.

5.

Listen to part of a lecture in a pedagogy class.

Professor: As an educator John Dewey revolutionized educational techniques and beliefs. The dominant school practice of his day was that students passively received information that had been packed and predigested by teachers and textbooks. Dewey strongly criticized this. He felt that schools were failing to provide genuine learning experiences and were instead feeding endless facts to students who soon forgot them. Dewey...

uhm... he argued teaching should emphasize learning through doing and experiencing. He suggested students learn best not by... by reading the "great books" in a closed room but by opening the doors and windows of experience. In other words, he thought... no, he believed important skills such as problem solving, language, and math concepts are developed as the students are allowed to move freely in and out of the classroom and explore their surroundings.

6.

Listen to part of a lecture in an art class.

Professor: So, the principal aim of Impressionist artists was to objectively capture a visual image and record the brief effects of light. They tried to capture an immediate impression of what the eyes see at a single glance with the light, rather than what the viewer knows or feels about the subject.

Student: Professor, you mean light played an important role for Impressionist artists?

P: Exactly! Impressionist painters put a lot of emphasis on the light and its variations. They were very interested in how light appeared on subjects in different weather and at different times of the day. You know, even when they painted the same natural scene, the painting took on a very different aspect according to the change of light. What I'm saying is... when painting landscapes and other outdoor scenes, they discontinued painting and came back again the next day at the same time to capture the same effects of changing light as the day before.

Dictation p. 36

1. was to blur the line between   2. make art accessible to everyone   3. was enjoyed by and available   4. they can reach up to   5. fierce predator of the seas   6. by filtering tiny organisms   7. shark uses gills   8. revolutionized educational techniques   9. The dominant school practice / that had been packed   10. learning through doing and experiencing   11. was to objectively capture   12. put a lot of emphasis on   13. how light appeared on subjects   14. took on a very different aspect

Listening Practice 01 p. 37

1. 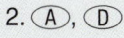   2.   3. Ⓐ

Listen to a conversation between a student and a professor.

Student: *[knocking]* Excuse me, Professor Duncan. I made an appointment with you today to discuss my first draft... umm... about endangered species. Did you have a chance to look at my report?

Professor: Yes, I've gone through it. You were looking at endangered elephants in Africa.

S: Right...

P: Well... it seems you've put lots of effort into finding information... I can see diverse data...

S: Well, I thought the richer the information, the better the report.

P: Hmm... that's true. To write a good report, it's necessary to have enough information. But there's a more important aspect you should pay attention to. That's what I want to point out about your report.

S: I see. Please go ahead.

P: All right. This report is a clearly written explanation of the information you found. But I don't see your personal ideas. I want you to analyze the material you research by reflecting your thoughts. Simply summarizing it is not sufficient.

S: I'm confused. Could you tell me more specifically what you want?

P: Okay. I mean... rather than just enumerating the information, you should classify and organize the data in terms of what causes African elephants to be endangered, and... what else?... yes, how the situation can be improved. But it should include your opinions.

S: Q3 🎧 I see. Actually, I didn't pay much attention to putting my ideas into the report. I've got a lot of work ahead of me.

P: **Yes, but you already have enough sources for your report.** It shouldn't take long to revise them.

S: I guess not. Thank you for your help.

Listening Practice 02 p. 39

1.   2.   3. Ⓒ

Listen to part of a lecture in an art class.

Professor: The next movement in the art world we're going to consider is Minimalism. As the name suggests, Minimalism is... or seems more basic than other types of art. Minimalist artists strived to reduce their work to the smallest number of colors, shapes, and lines, in a rejection of Abstract Expressionism.

Student: Was there a particular reason for that?

P: Well... Minimalist artists wanted to, essentially, remove themselves from the art. I mean... they rejected the idea that art should reflect the personal expression of its creator. Now the uhm... the common conception of art is that it represents an interpretation of the real world such as a landscape or a person. Or perhaps... perhaps that art reflects an experience such as an emotion or feeling. However, with Minimalism, artists consciously attempted to objectify their subjects and avoid abstract representation. Their aim was to... to kind of invoke a response from the viewer based only on what was in front of them. So Minimalist art did not refer to anything beyond its literal presence. For example, color... if used, was non-referential. Dark colors represented only dark colors and not some deeper emotional or philosophical mood.

Basically, with Minimalism, less is more. Minimalist artists didn't feel that by paring the work down to simple forms they were creating a poorer experience for the viewer. Quite the contrary, they believed that they were creating the possibility for a more direct and pure relationship between the viewer and the work.

Listening Practice 03 p. 41

1. B 2. C 3. D

Listen to part of a lecture in an environmental science class.

Professor: It should come as no surprise to anyone in this room that our planet is facing an unprecedented crisis, one that is being caused by our unrestrained consumer lifestyles. Put simply, we are, um, we are drowning the Earth in our trash. There was a point in time when people were confident that boosting our recycling efforts would be the answer, but, unfortunately, they were incorrect. Don't get me wrong, recycling is, is, um... well, it's essential. But as long as we keep generating the same enormous levels of waste, all of our recycling efforts amount to very little in the end. The bottom line, according to many experts, is that we need to start creating less waste, and that's where the concept of "zero waste" comes into play. It refers to the type of lifestyle in which absolutely no trash is created—in other words, we personally use, reuse or recycle everything we purchase or create. This might sound daunting, maybe even impossible, but you need to understand that it's, it's really just a goal to aim for. Even if we don't reach it, simply by foregoing plastic cups, paper towels, and things like that, we can become part of the solution rather than part of the problem. It's not like it's some kind of great inconvenience to use reusable mugs and cloth towels after all. Imagine living in a home where you don't even have a trash can, because... well, because you don't need one. Because everything you buy can be either recycled, composted or washed and reused. It's an interesting concept, and one that's well worth pondering.

iBT Practice 01 pp. 43~44

1. D 2. C 3. B 4. D

Note-Taking

Problem: going to Spain and my mail?

- 2 options ① Forward mail to Spain
            ② Hold mail here
            (both free for 4 months)
  → ①: Worried and not sure where to stay
    ②: OK

- Subscribe to any magazines? Yes, why?
  → Not enough space, so put it on hold

- Not back in 4 months? Email to us, charge $5 per week

⇒ Fill out form & bring it back before you leave

Listen to a conversation between a student and a clerk in a post office.

Clerk: Good morning! What can I do for you?
Student: Well, I have a few, um... I have a problem. I'm going away to Spain next semester as part of the school's international study program.
C: That's great. Spain's a beautiful country.
S: So I've heard. Q4 Anyway, I'm not sure what I should do about my mail while I'm away.
C: Oh, is that all? **We deal with this sort of thing all the time.** Generally, students choose one of two options when they go abroad for a semester. Either we can forward all of your mail to your new address in Spain, or we can hold your mail here until you get back. We'll be glad to do either of these free of charge for up to four months.
S: That's good to hear... I'm not so sure about having my mail forwarded. I'm sort of worried it won't get to me. I'm really not sure exactly where I'll be staying, but I hear it's a pretty small town.
C: I understand. So you'd prefer to have us hold your mail here?
S: Yeah... I think I would. It's not like I'm expecting anything important. I pay all my bills online.
C: All right. Holding your mail sounds like the best option, then. Um... do you subscribe to any magazines?
S: I get the *Campus Weekly*. Is that a problem?
C: Well, we can only hold letters. No periodicals or packages... we just don't have enough space. Why don't you call *Campus Weekly* and have them put your subscription on

hold?
S: That sounds like a good idea. But... well, I'm supposed to come back here when the semester is over, but I sort of like the idea of traveling through Europe a bit... so I might not be back in four months. If that's the case, what should I do?
C: Don't worry. You can access the school's website and send an email to us... I mean... let us know if your plans change. With your notice in advance, the service can be extended. But there's an extension charge... umm... $5 per week.
S: Oh, that's fine... So what do I do now?
C: Just fill out this form and bring it back here at least a couple of days before you leave.
S: All right. Thanks for all your help!
C: No problem.

iBT Practice 02

pp. 45~46

1. Ⓒ   2. Ⓑ   3. Ⓒ   4. Ⓓ

Note-Taking

Intro_ Placebo
; made of sugar, used when testing new medications

Positive effect... Why?
1. Power of suggestion (widest held belief)
   mental state influences on their physical well-being
2. Contrasting theories
   ① End of the symptoms is merely coincidence
      placebo effect – natural regression
   ② Interpretation change with expectation

⇒ Unverified. The exact physiological mechanisms remain mysterious.

Listen to part of a lecture in a psychology class.

Professor: A placebo refers to something that is given in place of actual medicine, often made up of nothing more than sugar. Originally, placebos were used by doctors as a way of dealing with hypochondriacs... people who always think they're ill. These days, however, drug companies that are, um, testing new medications most commonly use placebos. Patients are divided into 2 groups; one is given the medication, the other the placebo.

So the uh, well there is evidence to suggest that around 1 in 3 people who are given a placebo will actually report some positive results. Typically it's... uhm... it's taken for things like seasickness or a mild headache, but, of course, it's harmless and has no medically proven benefits. So uhm, why do you think people feel better?

Student: I'd say it's the power of suggestion... you know, you say something often enough and people will start to believe it... that kind of thing.
P: Right. Suggestion, the notion that something is working because you've been told it will. Currently that's the widest held belief. Good. Taking the placebo and expecting to feel better may soothe the autonomic nervous system and reduce the levels of stress chemicals, such as adrenaline. Also, placebos may trigger the release of the body's own natural painkillers, the uh... neurotransmitters known as endorphins. The placebo effect may suggest that a patient's mental state has a direct influence on their physical well-being. By convincing ourselves that we are recovering, our body may actually respond in kind.

There are contrasting theories about the effectiveness of placebos. Many illnesses or conditions will... you know, fix themselves in the fullness of time. Often modern drugs are ineffectual remedies for the common cold, but a placebo may fool a patient into thinking they've been cured. In reality, the end of the symptoms is merely coincidence. Furthermore, many disorders, pains and illnesses wax and wane. What is perceived as the placebo effect could, in many cases, be the measurement of natural regression.

Alternatively a person's interpretation of their symptoms may change with their expectation. For example, a sharp pain may be reinterpreted as an uncomfortable tingling. Also a feeling of tightness in the chest could be interpreted as indigestion or trapped wind.

All these theories remain unverified, though. The exact physiological mechanisms remain mysterious and whether the placebo effect is mainly psychological, misunderstood spontaneous healing, altered perception, or a combination of all three, hasn't been indisputably proven.

Vocabulary Review

pp. 48~49

A 1. physiological   2. predigest   3. enumerate
   4. accessible   5. daunting
B 1. Ⓓ   2. Ⓓ   3. Ⓒ   4. Ⓑ
C 1. Ⓓ   2. Ⓐ   3. Ⓐ   4. Ⓑ
D 1. forward   2. advance   3. indisputably
   4. unrestrained   5. through
E 1. Ⓒ   2. Ⓓ   3. Ⓑ   4. Ⓑ   5. Ⓐ
F 1. Ⓒ   2. Ⓑ   3. Ⓒ

Actual Practice Test 1

01
pp. 52~53

1. D 2. C 3. C 4. B 5. C

Note-Taking

Initial Purpose: to have a faulty laptop looked at
What was wrong? Screen went blank
→ Happened while writing an essay in a document
→ Nothing unusual occurred before the error

Secondary Purpose: to rent a laptop
→ Essay due tomorrow
Employee will contact the student in a day or two

Listen to a conversation in a computer shop.

Student: Hello? Is anybody here?

Repair Shop Employee: Hi. How can I help you today?

S: Oh, hi. I didn't see you there. I need to have someone look at my laptop. I was writing an essay last night when the screen suddenly went blank. I tried to find a solution online, but I couldn't find anything.

E: I see. Well, I'm sure I can help you with that. Can I see your laptop?

S: Sure. Here you go.

E: Thanks. And may I have your name, please?

S: Of course. It's Sam Martin.

E: Okay, Sam. I'll take a look at your laptop and figure out what caused it to malfunction. But I need to ask you a couple of preliminary questions first. And can I have your phone number? I'll need it to get in touch with you in a day or two.

S: Oh, sure. It's 616-822-6437.

E: Perfect. Now, how long have you had this laptop?

S: Approximately three years. Q4 It hasn't had any big problems. This is definitely the first major issue I've encountered.

E: **Good to know. Did you do anything out of the ordinary last night?** You know, maybe you opened a strange attachment or downloaded a new app.

S: No, nothing like that. I was just writing my essay in a document like I normally do.

E: Okay. Has the laptop ever gotten wet? Or has it been exposed to extreme heat or cold?

S: Nope, it hasn't.

E: All right. Well, that's all the information I need. Is there anything else I can help you with?

S: Q5 Well, I was wondering if you had any rental laptops available. My essay is due tomorrow, and I don't have easy access to the computers in the school library.

E: Yes, we have some laptops for rent. If you follow me, I'll show you where they are.

S: Excellent. Thanks a lot. *[They walk to the rental section.]*

E: So, they're all similar models. And they're all in excellent condition. Pick one you like, and I'll ring you up at the register.

S: Okay. Does this one have a fast processor? I'm in an engineering class, and I may need to download a certain program onto it for a project. Is that okay?

E: Yes, it does, and yes, that's fine. Once you return it, we'll perform a factory reset. Anything you do on the laptop will be erased.

S: Perfect. I'll rent this one then.

E: Awesome. Let's head over to the register. *[They go to the register.]* Okay, is that all for today?

S: Yep! So I should expect a call from you within a couple of days?

E: Yes, but I'll just text you. If I'm still working, it'll be a progress update. Otherwise, I'll let you know that your laptop is ready to be picked up.

S: Sounds good. Have a great day!

E: You too!

02
pp. 54~55

6. D 7. D 8. B 9. C 10. C 11. A

Note-Taking

Intro_ Separation anxiety of children
; anxious whenever away from parent or caregiver

1. Cognitive development between 7 months & 1 year
   → memories start to develop
   → recognize certain people
2. But why? They don't have any concept of time
3. Goes away when they learn & build trust that parents come back
   If not? Separation anxiety disorder (serious & not normal)

Listen to part of a lecture in a psychology class.

Professor: Class, we've been talking about cognitive development in children… the stages children go through as their minds develop. Today I'd like to cover an issue that's closely related to cognitive development… um, something called separation anxiety. It's when a child gets very anxious or frightened whenever they're away from their parent, or other familiar caregiver. Those of you who've spent time with young children have seen it, I'm sure. A parent tries to leave their child, who's maybe, oh, a year or so old… tries to leave that child with someone so they can go to work, or go out to dinner or something. And the kid is not happy about this, right? Q10 🎧 He or she cries, and screams, and tries to cling onto the parent. You know what I'm talking about? Anyone?

Student 1: Yeah, I know what you mean. But… how does this relate to cognitive development?

P: Ah. Well, separation anxiety is actually a very normal phase children go through. And it coincides with a specific period of their cognitive development. The age we're talking about is somewhere between seven months and one year… what's going on in a child's cognitive development during this time?

Student 2: Uh… I think that's when children's memories start to really develop, isn't it?

S1: Yeah, and since they can remember, children start to recognize familiar things… and people too.

P: Absolutely. See, babies younger than six months that haven't entered this stage… they can't really tell the difference between one adult and the next. They'll be happy with anyone who provides for their needs. But once the child learns to recognize certain people who're with them all the time… uh, usually the parents… once this happens, the child experiences separation anxiety when that familiar person leaves.

S2: But just because they can recognize people doesn't explain why young kids have this, this anxiety reaction. Do psychologists know the cause?

P: Well, let's think back again to the stages of cognitive development. Children around one year old can remember and recognize, but what's something they haven't developed yet?

S1: They don't have any understanding of time, right?

P: Yes. Q11 🎧 And since they don't have any concept of time, they can't understand that their parent will return in the future. Once the parent leaves, all the child knows is they're gone and may never come back. **Scary, right?**

　Now, as the child develops further, separation anxiety eventually becomes less intense… and then goes away altogether. The child learns its parent will only be away for a specific period of time… and develops trust in the parent or caregiver… trust that the person will in fact return. This may take a few years, but most children overcome their separation anxiety.

S2: Professor… what if they don't overcome it?

P: Hmm… well… this is really a topic for another class, but… in a small number of children, separation anxiety is very intense, and it continues… maybe even into the teens and beyond. We call this separation anxiety disorder. It's, it's something parents need to seek professional help to deal with. It's pretty serious and not a normal phase of development like separation anxiety is.

03　　　　　　　　　　　　pp. 56~57

12. Ⓒ　13. Ⓓ　14. Ⓐ　15. Horns - Ⓐ, Ⓓ / Antlers - Ⓑ, Ⓒ　16. Ⓑ　17. Ⓒ

Note-Taking

Intro_ Horns ≠ Antlers
1. Differences

	Horn	Antler
material	Skin (covered with keratin)	Bone
shape	Single point	Multiple points
growth	Continue to grow	Shed each year (grow quickly)

2. Similarities
Function: males – establish dominance, attract females
　　　　　(the bigger, the better)
　　females – protect themselves and their young
　　used for practical purposes

Listen to part of a lecture in a zoology class.

Professor: If I were to show you a picture of a bull, a goat, a deer, and a moose, you might say they all have something in common: they all have horns. But this is really a misconception. While bulls and goats do have horns, deer and moose actually have antlers… and yes, there is a difference. Despite what you might think, antlers are not simply a kind of horn.

　So, what are the differences? Let's start with the, er, the material they're made of. Antlers are made entirely of solid bone. Horns, however, are hollow projections of an animal's skin, covered in a material known as keratin. Keratin is a type of hard tissue that the body uses to form things like claws or hair. The kind of keratin that covers horns is similar to the keratin that forms our fingernails.

　There are other basic differences between horns and antlers. So let's see… While horns can come in all sorts of shapes and sizes – straight, curved, curled – they all have thick bases and narrow to a single point. Antlers, on the other hand, tend to branch off into multiple points.

　Also, horns are a, um, a permanent part of an animal, and they continue to grow throughout the animal's life. Antlers, however, are shed each year at the end of winter, at which time the animal begins to grow a new set. Because of this, antlers grow more quickly than horns. As the antlers grow, a soft material known as velvet, which contains nerves and blood vessels, covers them and helps them develop. After several months, the velvet falls off and the new antlers are, um… well, they're ready to be used.

　Now, when it comes to function, horns and antlers… well, they're fairly similar. Males use their horns and antlers mostly to, um... as a means of establishing dominance among other males of their own species. The size of an animal's horns or antlers serves to intimidate rival males. But if this fails, they'll resort to fighting, using their horns and antlers as weapons to determine which animal is more powerful. Also the size of horns and antlers matters for attracting females... because the males with the biggest ones are usually chosen by females during mating season. Q17 **If, as expected, large horns and antlers are an important survival advantage for males, then what about females?** Why do the females of a few species have horns or antlers? For these females, the primary function is generally to protect themselves and their young from predators.

In the course of their day-to-day activities, animals also use their horns and antlers for some pretty practical purposes, including such tasks as digging up food, peeling bark off trees or scratching themselves.

UNIT 03 Function

Basic Drills   pp. 62~63

1. Ⓐ   2. Ⓓ   3. Ⓒ   4. Ⓒ   5. Ⓑ   6. Ⓓ

1.

Listen to a conversation between two students in a college bookstore.

Student 1: Hi Rhonda. How's it going?

Student 2: Not great. I have to meet my professor in ten minutes, but this line is so long.

S1: Yeah, it's the beginning of the semester. Everyone's buying books. Plus the store is closing in twenty minutes. Why don't you wait until tomorrow?

S2: I can't. I have chemistry first thing tomorrow morning and that's the book I'm buying. I have to read a chapter tonight.

S1: I'll tell you what... why don't you let me get the book for you? **I have to wait in line anyway and I'm not in a hurry.**

S2: I appreciate that, but I don't have any cash on me. I was going to pay with my credit card.

S1: That's okay, I'll pay for it and you can pay me back later this evening when I bring it by your dorm.

S2: Really? That would be great. Thanks so much.

2.

Listen to part of a lecture in a zoology class.

Professor: Penguins, as we know, swim in the ocean's coldest and most food-rich currents. In order to survive the chilly temperatures of the southern oceans, warm-blooded penguins rely on feathers and fat for insulation. There're a number of ways they do this. First up, penguin feathers are small and densely packed, with up to um... about 70 per square inch. The feathers are stiff and form a tightly overlapping guard against wind, rain, and the cold ocean water. A special gland at the base of the tail produces oil that the penguin can spread across its feathers when it preens. So penguin feathers are like, um... like a waterproof outer coat. Another way is through fat. Penguins are insulated against the cold by a thick layer of fat under their skin. Typically, the... the colder the climate is, the fatter the penguin will be. At the same time, stored fat also enables penguins to go without food while they molt or brood their eggs. **Sometimes fatter is better, right?**

3.

Listen to part of a lecture in a medicine class.

Professor: MRI is widely used to capture internal images of a patient as a noninvasive method; it's not penetrating the body by incision or injection. However, it is associated with some risk in case of carelessness. A regular safety concern with MRI results from... uh, the machine's strong magnetic fields. The typical MRI is about, um... 30,000 times more powerful than the Earth's gravitational field. As such, any metal objects in the room can be drawn into the MRI unit at high speed. Actually, the magnetic attraction is so powerful that even small objects are potentially lethal if they exist on or er... worse still, in the patient's body. Metallic implants like surgical clips and pacemakers can be pulled into the magnetic field. If the implant is moved or malfunctions, serious injury or death can occur. Therefore, MRI rooms must be clear of any metal objects... and of course, patients are prescreened for the presence of any metal objects to prevent potential risk.

4.

Listen to a conversation between a student and a librarian.

Student: Excuse me, sir.
Librarian: Hello, there. How can I help you?
S: I'm looking for books with information on flow visualization. Do you know if the library has any?
L: **I'm sorry, that's not something I'm familiar with.** What's the subject? Is it related to engineering?
S: Yes, it is. Specifically, it's a term used in mechanical engineering.
L: I see. In that case, you should probably head over to row 2A on the first floor.
S: Is that where the engineering section is?
L: Well, we don't have a single section dedicated to engineering. But row 2A is where we keep all of our STEM books—you know, science, technology, engineering and mathematics. So if we have any books with the information you're looking for, you'd most likely find them there.
S: Perfect. Thank you very much.
L: My pleasure. If you need any more help, just let me know.

5.

Listen to part of a lecture in an art history class.

Professor: The Chauvet cave paintings, discovered in 1994 in Southeastern France, are fine black drawings and engravings depicting a wide range of animals such as horses, lions, and bison in lifelike poses – standing, running, or roaming in packs. Well, such sophistication led many people to assume that the paintings must be relatively recent. That's because, they thought... thousands of years of cultural development and artistic experimentation was behind those paintings. **However, the result of analyzing the animal drawings and various charcoal remains in the cave was rather surprising.** Radiocarbon dating, a um... precision form of carbon dating analysis, proved the Chauvet cave paintings to be between 29,000 and 32,000 years old. That's 10,000 to 15,000 years older than those at Lascaux.
Student: Lascaux, the cave that's famous for its paintings, right?
P: Yeah, it contains important ancient paintings that were thought to be the oldest. But, now the Chauvet paintings are the most ancient artworks ever found.

6.

Listen to part of a lecture in an environmental studies class.

Professor: Today's lesson is about "bio-remediation." You can probably guess that it has something to do with "remediate," which means to solve a problem. "Bio-remediation" is, um, a process of finding solutions to environmental problems by using biological organisms. So how does it work? In an environment that isn't polluted, bacteria and other microorganisms are continuously breaking down organic matter. But... if an organic pollutant such as oil contaminated this environment, a number of the microorganisms would be killed, um... while others would manage to survive as they are capable of dissolving such organic pollution. So umm... bio-remediation operates by giving these pollution-eating organisms uh... fertilizer, oxygen, and other conditions that promote their rapid growth. They can subsequently break down organic pollutants more quickly. Therefore, bio-remediation can be considered an inexpensive, environmentally sound strategy for particular types of pollution, like soil contamination and oil spill, by enhancing the same biodegradation processes that happen in nature.

Dictation p. 64

1. survive the chilly temperatures / rely on
2. produces oil / when it preens 3. are insulated against 4. stored fat / brood their eggs
5. it is associated with 6. implant is moved or malfunctions 7. clear of any metal objects
8. such sophistication led 9. cultural development and artistic experimentation 10. various charcoal remains 11. it has something to do with 12. an organic pollutant / capable of dissolving
13. subsequently break down

Listening Practice 01   p. 65

1. D   2. B   3. C

Listen to a conversation between a student and a registrar.

Registrar: Hello. Can I help you?

Student: Well, I hope so... I just came from lecture hall 3B and it's empty. Could you check which room the lecture on Modern Physics is in?

R: Hold on, let me check my computer, um... *[pause]* You're referring to the lecture by Professor Lee?

S: That's right... *[checking his schedule]* um, Professor Lee, 4 pm in Lecture Hall 3B. Is anything wrong?

R: I'm afraid so. The lecture was canceled, and the students were notified by email.

S: Canceled? You mean... canceled just for today? Or...

R: Completely canceled. Hold on... *[pause]* Here's the problem. Not enough students signed up for the lecture this semester, so it was automatically canceled.

S: That's... well, that's terrible. I was really looking forward to the lecture. By the way, why didn't I get an email?

R: Hmm. Let me check... What's your name?

S: Wallace Colby.

R: *[pause]* Q3 🎧 Okay. And your email address is WallyC@freemail.com?

S: Yes, it... No! No, that's my old email address. Oh boy, that's why... *[pause]* Hmm, I guess this is my own fault.

R: Well, you probably need to update your email address on the college system. Do you know how to do that?

S: Yeah. I'll take care of that tonight. Anyway, do you think this lecture will be offered next semester?

R: Oh yes, I believe they offer it every semester. As long as enough students are interested, you'll be able to take it then.

S: Okay. Thank you very much for your help.

Listening Practice 02   p. 67

1. D   2. B   3. C

Listen to part of a lecture in an economics class.

Professor: So, I think the relationship between price and sales is pretty clear. Q3 🎧 Imagine that you're a seller. If you lower the price of your product, you can reasonably expect your sales to go up. **Now, let's, um... let's make things a little more complex.** For nearly every product you'll find in the marketplace, you'll also find substitute products and complementary products. This is important because when the price of these related goods changes, it will affect the sales of your product.

  Let me give you an example... we can start with substitutes. A substitute product is one that can be used in place of your product, and vice versa. If you're selling chicken, for example, a substitute product might be pork. If the price of pork goes up, you can expect that some people will buy chicken instead. So when the price of a substitute product goes up, your sales go up.

  As for complementary products... well, they're sort of the opposite of substitute products. A person who buys a complementary product is likely to buy your product as well. For example, if you're selling CDs, a complementary product would be CD players. If the price of CD players goes down, we know the sales of CD players will go up... so will sales of your CDs, even if your prices stay the same.

  Alright, so these two mean that the sales of your product could be affected... um increase or decrease by the price changes of other products, though the quality and price of your product stay the same.

Listening Practice 03   p. 69

1. C   2. B   3. D

Listen to part of a lecture in an anatomy class.

Professor: Today we're going to talk about skeletal muscles, which are those attached to our skeleton. Q3 🎧 Well, there are three types of muscle: skeletal, smooth, and cardiac. **But you needn't worry about the last two types right now, okay?** Now, where was I? Ah, yes... skeletal muscles. These muscles create movement by providing strength to our bones and joints when they, um, contract. They can be divided into two distinct types: red muscle and white muscle. Red muscles are found in constantly-used muscles. And... as you know, muscles require oxygen during exercise. Therefore, red muscles need a steadier supply of oxygen. The fibers that make up red muscles contain an oxygen-storing chemical known as myoglobin. The presence of myoglobin allows these muscles to work for long periods of time and gives them their red or darkish color. White muscles, however, are only used occasionally and work best in short bursts, so they don't need as much myoglobin to store oxygen and thus appear white in color. If you think of them in terms of running, white muscles are good for sprinting short distances, while red muscles are better suited for a marathon.

Student: Then, for the same reason, do turkeys or chickens have some white meat and dark meat?

P: Absolutely. They don't usually fly but often run, so they have white muscles for short and quick flights in their breast and wings, and red muscles for constant use in their legs. If you cut into a, um, chicken or turkey at the dinner table, you can find their breast and wings are white meat and the legs are dark meat.

iBT Practice 01 pp. 71~72

1. Ⓑ 2. Ⓐ 3. Ⓓ 4. Ⓒ

Note-Taking

Purpose: get free student pass for gym

All free including the pool? Yes (excited)
Swimming lessons for free? No
 - free access but pay for classes
 - cost extra money to pay instructor (former national team member)
 - talk with her and decide: good
Should get tested? Yes, but just talk about your ability and level

Listen to a conversation in a school gymnasium office.

Student: Hello? Um… is this where I get my free student pass for the gym?

Employee: Yes, it is. I just need to see your student ID.

S: All right… *[pause]* Here you are.

E: Okay, good. Umm… Here is your gym pass.

S: Great. Thank you. *[excited]* This is all free, right? Including the pool?

E: That's right. As a full-time student, you have unlimited access to all the gym facilities, including the pool. I don't know if you've seen it yet, but it's just fabulous.

S: *[excited]* Yes, I came by to see it last week. It looks great! That's why I decided to join the gym this year. I've been meaning to learn how to swim for years, but I haven't had the chance. It's really great to be able to take swimming lessons for free! I plan on signing up for the class right away.

E: *[awkwardly]* Oh… I'm sorry, but I think you, um, misunderstood. The pass will give you free access to the pool, but if you want to take lessons… well, you still have to pay for those.

S: *[surprised]* You're kidding me. What good is a free pass if I have to pay for things?

E: Well… the pass just gives you access to the facilities. Any sort of training or lessons will cost extra. But it's still a really good deal. With your student discount, the lessons are pretty affordable. Let's see… umm, you're a full-time student, so it's going to be $80 for the nine-week term.

S: Oh… no. I thought the swimming lessons were available with the free pass card…

E: No, you're mistaken. The swimming lessons are another thing. Q4 The swimming instructor was hired specially for the new pool, so we need to charge for lessons to pay her salary. **And what's more, it's not like she's just some student volunteer.** Ms. Rossi is a former member of the national swim team and a professional swimming instructor.

S: Really?

E: Tell you what. She should be here in a few minutes. Why don't you wait and talk with her about what the lessons entail, and then you can decide whether to enroll in the swimming class or not?

S: Hmm. Sounds reasonable. Oh, one more question. I'm wondering if I should have my level tested for the swimming class.

E: Yeah, of course. Everyone gets tested before the first day of the class, since we have seven different course levels from beginner to advanced. But you don't have to get wet for the level test. You just talk to your instructor about your present ability and swimming experience before you register.

S: Oh, that's good. Thank you for your help.

iBT Practice 02 pp. 73~74

1. Ⓒ 2. Ⓐ, Ⓒ 3. Ⓓ 4. Ⓓ

Note-Taking

Modern architecture ≠ contemporary architecture
; used to be popular in the 1900s, Europe & US

1. Technology
- new materials: steel & concrete
- thin walls with large areas of glass etc.
2. Style
- simplify buildings, imitate machines
- function > form
3. Criticism
- too bleak and sterile, dehumanizing
- around 1980s, started to decline

Listen to part of a lecture in an architecture class.

Professor: At the end of the nineteenth century… um, and the beginning of the twentieth century, a new style of architecture was developing. Modern architecture.

Q4 Now, when I say "Modern architecture," I don't mean "contemporary architecture." That refers to the architecture that's being made in the present day. Modern architecture is a style that used to be popular. The height of its popularity was from about 1932 to 1984. Of course, it originated some time earlier. Around 1900. At that time, architects in Europe and the U.S. were designing structures in new ways. It was a new architectural style called Modern architecture. Eventually, it spread all over the world.

One of the major factors that shaped Modern architecture was… new technology. Specifically, two new building materials – steel and concrete. Together, these two materials made it possible to do things that had never been done before: extremely thin walls with

197

large areas of glass, enormous spans without supporting columns, and corners formed of glass rather than stone, brick, or wood. So, steel and concrete became the standard building materials, along with glass.

Modern architecture was influenced by new technology. Um, but that wasn't the only factor that affected the look of Modern architecture. See, many architects working in this style were, um, trying to get away from the architecture of the nineteenth century. They thought it borrowed too much from the past. To them, it was too ornate… and outdated. So they tried to make structures that represented values that were current. They got rid of extra ornamentation and simplified their buildings. They also tried to imitate machines by making their designs sleek, elegant, and powerful. The primary principle of this change was that "Form follows function." They thought, um… the form and design of the building should be determined only by functional requirements… not by a traditional style or, um, an aesthetic choice. In short, they valued function over form.

But not everyone embraced Modern architecture. Some people looked at the architecture and saw boring rectangular boxes. Meaningless. They felt like Modern architecture was too bleak and sterile. Some even suggested that it was dehumanizing. They didn't want architecture to imitate machinery… because humans aren't machines. And many humans don't want to live in machines. These critics of Modern architecture wanted to see architecture that was human and accessible. More and more people began to support this viewpoint. So, around the 1980s, Modern architecture began to decline. It certainly hasn't disappeared, though. We can still see Modern architecture and its influences are, um, evident all around us.

Vocabulary Review   pp. 76~77

A 1. brood   2. sprint   3. fertilizer
    4. microorganism   5. layer
B 1. Ⓒ   2. Ⓒ   3. Ⓐ   4. Ⓒ
C 1. Ⓐ   2. Ⓑ   3. Ⓓ
D 1. injection   2. fabulous   3. subsequently
    4. advanced   5. aesthetic
E 1. Ⓐ   2. Ⓒ   3. Ⓓ   4. Ⓑ   5. Ⓓ
    6. Ⓒ
F 1. Ⓐ   2. Ⓒ

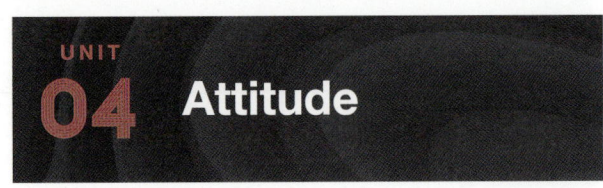

UNIT 04 Attitude

Basic Drills   pp. 82~83

1. Ⓒ   2. Ⓐ   3. Ⓑ   4. Ⓓ   5. Ⓓ   6. Ⓐ

1.

Listen to a conversation between a student and an employee in a Student Help Center.

Student: Hi, I have a problem. It's my roommate… I requested to be placed with my friend. But I was assigned a room with someone else.

Employee: That's a shame. I'm afraid the deadline for switching roommates has passed. You're going to have to live with the situation.

S: *[a little angry]* I know about the deadline. But the thing is, um, it's not my fault this happened. I certainly made a request before the time limit and the office made a mistake.

E: I'm sorry but it's not an easy thing to change roommates. We have to find a new place for your current roommate.

S: Look, I know the rules. I also know that the dormitory makes exceptions in certain cases. This is a situation where they should make an exception.

E: Hmm… the best I can do for you is to tell the director about the situation. If she says it's okay, I'll let you know, okay?

S: Alright.

2.

Listen to part of a lecture in an art history class.

Professor: The close resemblance between Roman art and Greek art can be seen in their concentration on sculptures. Actually, a lot of famous Roman sculptors drew their inspiration from their Greek predecessors. At that time, many rich Romans commissioned copies of Greek statues to embellish their villas and gardens. However, there was more to Roman sculpture than just copying Greek styles. As time passed, it became distinguishable from Greek art. Well umm… the Greeks were known for their idealistic portrayal of people and attempted to capture a person's youth. Roman sculpture, in contrast, attempted to represent a more realistic view. Roman artists tried to recreate what the person really looked like as opposed to showing some ideal. So, portraits of those Romans show every blemish and wart.

Consequently, the Romans' most important contribution to the art of sculpture was realistic portraiture.

3.

Listen to part of a lecture in a geology class.

Professor: Glacial movement, known as basal sliding, occurs when the growing ice mass becomes too heavy to maintain its rigid shape and begins to flow. It is enhanced by pressure melting in which immense pressure of the overlying glacial mass causes the ice making contact with the ground to melt. The melting ice then forms a layer of water that reduces the friction between the glacial ice and the uh… the ground surface. This water works as a lubricant. Naturally, basal sliding depends much on the seasons… because the relatively high temperatures melt away some of the glacier. So, as we can imagine, it happens much faster in summer… while average rates of basal sliding are less than 1 meter per day, some glaciers move up to 50 meters in one summer day.

Student: *[surprised]* 50 meters? That's a pretty big increase.

P: That's right. Daily movement can cover up to 50 meters. The temperature does… um quite a lot, doesn't it?

4.

Listen to a conversation between a student and a basketball team coach.

Student: Hi, coach. Listen, I'm sorry I missed practice last weekend. I forgot to tell you… my sister got married that day.

Coach: Oh, how nice. Congratulations to your sister. I actually have some news for you.

S: Oh?

C: Well, Carey quit the team.

S: She did? But she was the captain.

C: I know. But she said her schoolwork was suffering so she had to quit.

S: I guess we'll have to pick a new captain. How about…

C: *[interrupting]* Well that's what we did on Saturday. Congratulations!

S: What? What do you mean?

C: You were elected the new captain. We all agree that you have the leadership skills necessary.

S: *[surprised]* Wow… but, I'm only a sophomore. Wow, I never would have expected that. Thanks. But… why didn't they tell me?

C: I asked them to wait so I could tell you the good news myself.

S: Wow, I'm honored. And I'm going to get to work right now.

5.

Listen to part of a lecture in an acting class.

Professor: Okay, method acting, or simply the Method as it's known… is an acting technique in which actors draw on their own emotions and experiences to portray a realistic performance of their characters. Well, you might think it's absolutely natural. But conventional acting before the Method was quite different. For example, to uh… express the extreme anger of the character, an actor used to… swing his fist or stamp his feet. When depicting love, he would clasp his hands together on the chest. It was like um… an um… demonstration of wooden actors. So when actors began to draw upon their personal memories of an incident, their performances became much more realistic. They fully immersed themselves in the character in order to sense all of the experiences the character would and… and then used real emotions in portraying their character. Therefore, the audience does not simply understand what the character is experiencing, they also experience it.

6.

Listen to part of a lecture in a psychology class.

Professor: When you are talking with someone, you might often find yourself mirroring their behavior, you know, like um… copying the words they use or mimicking their gestures. Well… interestingly, the same thing appears to apply to laughter, at least at the level of the brain. According to scientists, positive sounds, such as laughter, trigger a strong response in the listener's brain. The response occurs in the same area that's activated when we smile, just like when we prepare our facial muscles to laugh.

Student: How about unpleasant sounds? Don't they also influence the facial muscles?

P: True. Unpleasant sounds such as screaming are also found to trigger similar activity in the same region of the brain. But positive sounds provoke a much more powerful reaction, which um… er, suggests that these were more contagious. So we tend to laugh along with others. Now, it is absolutely true to say "Laugh and the whole world laughs with you."

Dictation
p. 84

1. The close resemblance between 2. drew their inspiration from 3. as opposed to showing some ideal 4. becomes too heavy to maintain 5. enhanced by pressure melting 6. that reduces the friction 7. portray a realistic performance 8. clasp his hands together 9. draw upon their personal memories 10. trigger a strong response 11. that's activated / facial muscles to laugh 12. these were more contagious 13. it is absolutely true to say

Listening Practice 01
p. 85

1. B 2. C 3. D

Listen to a conversation between a student and a professor.

Student: *[apologetic]* Q3 🎧 Sorry I'm late. I had a printer problem.

Professor: Don't worry about it. **I know how troublesome printers can be.** So, you wanted to talk to me about your paper?

S: Right. I've decided on a topic, but I don't know where to begin. I want to write about Evolution vs. Creationism. I've done a lot of research on both sides and I have a lot to say… but, I'm just having trouble figuring out how to start.

P: Okay, what you need to do before you try to write the paper is make an outline. Organization is so important when writing a paper. If you write an outline first, it will help you stay organized. That way you won't get off topic.

S: An outline? Is that the same thing as a road map?

P: No, they're similar, but the difference is that a road map presents different paths you could take. It could be useful when you set every possible plan or guideline for a goal, but when it comes down to writing the paper, you really need an outline.

S: I see.

P: And there's one more thing I want to emphasize. When writing papers for any class, try to be creative. We professors get so bored reading virtually the same paper over and over again. If your paper stands out from the rest, it makes it more enjoyable to read and, provided everything else is okay, you'll probably get a better grade. So, be creative by… um, by approaching your topic from new perspectives.

S: I'll keep that in mind. Thanks.

Listening Practice 02
p. 87

1. B 2. D 3. B

Listen to part of a lecture in a biology class.

Professor: Most of you have probably heard of melatonin. Well, melatonin is the hormone that our body uses to regulate its sleep cycle. It is produced by the pineal gland, a small organ located in our brain, and its production has to do with light… well, to be precise, changes in light. At night, our body increases melatonin production, which induces sleepiness. When the sun comes back up, the light causes production to decrease, helping us to, um… to awaken. So it maintains our circadian rhythm, which is um… an internal 24-hour timekeeping system.

However, when we're exposed to excessive light in the evening or too little light during the day, our normal melatonin cycle can be disrupted and we can experience a temporary sleep problem. For example, night shifts or jet-lag. In these cases, people can take synthetic melatonin as a dietary supplement to help them regain natural sleep cycles. And this has become common. It's also taken by people with more serious sleep disorders, such as insomnia.

But now… it's important to note that there are questions about whether taking melatonin is safe and effective. Studies show that it does have a helpful effect in fighting minor disruptions of sleep patterns in the short term, but we're still not sure what the long term effects might be. Furthermore, taken at the wrong time or in the wrong dosage, it can further disrupt sleep patterns rather than correct them. Definitely more research is needed on the use of melatonin for these treatment purposes.

Listening Practice 03
p. 89

1. C 2. A, D 3. B

Listen to part of a lecture in an art class.

Professor: Fresco is one of the oldest forms of painting. In painting a fresco, wet plaster is used as the base and the artist mixes pigment with water to paint directly onto this wet surface. As it dries, the surface absorbs the paint, and the painting literally becomes a part of the surface. This is what we call buon fresco, or true fresco. Buon means "good" in Italian, but we can think of it as "pure" or "true." Q3 🎧 Besides this, there is also secco fresco. Now, can anybody tell me the difference between the two? It may be easier if you know that secco is Italian for "dry."

Student: Um, you mean… secco fresco uses dry plaster instead of wet plaster?
P: Exactly. But, secco fresco is not considered quite as authentic because dry plaster does not absorb and integrate with the paint. Now, let's talk about the process and the difficulties associated with buon fresco. Buon fresco is difficult to create because of the deadline for the drying time of plaster. An artist needs to meticulously prepare what he or she wishes to accomplish before the plaster dries, dividing the piece into sections that can be expediently completed. A second somewhat more challenging feature is the fact that mistakes are very difficult to cover up. Normally, a painter can disguise mistakes by simply painting over them, but this is not the case with buon fresco where the pigment is absorbed. Once dried, no more buon fresco can be painted without removing the dried plaster from the wall.

iBT Practice 01   pp. 91~92

1. Ⓓ   2. Ⓒ   3. Ⓑ   4. Ⓐ

Note-Taking

Find a book for art class
- Buy your text book now? Because I lost mine
- No copies left

Options
① Can special order but have to ask professor (x)
② Go to big bookstores downtown (△)
③ Check message board: buy & sell used books (o)

Listen to a conversation between a student and a college bookstore clerk.

Student: Excuse me, can you give me a hand?
Bookstore Clerk: Sure. What can I do for you?
S: Q3 🎧 I'm trying to find a book for my Intro to Art History class, but it doesn't seem to be here.
C: Well, you're in the right place. This is the Art section... Did you say Intro to Art History? With Professor Goldman?
S: That's right.
C: [surprised] And you've just come to buy your textbook now? **That class started more than a month ago.**
S: I know. I lost my copy last week. I tried to find it, but I couldn't... it wasn't in the Lost and Found, either.
C: Oh, that's too bad. So now you need to get a new one.
S: Uh-huh. But... it looks like there aren't any copies left.
C: That's right, there aren't. It's been out of stock for weeks.
S: Oh, no... Is there any way I can get one?
C: Q4 🎧 Well, actually, you have a few, um, options. I can special order a copy for you, but you'd have to ask Professor Goldman to come down to the bookstore. We can only make special orders at the direct request of a professor.
S: [hesitantly] Oh... I see. I'll erm... I'll think about it... but, I wish there was another way.
C: You could also go downtown to one of the big bookstores in the, er, mall and see if they have a copy. But I'm not sure if they'd have what you need. You know, the situation wouldn't be much different there. And, you know... there's always the message board. Unless, of course, you've already checked it.
S: The message what?
C: The message board. It's down the hall, across from the cafeteria. You don't know about it?
S: No. What is it?
C: It's just a big bulletin board where students can buy and sell used textbooks. Check to see if anybody is selling the book you need. If not, you can put up your own note saying you're looking for a copy. If anyone has one, they'll give you a call. I think there's a good chance you can get the book because so many students use that board.
S: Cool. That sounds great. I'll check out the board first before I make the trip downtown. Thanks for your help.
C: Good luck.

iBT Practice 02   pp. 93~94

1. Ⓐ   2. Ⓒ   3. Ⓑ, Ⓓ   4. Ⓓ

Note-Taking

The BCG Growth-Share Matrix
- relative market growth & relative market share
- market share ↑ → cash generation ↑
  → cash consumption ↑ (investment ↑)

1. Dogs
   growth ↓ share ↓, cash consumption & generation ↓
2. Cash Cows
   growth ↓ share ↑, cash generation > consumption
   (invest in Stars)
3. Stars
   growth ↑ share ↑, cash generation & consumption ↑
   (become Cash Cows)
4. Question Marks
   growth ↑ share ↓ (become either Stars or Dogs)

Limitation: ignores other factors, overlooks
           interrelatedness among units
→ But still used

Listen to part of a lecture in a business class.

Professor: The BCG Growth-Share Matrix is a sort of planning model that can be used to determine the importance of business units within a corporation or the products within a single unit. It breaks them down into four basic categories based on, um, two factors: relative market growth and relative market share. The BCG Matrix is based on the assumption that an increase in relative market share will lead to an increase in cash generation and that a growing market will lead to an increase in cash consumption, due to a need for increased, um... increased investment. Got it? Good. Now, does anyone know what the four categories are?

Student: Well... I've heard about the names and I remember each category has an interesting name. But all I remember is that Cows are good and Dogs are bad.

P: Well... that's basically correct. But it really requires some elaboration. Dogs are units that have a low growth rate and low market shares, signifying low levels of both cash consumption and generation. Basically, they are unprofitable and undesirable. On the other hand, Cash Cows are part of a low growth industry, but have a high market share. They generate more cash than they consume and are the source of cash for other units. Stars are units with high growth and high market shares that generate and consume large amounts of cash, eventually becoming valuable Cash Cows. And finally, Question Marks are high growth, low market share units. As they mature, these units have the potential to become either Stars or Dogs. So to put it all together, Cows provide the cash to invest in Stars, which represent future potential. Dogs are bad for a business, and Question Marks, as the name implies, can go either way.

As you can see, the BCG Matrix is simple and easy to understand. However, it has its limitations. It ignores many other influences on profitability. Market growth rate is just one of many factors relating to industry attractiveness, as is relative market share in relation to competitive advantage. In addition, the BCG matrix overlooks the impact of interrelatedness among units. In some instances, a business unit that is a "dog" may be aiding other units to gain a competitive advantage.

Well... its importance may have diminished, but the BCG matrix can still be used as a snapshot of a corporation's business portfolio and can act as a starting point for considering resource allocation among strategic business units.

Vocabulary Review — pp. 96~97

A 1. perspective 2. distinguishable 3. mimic 4. portrayal 5. swing

B 1. Ⓐ 2. Ⓓ 3. Ⓒ 4. Ⓓ

C 1. Ⓑ 2. Ⓐ 3. Ⓑ 4. Ⓒ

D 1. draw 2. get 3. rigid 4. stock 5. competitive

E 1. Ⓓ 2. Ⓐ 3. Ⓒ 4. Ⓒ 5. Ⓑ

F 1. Ⓑ 2. Ⓑ 3. Ⓓ

Actual Practice Test 2

01
pp. 100~101

1. Ⓒ 2. Ⓑ 3. Ⓐ 4. Ⓒ 5. Ⓑ

Note-Taking

Final report
- terrific!
- will make excellent presentation at seminar 'cause topic fits

How about giving presentation?
- (student) need time to think
- (prof.) ok, but good opportunity
  (meet influential people & look great on resume)
→ Will try

Plans after graduation?
- teach at high school → college
- grad school? not sure
→ very promising future!

Look over the material?
- come back Mon. 2 pm

Listen to a conversation between a student and a professor.

Student: You wanted to see me, Professor Park?

Professor: Yes, Mario. Come in and have a seat. I wanted to talk to you about your final report.

S: Oh... I hope it was okay.

P: It was more than okay, Mario. I honestly think it may have been the best report I've read this semester. You did a terrific job with it.

S: *[happily]* Oh, thank you.

P: In fact, the reason I wanted to talk to you was that I think the material you cover in your paper would make an excellent presentation at the upcoming teaching seminar the Education department is hosting on campus. Your paper, the, um... what was its exact title again?

S: "How to Increase Students' Intrinsic Motivation in the Classroom."

P: That's it. The topic is a perfect fit with one of the sessions I plan on attending. How about giving a presentation on your paper there?

S: *[surprised]* Can I?

P: Yes, you can make it as a student speaker...

S: Q5 🎧 Oh... I'm really honored that you'd ask me. But... this is sort of unexpected... I'm not sure I could do it well enough. Is it okay if I take a little time to think it over?

P: Sure. The choice is yours, Mario. **I will say, however, that this is a tremendous opportunity.** You'll meet a lot of influential people in the education field and it will look great on your resume.

S: Well... considering what you said, I guess it would be a good experience.

P: No doubt! If necessary, I'd be willing to help you.

S: Okay, I'll give it a try. Now I need to refine my report for the presentation.

P: Good! I'll write down the website of the conference. If you're online, look it over. You can see which other papers will be presented, and it should give you a better idea of what it's all about.

S: Thank you for your help.

P: No problem! Anyway... can I ask what your plans are after graduation?

S: Well, I've got another whole year before I graduate, but I'd really like to teach... maybe at a high school at first, but eventually at the college level.

P: Excellent. Have you given any thought to attending graduate school right away?

S: I've thought about it a little... but... well, I'm still not sure.

P: OK. I was just curious about your plans. I think you have a very promising future in the field of education.

S: It means a lot to hear you say that, Professor Park. So I guess I can prepare the material for the presentation this weekend. Could you look it over?

P: Of course! Let me see... Why don't you come back next Monday at... umm... 2 pm?

S: I only have one class on Monday. It's in the morning, so that's fine.

P: Great! See you then!

02
pp. 102~103

6. Ⓐ 7. Ⓑ 8. Ⓓ 9. Ⓓ 10. Ⓒ 11. Ⓑ

Note-Taking

Intro_ similarity in sleep patterns (4 stages)
- REM? final stage, Rapid Eye Movement
- Non-REM? 1-3 stages

1. half awake: body contracts
2. light sleep: brain waves & heartbeat slow down
3. light → deep sleep: delta waves
4. deeper sleep
5. REM: dreaming, brain & eye ↑ , heart rate & breathing ↑

Cycle: 1-2-3-2-REM
- grow older → shorter deep sleep
- can be disrupted by stress

Listen to part of a lecture in a psychology class.

Professor: Along with food, air, and water, a basic requirement of all humans is sleep. How long do you sleep on average? Umm... about 8 hours? 7 hours? Well, in my case... 6 hours. And I'm pretty sure some of you are early birds, and others are not. Now, as you can see, how much sleep we need is different from person to person. However, there's a certain, um... basic similarity in our sleep patterns that we all share. When we sleep, we progress through a cycle of stages... with four stages in total. So... can anybody identify any of these stages?

Student: Um... REM is one of the stages, isn't it?

P: Yes, it is. REM is the fourth and final stage of sleep. Do you happen to know what the acronym REM stands for?

S: Actually, I don't.

P: Q10 REM stands for Rapid Eye Movement, named for the way our eyes react when we dream. Then, what about the other three stages? They don't involve this kind of movement. **And you probably inferred this, but the first three stages of sleep are known as non-REM sleep.**

Let's briefly run through the four stages of sleep. Stage one... this is the very beginning of sleep, the period when you're half awake and half asleep. As you begin to relinquish control of your muscles, you might feel your whole body suddenly contract for no apparent reason. Although your body has begun to sleep, you remain partially aware of your environment.

The next stage, stage two, is a period of light sleep. Your body relaxes, and your brain waves and heartbeat slow down as you begin to drift toward deep sleep. Okay? Is everybody still with me? Good.

From here, we move to the third stage, when you make the transition from light to deep sleep. Your brain... umm... your brain begins to produce slow waves known as delta waves, and your eyes and muscles stop moving. Sleepwalking also tends to occur most often during this stage of deep sleep.

Finally, the fourth stage is when we experience REM sleep. The REM or Rapid Eye Movement stage is when, um... well, it's when a change in physiological state really begins to kick in. During this period, dreaming occurs. Because of this, brain activity increases dramatically, as does eye movement. Also, your heart rate and breathing speed up. Although your body is basically paralyzed at this point, your hands and feet may begin to twitch.

Now... healthy sleep generally occurs in cycles, moving forward through the first three stages, then back to stage 2, before slipping into the REM stage. Non-REM stages tend to last about 5 to 15 minutes each, while we get about an hour and a half to two hours of REM sleep per night.

These cycles are altered as we grow older, with a decrease in the length of stage three, where deep sleep occurs. They can also be disrupted by factors such as stress or depression. Q11 But if your body is allowed to go through the cycles uninterrupted, you'll generally wake up feeling rested and refreshed.

03   pp. 104~105

12. Ⓐ 13. Ⓓ 14. Ⓑ, Ⓒ 15. Ⓑ 16. Ⓒ
17. Ⓑ

Note-Taking

Intro_ Mayan civilization
; Pre-Columbian times
  Hunter-gatherer lifestyle? No, quite advanced

1. Math
- had the concept of zero
- base twenty number system
- 3 glyphs → create large numbers

2. Astronomy
- observed motions of the Sun, stars, planets
- created 365-day calendar

3. Architecture
- beauty & astronomical markers
- pyramids & cities: use as calendar

4. Writing system
- used symbols, represented spoken language, depicted human shapes...

Listen to part of a lecture in a history class.

Professor: The Mayan civilization spanned Southern Mexico and Northern Central America. So... what is today Guatemala, Belize, Western Honduras, and El Salvador as well as some of the southern states of Mexico... that was the region of the Mayan people. So we're talking Pre-Columbian times, right? Now, often when we imagine the Americas before Christopher Columbus arrived we think of tribal peoples living a hunter-gatherer lifestyle. That was common in North America. But the Mayans were very different. They had a large population, they stayed in one place, and most importantly... were quite advanced.

For starters, they were excellent mathematicians. They had the concept of zero by as early as 36 BC. Over in Europe they didn't understand "nothing" as a number for another thousand-odd years. And the Mayans developed a numerical system and used a base twenty number system. It incorporated 3 glyphs: a dot for one, a bar for five, and zero was represented by a shell. By um... simply changing the arrangement of the symbols, they were able to create larger numbers... reaching the hundreds and millions... and perform complex mathematical operations.

Math was a stepping stone to achievements in other fields. I mean, the Mayans used the mathematical system to develop astronomical knowledge. They were especially interested in observing the complex motions of the Sun, the stars, and the planets. From these observations, they created a 365-day calendar. The accuracy of their calendar was almost flawless, so neighboring nations such as the Aztecs adopted its mechanics. Now, remember... this was before any telescopes. That's pretty impressive.

Next, advanced astronomy was applied to architectural constructions. Mayan architecture is famous and valued not only for its beauty but also for being astronomical markers. For example, the fantastic stepped pyramids were built basically for religious purposes. But, they were also used as a calendar: just like the number of days in a year, there were a total of 365 steps, with one platform atop 4 stairways each containing 91 steps. This is not all. Q17 🎧 Actually, Mayan cities ended up being monumental records of the planetary movements through the skies. The orientation of the buildings coincided with the movements of the Sun and actually functioned as a calendar. **How?** By building structures in that way, the shadow they cast would give people an idea of how far they were from the solstices and equinoxes.

Last, but certainly not the least, they had a writing system. In fact, they were the only ones in the Americas to have a fully developed writing system in the Pre-Columbian era... as far as we know, anyway. They began writing over 2300 years ago and their writing system consisted of symbols that are known to completely represent the spoken language of its community. Arranged to depict human shapes and forms, the symbols also included a few abstract figures. The Mayans wrote using individual signs or glyphs, paired in columns that read together from left to right and top to bottom just as we do today. So anyway, it's been pretty much deciphered and we can see that the ancient Mayans used this writing system to keep records of all kinds of things... dates, history, and of course, observations of the sky.

UNIT 05 Organization

Basic Drills

pp. 110~111

1. Ⓒ   2. Ⓐ   3. Ⓓ   4. Ⓑ   5. Ⓓ   6. Ⓒ

1.

Listen to part of a lecture in a geology class.

Professor: Okay, so we know that glaciers begin to form when snow remains in the same area year-round, and where enough snow accumulates to transform into ice. Now, each year brings new layers of that snow cover that compress the previous layers. This compression... uh... forces the snow to re-crystallize, into a shape and size similar to a grain of sugar. Gradually the grains grow and squeeze out air pockets between them, causing the snow to slowly compact and increase in density. After about... maybe two winters, the snow turns into firn – an intermediate state between snow and glacier ice. At this point, it is about half as dense as water, but the process isn't complete. Over time, larger ice crystals become so compressed that there are almost no air pockets between them. In very old glacier ice, crystals can reach several inches in length. For most glaciers, it takes over a hundred years to reach this state.

2.

Listen to part of a lecture in a biology class.

Professor: All right. As you know, the body organs used for tasting are the tongue and the palate in the mouth, but the real detectors are the taste buds, of which there are about 10,000 on the tongue. Now, you might think the bumps on your tongue are the taste buds. But in fact they are called papillae, and your taste buds are located on them. Each uhm... taste bud is made up of er... receptor cells or taste cells that respond to taste. Basically a receptor can respond to all tastes, but it responds strongest to a particular taste... sweet, sour, salty, or bitter. So, when recognizing taste, the flavor dissolved in your saliva gathers in tiny pools at the bottom of all the taste buds. The receptors then change these chemical erm... signals I guess, into an electrical stimulus, which travels through the nervous system to the brain.

3.

Listen to part of a lecture in a psychology class.

Professor: So now, let's talk about stress and trauma. First, what causes stress?

Student: Something like an exam, deadline, or job interview.

P: Absolutely. Like you said, stress is a reaction to less dramatic and often daily events. Meanwhile, trauma is when a sudden event overwhelms the individual's ability to cope… uhm… such as a terror attack or a car crash. Now, as you can guess from those examples, the degree of shock and anxiety differs greatly between stress and trauma. Most people will understandably feel nervous when facing an important exam, but wouldn't lose their self-control. However, people who go through… erm… a traumatic experience are vulnerable to loss of control because of the severity of the event. Now in some cases, the trauma is so severe that they suffer repeated memories of the event and feel completely insecure and helpless. The traumatic event is relived repeatedly in their minds and impedes their ability to live their lives.

4.

Listen to part of a lecture in an astronomy class.

Professor: Currently the… the accepted explanation of the beginning of the universe is the Big Bang theory. It uh… now let's see, it… uh… proposes that the universe was once extremely compact, dense, and hot and that… uh… some original event, a cosmic explosion called the Big Bang, occurred about 13.7 billion years ago, and the universe has been expanding and cooling ever since.

Student: Oh, you mean our universe was not as big as it is now?

P: Exactly. According to the theory, initially all of the matter and energy of space was contained, erm… condensed at one point, like a fireball. Then, with the Big Bang, all of the particles of the embryonic universe filled the space. Think of the universe as a fruitcake in an oven. As it bakes, the cake rises and all the bits of fruit move further and further away. See, this is what has been happening to our universe.

5.

Listen to part of a lecture in a literature class.

Professor: Okay. Autobiographies and memoirs take very different approaches in their representations. As a rule, they differ in time and focus. I mean… while an autobiography tends to follow chronological order through a person's life, a memoir usually doesn't adhere to a chronological timeline. And while an autobiography focuses on specific events, awards, or accomplishments of the author with an objective viewpoint, a memoir has…uhm… how can I say… more intimate focus on his or her own memories, feelings, and emotions. So memoirs are more subjective and resemble fictional novels. Let's take an example… umm… from the Civil War. The autobiography of a Civil War general might include sections on the nature of slavery, the origins of the War, and the political career of Abraham Lincoln. But his memoir would focus on personal reasons for joining the battle, the effect of the war on his mind, and the joy and fear he felt on the battlefield.

6.

Listen to part of a lecture in a physics class.

Professor: Because of a gamma ray's high energy, it can travel a great distance and pass through many kinds of material, including human tissue. This penetrating property is what makes gamma rays a primary hazard. Once they penetrate human tissue, they can cause DNA to change by messing around with the genetic material of the cell. Actually, it is more of an alteration. To be exact, it's damage that correlates with an increased risk of developing a variety of cancers… leukemia, lung, liver, skeletal, and other cancers. Also, the… uhm… the gamma rays produce thermal burn injuries on human skin. So, the term "radiation sickness" describes the effects of large exposures to radiation in a short period of time, the most severe damage almost certainly resulting from gamma radiation.

Dictation   p. 112

1. accumulates to transform into ice   2. squeeze out air pockets   3. half as dense as water
4. responds strongest to a particular taste
5. gathers in tiny pools   6. vulnerable to loss of control   7. is relived repeatedly   8. condensed at one point   9. follow chronological order / adhere to
10. resemble fictional novels   11. a primary hazard   12. by messing around with   13. produce thermal burn injuries

Listening Practice 01   p. 113

1. Ⓐ   2. Ⓑ   3. Ⓒ

Listen to part of a lecture in a zoology class.

Professor: In the past, people had a very different attitude toward household pets than most of us do today. In essence, they were viewed as little more than possessions. It's not that people didn't form emotional attachments to them, but they were generally valued more for, um, practical purposes.

Student1: Do you mean like the fact that dogs could protect your house?

Professor: Yes, exactly like that. Dogs had value because they can scare away intruders or help control livestock. And cats would keep the household free of rats and other vermin. Today, however, pets primarily serve a very different role. What do you think that is?

Student1: Um... companionship? I mean, it seems like people enjoy spending time with their pets. You know, just taking them for walks or playing with them.

Professor: Correct. Almost as if they were members of the family, right? Which is exactly the way many modern people view their pets. They treat them like children, and in return they receive friendship and loyalty. Also, as any parent can tell you, pets are great with kids. They keep kids engaged and happy, and taking care of them can teach a child important lessons about responsibility. What's more, pets can help people connect with other people in their community.

Student2: I'm sorry, but I don't understand. How can pets do that?

Professor: Well, for example, dogs love going to the park, but their owners also benefit by getting a chance to meet and chat with other dog owners. So, ultimately, welcoming a pet into your home is a win-win situation. Interestingly, Gandhi once commented about that. He wrote that the relationship between man and beast should involve "mutual aid" rather than one taking advantage of the other. Like many great thinkers, he recognized the importance of the social bond between humans and animals.

Listening Practice 02   p. 115

1. Ⓑ   2. Ⓒ   3. Ⓐ, Ⓒ

Listen to part of a lecture in a modern dance class.

Professor: Isadora Duncan was perhaps one of the most important dancers in the early twentieth century in America. People called her the mother of modern dance because she revolutionized dance through ballet. In the 1920s, ballet lacked the grace it has today – it was, umm... all acrobatics and gymnastics. Ballet dancers also endured torturous restrictions to their bodies such as corseted costumes and shoes that were too small. Duncan criticized these conventions for making dancing inexpressive and unnatural. So she literally kicked off her toe shoes and wore a long, flowing Grecian gown to enhance the expressiveness of the human body.

Duncan also brought a new perspective to the use of music. Traditionally, ballet scores like waltzes and polkas were the means of creating dances which dancers simply danced to. However, Duncan believed dancers shouldn't think about music but should feel it with their soul. For her, music was an inspirational element that brought excitement and emotional energy. So she turned to the finest music of the master composers – Beethoven, Chopin, Bach, and Schumann. Her unique approach certainly paved the way for future dancers and opened up the world of interpretive dance.

Isadora Duncan also emphasized moving dance away from strict formal structures and toward more free-flowing forms of personal expression. She employed everyday human movements such as skipping and running, in her dance. With such motions she imitated nature in her dancing. For example, she and her fellow dancers would move together in such a way as to imitate a person or animal breathing, making the whole stage seem alive. That's what made her dancing truly unique.

Listening Practice 03   p. 117

1. Ⓐ   2. Ⓑ   3. Ⓓ

Listen to part of a lecture in an ecology class.

Professor: The food chain is a graphic representation of the feeding relationships between species in an ecological community. Today we'll examine some of the features that comprise a typical food chain. Okay, let's start with the producers, which are at the bottom of the food chain. They... uhm... they can make their own food and include such organisms as plants and vegetables. The producers obtain energy by converting light into sugars and starches through photosynthesis.

The... uhm... next link in the chain are the consumers. They cannot make food for themselves so instead survive by feeding off other organisms. Scientists have classified three sublevels of consumer, the first of which, the primary consumers, are the herbivores. As no doubt the name suggests, herbivores eat only plants. Secondary consumers eat the primary consumers. They are also called carnivores, which means "meat eater." Lastly, the third consumers are called omnivores.

207

Omnivores are organisms such as humans that eat both plants and animals.

Completing the ecosystem are the decomposers. These are mainly... uhm... bacteria and fungi that convert... uh... dead matter into gases such as carbon dioxide and nitrogen to be released back into the air, soil, or water. In other words, they play an important role in recycling nutrients to be used again by producers.

Now, as you may have noticed, the food chain is depicted as a pyramid. There are far more producers than consumers, and far more herbivores than omnivores. This pattern is crucial to sustain life.

iBT Practice 01   pp. 119~120

1.   2.   3.   4. Ⓐ

Note-Taking

Defense of human body: immune system
Allergy: an exaggerated reaction by our immune system
Allergen: substance causing allergic reaction
  1. breathe in (eg. dust mites, pollen: runny nose, itchy eyes)
  2. eat (eg. peanut: could die)
  3. contact with skin (eg. plants, metals: itchy rash)
  4. be injected (eg. bee sting: fatal reaction)
Cause? Heredity (but not necessarily)

Listen to part of a lecture in a biology class.

Professor: The human body is designed to defend itself against substances that enter it. This defense is called an immune system. For example, a virus enters your body, you get sick. Now... hopefully, with some rest and some medicine, you will get better. That is because your immune system fights the virus. However, sometimes our immune system is kind of... mobilized to fight off what's not a virus. Allergies are related to this phenomenon. In other words, an allergy is an exaggerated reaction by our immune system in response to bodily contact with certain foreign substances. The reason why I use the word "exaggerated" is because the immune system is turned on the foreign substances, which are usually seen by the body as harmless and cause no response to non-allergic people. The... the substance that causes an allergic reaction is called an "allergen."

Now, let's look over a few sources of allergens. First, some allergens enter the body when we breathe them in, such as dust mites and pollen. People who are sensitive to them exhibit such symptoms as a runny nose and itchy eyes. Other allergens, such as food allergens, enter the body when we eat them. For example, while most people can enjoy peanuts, there are some people who react so severely that they could die if they ingest the nut. Next, some allergens affect people when they have contact with their skin. Plants such as poison ivy or oak and metals like nickel are examples. Allergic reactions to them involve an itchy rash on the skin. Finally, let's see here... allergens can enter the body by being injected, like when a bee stings a person. Also vaccines and hormones like insulin can be the allergens in this case. Those who are allergic can have a fatal reaction because the allergen goes directly into the blood stream.

So why is it that some people have allergies and others don't? The major factor appears to be heredity. Q4 🎧 I mean... your risk of developing allergies is related to your parents' allergy history. If neither parent is allergic, your chance of having an allergy is about 15 percent. If one parent is allergic, your risk increases to 30 percent and it's greater than 60 percent if both parents suffer. However, although you may inherit the uhm... tendency to develop allergies, you may never actually have symptoms. Nor uh... would you necessarily inherit the same allergies or diseases as your parents. It is unclear what determines which substances will trigger a reaction in an allergic person.

iBT Practice 02   pp. 121~122

1.   2.   3.   4.

Note-Taking

Climate change caused by external factors
1. Earth is tilted
   - season, different length of day & night
   - inclination changes: greater tilt → extreme weather
2. Shape of Earth's orbit
   - not circular
   - orbit shape change: more elliptical → extreme weather
3. Orientation of tilt of the Earth
   - moves in circle: precession
   - winter and summer were reversed
⇒ natural occurrence

Listen to part of a lecture in a climatology class.

Professor: Today, I want to talk about climate change. It has become clear that the climate of our Earth is changing, and scientific evidence suggests that humans are partially to blame. But it's important to understand that the Earth's climate has changed before. There are many reasons for that. Okay, let's start with some external factors... things that cause climate change.

First above all, if the Earth did not tilt, there would be

no seasons and day and night would be the same length all year. However, the Earth is tilted at an angle of 23.5°. When the northern hemisphere is having its summer, umm… beginning in June, there is more sunlight in northern latitudes than in the southern hemisphere. During this phase, the days are longer and the Sun is at a higher angle. At the same time in the southern hemisphere, winter has arrived – umm… with shorter days and the Sun at a lower angle. The more important fact is… according to theory, the Earth's inclination on its axis is not always set at 23.5°. During a 41,000-year cycle, this tilt is calculated to alter between 22.1° and 24.5°. A lesser tilt results in cooler summers and milder winters. A greater one leads to more extreme seasonal weather.

The second factor we should consider is the shape of the Earth's orbit around the Sun. It is not quite circular, as you know. The Earth is slightly nearer to the Sun during some times of the year than at other times. But the shape of the Earth's orbit is also changing in cycles of between 90,000 and 100,000 years. So, when it is more elliptical than it is now, some parts of the Earth will have to undergo extremely hot summers or cold winters.

But there is another complication. The orientation of the tilt of the Earth's axis changes over time. Like a spinning top that is winding down, the axis moves in a circle. This movement is called precession. Taking place on a 22,000-year cycle, this causes the seasons to move very slowly through the year. Umm, in fact, if you go back 11,000 years, the northern hemisphere was inclined toward the Sun in December, not June – that is, winter and summer were reversed. In 11,000 years time, they will have switched again.

These three factors – tilt, orbital shape, and precession combine to create immense changes in climate. But well, it is sort of a natural occurrence. As I said, this kind of change happens outside the Earth at least every um… every 10 thousand years. We can't change those causes. Now, let's move on to the internal factors that have more to do with human activities.

Vocabulary Review pp. 124~125

A 1. subsequent 2. elliptical 3. chronological 4. embryonic 5. inherit
B 1. Ⓓ 2. Ⓒ 3. Ⓓ 4. Ⓑ
C 1. Ⓒ 2. Ⓑ 3. Ⓓ 4. Ⓐ
D 1. away 2. around 3. terms 4. system 5. paved
E 1. Ⓐ 2. Ⓑ 3. Ⓓ 4. Ⓑ 5. Ⓓ 6. Ⓐ
F 1. Ⓐ 2. Ⓒ

UNIT 06 Connecting Content

Basic Drills pp. 130~131

1. Ⓒ   2. Non-El Niño condition – Ⓑ, Ⓓ / El Niño condition – Ⓐ, Ⓒ   3. Ⓓ – Ⓒ – Ⓐ – Ⓑ   4. Ⓓ   5. High N score – Ⓐ, Ⓓ / Low N score – Ⓑ / Neither – Ⓒ   6. Larva – Ⓑ / Pupa – Ⓐ / Adult – Ⓒ

1.

Listen to a conversation between two students.

Student 1: You don't look so good. Are you feeling alright?
Student 2: *[voice is hoarse]* No, I've got a bug. My throat is sore and I have a fever.
S1: It sounds like you should see a doctor.
S2: I can't afford to see a doctor.
S1: What do you mean you can't afford it? What about the school insurance policy?
S2: I don't have insurance through the school.
S1: Of course you do. It's included in your tuition.
S2: Well, last semester I tried to see a doctor and they told me I wasn't covered.
S1: That's strange. Wait… how many credits did you take last semester?
S2: Just 8.
S1: Oh, that explains it. You have to be a full time student. You're only part time.
S2: But I'm full time now.
S1: In that case you should be covered. You should go to the Student Health Center and check it out. You need to get some medicine.
S2: That's a relief. Thanks.

2.

Listen to part of a lecture in a meteorology class.

Professor: So, in normal, um… in non-El Niño conditions, the tropical trade winds blow toward the west across the tropical Pacific. These winds pile up warm surface water in the western Pacific, so that the surface level in the west is a half meter higher than in the east. Also, in the eastern Pacific… around South America, westerly trade winds promote an upwelling, you know, the wind-driven motion of deep and cooler water toward the ocean surface. This cold water is nutrient-rich and supports diverse marine ecosystems. But, um, during El Nino, this situation is disrupted and the trade winds weaken, which means the upwelling of cool waters in the eastern Pacific reduces and uh... as such the pool of warm water in the west drifts eastward toward South America.

3.

Listen to part of a lecture in an art class.

Professor: The first step in appreciating art is identifying what is actually in the work. What I mean is, we should examine every aspect of it, including specific shapes, colors, and textures. Then it's time to analyze how the work's qualities are arranged. For example, we can think of questions like these: Is the work visually symmetrical or asymmetrical? Are there any clearly prevailing colors? After analyzing... the uh... next step is interpreting what the work expresses. Now we include our emotions and thoughts, based upon what we observe... so our judgment shouldn't be clouded by prejudice, you know? Instead, we must discover the meaning of the work and the intention of the artist from the apparent features of the work. Finally, we evaluate the artwork. Now, this requires a background that is related to what's being evaluated. For example, questioning whether a work is an extraordinary example of a particular artistic style needs some acquaintance with other works of the same style.

4.

Listen to a conversation between a student and a professor.

Student: Excuse me, sir. Would it be possible for me to take Friday's test another time?
Professor: May I ask why?
S: Well, I'm actually going to France this weekend.
P: France! In the middle of the semester! Don't you think you should wait till school's out?
S: Oh, it's not a vacation. I have a job interview.
P: A job interview in France? That's interesting.
S: Yes, the interview is for a management position at a company in Paris.
P: Wow, that's exciting. I wish you the best of luck. Now, the test... it won't be a problem because I was planning to make it a take-home. You can probably do it on the plane.
S: Perfect. When can I pick it up?
P: Come by my office on Thursday. I'll have it ready by then. And I'd like you to get it back to me by class on Monday, okay?
S: Sure, thanks.

5.

Listen to part of a lecture in a psychology class.

Professor: Okay, so the last factor of the "Big Five" personality traits is neuroticism or negative emotionality, known as N by psychologists. This uh... this trait is about the tendency to experience negative emotional states. Individuals who score high on neuroticism are more likely than the average to experience such feelings as uh... let me see... such feelings as anxiety, anger, guilt, and depression. In other words, such people are more likely to interpret ordinary situations as threatening, and minor frustrations as hopelessly difficult. So they get stressed out very easily.
Student: Umm, professor. If some people get low scores on neuroticism, does it mean that they feel happy with their circumstances?
P: Well, it's not like that. Freedom from negative feelings does not always mean happiness. Instead, those people show a relatively stable and calm state of mind.

6.

Listen to part of a lecture in a biology class.

Professor: Alright, complete metamorphosis takes place in most species of insects, including butterflies, beetles, bees, and ants. All these insects go through four developmental stages. So let's take a look. First, an adult female lays a tiny egg from which a small worm-like creature called a larva hatches. Most insects with complete metamorphosis spend the majority of their lives in this humble larval form, doing little more than eating and growing. A nice easy life, huh? When the larva completes its growth, it stops eating and becomes a pupa. Okay, to prepare for this stage, some larvae spin a cocoon or form some other protective cover around their bodies. While in this state, the larval structures are broken down and reformed into adult organs. Once the change is complete, the pupa cover cracks open and the adult insect crawls out.

Dictation p. 132

1. pile up warm surface water 2. supports diverse marine ecosystems 3. examine every aspect of it 4. be clouded by prejudice 5. needs some acquaintance with 6. make it a take-home 7. negative emotional states 8. more likely to interpret / hopelessly difficult 9. calm state of mind 10. four developmental stages 11. lays a tiny egg / hatches 12. the majority of / doing little more than 13. cracks open / crawls out

Listening Practice 01   p. 133

1. Ⓒ   2. Ⓑ   3. Ⓐ

Listen to a conversation between a student and an academic adviser.

Academic adviser: What can I help you with?
Student: I was wondering if you knew of any student exchange programs... for Spain I mean. I'm doing pretty well in my Spanish class and I want to become fluent.
A: Yes, there are a couple, but you'll need to see Dr. Sullivan about that. He's in charge of the language department and he'd be the one with the application forms. Let me ask you... what year are you in?
S: I'm a sophomore.
A: Good. It's best to apply in your early years rather than when you're getting close to graduation.
S: That makes sense.
A: Well, as far as I know, there are two options. One is the structured program. This is where you go to study at a sister school and you are provided with housing and all your meals.
S: What's the other option?
A: With the other option we hook you up with the sister school, but you have to find your own place to live and pay for your own meals. Of course, this is the cheaper option.
S: I see. I think it would be worth it to pay the extra money for the structured program. After all, I've never been to Spain before. It might be hard to find housing and stuff, especially before I get the language down. What is the difference in price, anyway?
A: Unfortunately, I don't know the details. You'll have to talk to Dr. Sullivan for more information because he has a lot more experience than I do with the exchange programs.
S: Okay, well, I really appreciate your help.

Listening Practice 02   p. 135

1. Ⓑ   2. Ⓑ   3. Coloration – Ⓒ / Countershading – Ⓐ / Disguise – Ⓑ

Listen to part of a lecture in a biology class.

Professor: Another common survival technique is camouflage. Some animals use it to sneak up on prey, while others use it to avoid predators. Generally, camouflage works by, um... by allowing an animal to blend in with its environment. So... who can give me an example of an animal that uses camouflage?
Student: How about leopards? The dark spots on their fur sort of blend in with the light and shadows of the grass. It makes them really hard to see.
P: Right. That's called coloration and many animals rely on their coloration for camouflage. You know, animals that live in the snow are often white, while ones that live in the desert are the color of sand. Other animals, like leopards, rely on multi-colored patterns... sometimes spots, sometimes stripes... to make their bodies resemble the texture of the world around them.
   Another type of color-based camouflage is something known as countershading. Many fish, for example, are darkly colored on top and lighter underneath. By offsetting the light underwater – with sunshine above and dark shadows below – this type of coloration makes fish difficult to detect from a distance.
   And some animals use disguises as camouflage, a technique we call mimicry. This means they appear to be something they are not, either an object or another kind of animal. In trees, for example, you'll find some insects that resemble leaves and others that resemble twigs. By keeping still when predators approach, they seem to be part of the tree.

Listening Practice 03   p. 137

1. Ⓓ   2. Ⓑ   3. Chansons de geste Ⓐ, Ⓓ / Chivalric romances – Ⓑ, Ⓒ

Listen to part of a lecture in a literature class.

Professor: During the medieval period, French literature was dominated by a genre that we refer to as chivalric literature. Now, can anybody tell me what the two, um, predominant forms of French chivalric literature were?
Student: Um, I'm not sure but... romance?
P: Yes, chivalric romance. That's one... but do you know what came before chivalric romances? Anybody? [pause] Before chivalric romances, there were the chansons de geste, which means "songs of heroic deeds" in old French. These epic poems date back to the late eleventh century, with chivalric romance coming along about... well, about one hundred years later. Now, the, um, line between these two styles is loosely defined and sometimes blurred, but we can identify some basic contrasting characteristics.
   For example, the chansons de geste were written to be sung by performers known as troubadours, but chivalric romances were designed to be read in private rather than performed publicly. And while the writers of these chivalric romances were mostly well-known figures, most early chansons de geste were written anonymously.
   And as for theme... well, chansons de geste usually concerned battles fought by knights and their courage, perhaps because there were major wars in French military history, such as the Crusades. The intent was

to inspire patriotism among their listeners, but as the Crusades ended, romance took over as the primary theme. While the, um... the chivalric romances also revolved around valiant knights, the genre focused more on themes of courtly love and emphasized emotions over actions.

iBT Practice 01　　pp. 139~140

1. Ⓑ　2. Ⓒ　3. Yes - Ⓒ, Ⓔ / No - Ⓐ, Ⓑ, Ⓓ　4. Ⓓ

Note-Taking

Problem: can't go inside, ID card needed
- I lost it
- a lot of people entered without ID
  ⇔ only at the beginning of the semester for new students

What to do now?
1. Show photo ID - Can't! Lost wallet with other IDs
2. Memorize student ID No.? Yes, on class schedule

Thanks and sorry... so stressed out
- I understand
- get temporary ID & reissue cafeteria card

Listen to a conversation between a student and a security guard.

Security Guard: Excuse me, ma'am? You can't go inside until I see your college ID card.

Student: Sorry, but... I don't, um... I don't have it.

G: I'm sorry, but you can't enter this building without an ID.

S: I know, but I lost it. That's why I'm here. I need to get inside so I can get a temporary one.

G: Oh... well, then...

S: Come on, I know a lot of people who got into the building without having an ID at the beginning of the semester.

G: That's an exceptional case. We weren't checking IDs at the beginning of the semester because many of the new students hadn't been issued one yet. But everyone has one now, and you need it to get inside. That's the rule now and you have to follow it.

S: Okay, I got it. But the problem is... I have to get inside first to get a new ID. So, please tell me what I should do now.

G: If you can just show me some form of photo ID... a, um, driver's license or a passport, maybe... that'll be good enough.

S: I don't have my ID card because my wallet was stolen this morning while I was working out at the gym. All of my identification was in it. And my passport is in my dorm room... and they won't let me in the dormitory without my ID card.

G: Oh, wow... I'm really sorry to hear that. Don't worry, I'll help you get through this mess. Have you, by any chance, memorized your student ID number?

S: Um, no... but hold on, I think it's on my class schedule. [pause] Here it is. 715-42518.

G: Great. I'll just punch this into the computer and see if I can confirm your identity. Your name is?

S: Sara. Sara Caruso.

G: Okay. It'll just take a minute or two for the system to verify your identity.

S: Thanks for being patient with me. I'm sorry for bothering you. I'm just so stressed out by all of this...

G: Don't worry, it's OK. I understand how you feel.

S: I couldn't even get any lunch since all my money and cafeteria card were in my wallet.

G: Oh, really? That's too bad. You know what? When you go inside, just head straight for the Identification office. They'll give you a temporary ID card, and then they can reissue your cafeteria card. [pause] All right, Ms. Caruso. Looks like your identity has been confirmed. You're free to go inside.

S: Q4 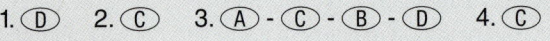 Great. Thanks again for your help.

G: No problem. I'm just glad I could help you.

S: Me too!

iBT Practice 02　　pp. 141~142

1. Ⓓ　2. Ⓒ　3. Ⓐ - Ⓒ - Ⓑ - Ⓓ　4. Ⓒ

Note-Taking

Intro_ Atolls
; not islands, in tropical waters

Formation process (theory by Darwin)
- Volcanic islands → Barrier reef islands → Atolls

Volcanic islands surrounded by fringing reef
→ volcanic activity ends, islands sink
→ reefs grow upward ⇒ barrier reef islands
→ islands disappear, only reef & lagoon ⇒ atolls

Listen to part of a lecture in a geology class.

Professor: When studying the geology of the islands of the South Pacific, the first thing you must understand is that many of these islands aren't actually islands. Instead, they are something known as atolls. Atolls are generally small, sandy and shaped like... well, a bit like a broken ring. This ring encloses... or partially encloses... a body of water known as a lagoon. Atolls are found in tropical waters all around the world, and although they may appear to be quite similar to islands, the process by which they form is very different.

Now... although the formation of atolls remains a bit of a geological mystery, a widely-accepted theory was put forth by Charles Darwin back in, um, 1842. He believed that the three types of island-like formations he encountered during his voyage through the South Pacific were simply different stages in a single process taking place over millions of years. The first type were volcanic islands, the second were barrier reef islands, and the third, atolls.

A volcanic island represents the earliest stage of the process, formed by a volcano rising up from the ocean floor. Over thousands of years, this new island will eventually be surrounded by something known as a, um, fringing reef. Reefs, of course, are rock-like living organisms formed by a special type of coral that lives only in tropical waters. In fact, reefs commonly form around these islands because reef building coral is one of few forms of life that can exist in warm surface water, which offers little in the way of nutrients. **Q4**
🎧 Anyway... um... eventually, as the volcanic activity beneath it comes to an end, the island begins to undergo subsidence... **meaning it begins to gradually sink into the earth's crust.**

Meanwhile, as the island sinks downward, the reef continues to grow upward, constantly forming new living layers atop the, um... the skeleton of dead sections of the reef. Eventually, the fringing reef grows large enough to be considered a barrier reef... and the island, a barrier reef island. This means that it has been encircled by a wall of coral, with the open ocean on the outside and a placid lagoon within. Finally, after millions of years, when the sinking island has completely disappeared beneath the sea, only the reef and lagoon remain. And they have now become an atoll.

Vocabulary Review   pp. 144~145

A	1. subsidence	2. extraordinary	3. offset
	4. interactive	5. skeleton	
B	1. Ⓐ	2. Ⓑ	3. Ⓑ	4. Ⓒ
C	1. Ⓐ	2. Ⓓ	3. Ⓑ	4. Ⓓ
D	1. through	2. revolves	3. blends	4. atop
	5. chance		
E	1. Ⓑ	2. Ⓐ	3. Ⓑ	4. Ⓓ	5. Ⓒ
F	1. Ⓓ	2. Ⓐ	3. Ⓑ		

UNIT 07 Inference

Basic Drills   pp. 150~151

1. Ⓒ   2. Ⓒ   3. Ⓓ   4. Ⓑ   5. Ⓒ   6. Ⓐ

1.

Listen to a conversation between a student and a professor.

Student: Dr. Goodman, I need to discuss the group project. The deadline is next week, and Peter hasn't done anything.
Professor: Have you spoken with him yet, Matt?
S: Yes, but he doesn't seem to care.
P: I see. Well, if you'd like, I can talk to him, and if he fails to present a reasonable explanation, he'll be graded separately from the group.
S: That would be great, but wouldn't it be better to evaluate students individually for every group project? That would prevent these kinds of issues.
P: Well, that would make the grading process fairer, but I have a reason for not doing it that way. Once you enter the workforce, you'll constantly be assigned to work in groups, and only the final results will matter to your employer.
S: That's true.
P: Motivating others to do their best is part of what I want you to learn from this project.
S: I see. I guess the entire group should get together and try to find a solution before you get involved.
P: Excellent. In the meantime, don't be anxious about your grade—his lack of effort won't affect it.

2.

Listen to part of a lecture in a geology class.

Professor: Okay, so uhm... Dr. McElwain, a field museum scientist, has developed a new method of understanding the past elevation of land surfaces by observing the stomata of plants. Stomata, which as we know are tiny openings on the surface of leaves, help plants absorb necessary gases, including uhm, carbon dioxide for photosynthesis. And as we know, carbon dioxide and other gases are less dense at higher altitudes, which means that the er... the plants in the higher mountains have more stomata to survive. So, what Dr. McElwain came up with is... um, by counting fossil plant stomata, we can estimate the elevation at which the fossil plant once lived. With historical and modern collections of uhm, let me see... oh yes... California black oak leaves, which grow at a wide range of altitudes, she proved her new method is effective with a much lower error rate than existing methods.

3.

Listen to part of a lecture in an ecology class.

Professor: Let's begin, shall we? Although the salmon fishery creates economic benefits in rural coastal areas, there're other things we have to know. First, salmon in fish farms are fed diets containing large amounts of fish caught from the wild. It is estimated that more than 3 tons of wild-caught fish are needed to produce 1 ton of farmed salmon. And uhm... or rather besides, the more important thing is that salmon farming introduces foreign salmon and creates genetically modified species. When these new kinds of salmon escape from the farm, they have harmful effects on the ocean's ecosystem by transmitting diseases or attacking original species. Furthermore, keeping large numbers of fish concentrated in a small area has led to the pollution of the surrounding area. Fish waste and farm chemicals settle and er... form sediment beneath the salmon cage and in the surrounding area, killing underlying marine life. Now we can er... we can understand the old saying "You can't have your cake and eat it."

4.

Listen to a conversation between a student and a cafeteria employee.

Student: Excuse me, there seems to be a problem with my meal plan bill.

Employee: Oh? What's the problem?

S: Well, I've only been having two meals each day, but I was billed for a three-meal-per-day plan.

E: That's strange. Did you sign up for a two-meal-per-day plan?

S: Well, originally I signed up for the three-meal plan, but then I changed my mind. I don't eat big breakfasts anyway, so I sent an email to the office to change plans, and I've only been eating two meals at the cafeteria each day.

E: When did you send the mail? If it wasn't received by the 5th of the month, it won't be changed until next month.

S: Oh really? I didn't realize that. Is there anything that I can do to get my money back?

E: I wish I could help you, but sorry. I have to follow the regulations.

5.

Listen to part of a lecture in a literature class.

Professor: Now let's think of Aristotle's ideas about tragedy shown in his influential book *Poetics*. So what do you know about tragic heroes according to Aristotle?

Student: Tragic heroes must all be noble men and umm, admirable.

P: Correct. Aristotle suggested tragic heroes must be essentially admirable to draw out our genuine compassion or emotional cleansing, like a catharsis. As a rule, the nobler and more truly admirable a person is, the... the greater our... our anxiety or grief at his or her downfall will be. And let's think about the causation of the tragedy. What caused the tragic consequences?

S: Well, I think the heroes themselves have responsibility for their situations.

P: Yes, that is... authentic tragedy must always be the result of some fatal choice or action of the heroes. After all, a genuinely tragic downfall can't ever really be purely a matter of blind accident or bad luck.

6.

Listen to part of a lecture in a history class.

Professor: So, today we're going to study early French feudalism in detail. In feudal systems, a ruler offered fighters control of a unit of land in exchange for military service. The individual or individuals who accepted this land became a vassal, and the man who granted it became his lord. Feudal government was based on this basic contract. According to this relationship, individual lords divided their lands into smaller and smaller sections to give to lesser rulers and knights. Each knight then uhm... swore his loyalty to the one who gave him land, but... and this is important; this was not necessarily the king. Actually, feudal government was always an arrangement between individuals, not between nation-states and... uhm, their citizens. This means that while individual barons, dukes, earls, and so forth might be loyal in theory to the king or a centralized noble family, there was no strong legal tradition to prevent them from having more power than the king.

Dictation p. 152

1. past elevation of land surfaces   2. tiny openings / help plants absorb   3. at a wide range of / lower error rate   4. fed diets / caught from the wild   5. by transmitting diseases   6. draw out our genuine compassion   7. blind accident or bad luck   8. in exchange for military service   9. who granted it   10. might be loyal in theory / legal tradition

Listening Practice 01   p. 153

1. Ⓓ   2. Ⓐ   3. Ⓑ

Listen to a conversation between a student and a professor.

Student: *[knocking]* Can I come in, Professor Ryan?

Professor: Of course, Rachel. Have a seat.

S: Thank you. I, um, I wanted to talk to you about my internship this summer. I have a couple of offers, but I'm not sure which way to go.

P: What are your options?

S: Well, they're both marketing positions, but one is with an advertising firm and the other is with a car company. Right now I'm leaning toward the advertising firm.

P: Why's that?

S: Because I'm really interested in advertising. It's such an exciting field, and there're so many interesting components to it... It's really something I'd like to get involved with.

P: That sounds reasonable to me. So, er... why are you hesitating to accept their offer?

S: Well... because the car company is National Motors. They're one of the biggest companies in the country. And it would look really great on my resume after I graduate.

P: I see. But... well, I'd advise you to follow your heart. Just talking to you for a few minutes, I can see that you're really passionate about advertising.

S: I am. But it's a... small firm and not very well-known.

P: I understand, Rachel, but you shouldn't be so, um, so concerned about filling your resume with impressive names. This might be your last chance to get directly involved in advertising. What if you regret blowing your chance?

S: You're right. I've made up my mind. Thanks for your advice, Professor.

P: I'm glad I could help.

Listening Practice 02   p. 155

1. Ⓑ   2. Ⓒ   3. Ⓒ

Listen to part of a lecture in an ecology class.

Professor: Another animal that inhabits our region and plays an important ecological role is the beaver. Beavers, of course, are large rodents that spend a great deal of their lives in the water. They are best known as ecosystem engineers because of their natural trait of building dams in rivers. These dams create ponds, which give beavers a place to live that is safe from predators and near food sources.

Because of their dam making, beaver populations have a heavy impact on their environments. Introduced to a foreign ecosystem, they could potentially cause great harm. But in their natural habitats of North America and Europe, beaver dams and ponds play a vital role in the health of our rivers and streams. For instance, when heavy rains occur, beaver ponds impound water, and then the dams gradually release the stored water. In this way, beaver dams help reduce the flood damage just like human dams. Additionally, they slow down the flow of water, which eventually minimizes erosion of the land surrounding rivers. And most importantly, beaver dams play a role in forming wetlands. These wetlands develop in and around abandoned beaver ponds, creating a type of habitat for many rare as well as common species. And that is crucial to biodiversity and the well-being of the entire ecosystem.

Q3 Well, of course, the beaver dams don't always fit in with the plans of humans; they occasionally affect property and disrupt transportation. But because of their importance to our ecosystem, it is necessary we, er... we should value their contributions.

Listening Practice 03   p. 157

1. Ⓒ   2. Ⓐ   3. Ⓓ

Listen to part of a lecture in a literature class.

Professor: The novel we'll be looking at today is largely considered to be the forerunner of the modern detective story. It is of course Wilkie Collins' *The Moonstone*, written in 1868. It revolves around a young English woman who is given a large valuable diamond for her eighteenth birthday. During her birthday party the diamond is stolen. It is later revealed that it was originally taken from India and that... um, the jewel is cursed and disaster will strike anyone who possesses it.

The significance of the novel is that it introduced a number of aspects that are now considered standard features of modern mystery novels. For example um... heroes and villains that are now stereotypical characters of the genre. It also featured so-called common plot settings and situations... you know, like mistaken identities and a large number of suspects.

Student: Q3 I'm sorry, Professor Irving, but a book about a cursed jewel? I've read that kind of story a million times.

P: **Well... cursed jewels weren't a cliché until Collins wrote this novel,** and really... he was the first to use many ideas that have become common. And *The Moonstone* is far more than just a story about a cursed jewel. We must take into consideration when this book was written and what was going on in the world. The age of colonialism had reached India, where the British were taking **all that they wanted**. The moonstone symbolizes one of those Indian assets taken by the British, so its curse can be thought of as **revenge upon** the imperialist invaders.

iBT Practice 01   pp. 159~160

1.   2.   3.   4. Ⓒ

Note-Taking

Look over grant application form
- Topic: traffic of Chicago (appealing!)
- Will analyze factors & suggest plan (good!)

But need improvement
- How? Change the order (project info → personal info)
- Write a new one? No, just reorganize

⇒ Bring it back tomorrow (but don't worry, a little adjusting)

Listen to a conversation between a student and a professor.

Professor: Hello, Melissa. Come on in.

Student: Hello, Professor Morris. I'm not early, am I?

P: You're right on time. Um... I just finished looking over the grant application form you gave me yesterday.

S: Great. I was hoping that you could give me some insights. What did you think of it?

P: Well, I think it was an excellent idea to choose "The Traffic of Chicago" for the topic of your project... to deal with the safe and efficient pedestrian environment in the city. Chicago has a national reputation for being pedestrian-friendly, so I think your topic is very appealing.

S: Thanks. I'm relieved to hear that. I'm going to analyze the factors which make Chicago such a walkable city, and I'd like to suggest a possible plan that could be applied to other cities.

P: Good. Sounds like your project has great potential. It would be invaluable to the university's Urban Planning department. But, one thing... your application form needs a few improvements.

S: Improvements? Could you explain what the problem is?

P: Well... look at this. In your proposal, you lead with your personal background information and your academic plan. Then, after a few paragraphs, you explain what you will deal with, why you need the amount of money you're requesting, and how you intend to go about gathering the data. This is, um... I have to tell you, I would do it the other way around.

S: OK. So change the... um, the order, right?

P: Yes. I used to be on the grants committee, as you know, so I know from personal experience that they don't have a lot of time to go through all these applications. So, I suggest you put your project information first. This can make a big difference because they can find the essential part quickly and won't miss it.

S: Okay. I get your point. *[disappointed]* I guess I should really write a new application.

P: I don't think that's necessary, Melissa. Just reorganize it. Focus on your project, not yourself.

S: *[relieved]* That'll be enough? Then, can I bring it back tomorrow for one last look?

P: Sure. Don't worry, you're on the right track... it just needs a little adjusting. Drop it off at my office when you're done and I'll look at it the first chance I get.

S: Thanks, I really appreciate it.

iBT Practice 02   pp. 161~162

1.   2.   3.   4.

Note-Taking

Crocodile skin
- Looks threatening, gives camouflage
- Spots? ISOs (sensory organs)

Experiments to explain function (Alligators & crocodiles have them)
① Light? No
② Electricity? No
③ Taste or odor? No
④ Screwdriver? Yes... Why? Water waves were lapping
∴ ISOs = motion detector
  + Because they live in swamp, muddy water ⇒ ISOs help see like eyes

Listen to part of a lecture in a zoology class.

Professor: Now, many people are aware that crocodiles have strong, thick skin. Take a look at the picture in the book. Well, it looks quite threatening, doesn't it? How about the color? Its colors – green and brown, with some black coloration – give it great camouflage in the wetland.

However, the most interesting thing about their skin is... small spots or dimples that you've probably seen before in a picture or something. These are the special part, "ISOs – integumentary sensory organs." As you might notice from their name, ISOs are sort of sensory cells in the skin. So, what's the role of these spots? It's been suggested that they may detect saltiness of water. But this has never been confirmed.

Q4 🎧 There was one experiment that discovered the main function of the dark ISO spots. Scientist Daphne Soares used an American alligator in her research; well, in fact, umm... both alligators and crocodiles have these spots in their skin although they are not exactly the same. I'm going to explain the difference later. **Okay… Let's get back to the experiment.**

After recognizing ISOs on the alligator's skin have a special function, Soares desperately wanted to know exactly what these spots do. Firstly, she illuminated the alligator's skin with light, but the alligator didn't perceive any changes. The next observation was to see if they can detect electricity; the scientist stimulated its thick skin with electricity, but the animal didn't react. She also threw ground-up fish over the spots to see if they were sensitive to taste or odor. But nothing happened. One day, she accidentally dropped a screwdriver into the water tank in which the alligator was kept, and the animal quickly recognized and attacked it. What made the alligator react? *[pause]* The reason is that when something was placed in the water, the waves lapped against the alligator's skin, especially the ISOs. With additional experiments, she confirmed that they're motion detectors.

Okay. We've learned the function of the dark spots, and now I have a question for you. How come the alligators or crocodiles have such special cells in their skin? Well, Daphne Soares also came to a certain conclusion about this. Where do alligators and crocodiles live? They live in swamps where they can't see clearly, you know, the water is muddy and blurry. So, the alligators and crocodiles need other organs to help them see in the water. Therefore, we can say the ISOs act like eyes for crocodiles and alligators.

Vocabulary Review pp. 164~165

A	1. volume	2. abandon	3. catharsis		
	4. stimulate	5. stereotypical			
B	1. Ⓒ	2. Ⓐ	3. Ⓒ	4. Ⓓ	
C	1. Ⓐ	2. Ⓑ	3. Ⓑ	4. Ⓓ	
D	1. track	2. exchange	3. genetically		
	4. blew	5. with			
E	1. Ⓐ	2. Ⓒ	3. Ⓑ	4. Ⓑ	5. Ⓐ
F	1. Ⓓ	2. Ⓒ	3. Ⓓ		

Actual Practice Test 3

01 pp. 168~169

1. Ⓑ 2. Ⓓ 3. Ⓐ 4. Ⓐ 5. Ⓓ

Note-Taking

Problem: need help with the project

1. Conducting interview? Fine, I was a reporter
2. Then what? Can't find a successful businessman
   Introduce someone, plz
   → No, it wouldn't be fair
3. Advice
buy a newspaper & find a story about a businessperson, then contact them
But, they are too busy
   → Be positive! They'll do. If not, try someone else
+ Good opportunity for plan on owning business
   → So, learn from them

Listen to a conversation between a student and a professor.

Student: Professor Blair, may I come in?
Professor: Oh, sure, Gary. How are things going? I thought you'd be very busy with your final research project.
S: Yes, actually I need some help with the project, and… I was wondering if you could help me.
P: No problem. I understand learning about conducting an interview and doing a real one are quite different.
S: Oh, it's not that. I think I can… I mean, I think I can easily interview somebody because I was a reporter for my school newspaper back in high school. I've done plenty of interviews before.
P: Well, good for you. So what's the problem?
S: I just can't… *[sighs]* I can't seem to find anyone worthwhile to interview. I mean… the subject should be a successful businessperson, and unfortunately, there's nobody like that around me. So I was sort of hoping you could introduce me to someone you know…
P: But I can't help you with that. Part of the assignment is finding an appropriate interview subject, and then convincing them to meet with you. So it wouldn't be fair to the other students if I help you with that.
S: Yes, I understand. But… what am I supposed to do now?
P: I'll give you some advice. Don't try to find the right subject among your acquaintances.
S: Oh, okay, but how can I meet somebody I don't know?
P: Why don't you buy a local newspaper and flip through all the articles? When you find a story about a

businessperson who is doing something noteworthy, contact them about an interview.

S: Someone from the newspaper? If somebody is famous enough to have articles written about them in the newspaper, I'm pretty sure they'll be too busy to talk to some college student.

P: I think you should be more positive, Gary. Most people would be glad to give half an hour of their time to a young student who looks up to them. I think they'd be flattered. What's the worst that could happen?

S: Well... *[pause]* they could say no.

P: Exactly. And if they do, you just thank them politely and then try someone else. Q5 🎧 Well, if you are still nervous, remember this could be a great opportunity for you. You've mentioned in the past that you want to get involved in business, haven't you?

S: *[excitedly]* I sure have. I plan on owning my own small business by the time I'm thirty.

P: That's a great goal to have. And if you interview one of our community's business leaders, you'll have a chance to learn all kinds of things about what it takes to be successful.

S: I guess you're right.

P: Now, grab a newspaper and get started. You don't want to fall behind on the assignment.

S: All right, I will. Thanks for the encouragement, Professor Blair.

P: That's what I'm here for. I'm looking forward to reading your interview.

02
pp. 170~171

6. ⓓ 7. ⓑ, ⓒ 8. ⓑ 9. ⓓ 10. ⓒ
11. ⓑ

Note-Taking

Behavioral leadership model_ managerial grid
; 2 aspects – people & production

1. Production(↑) people(↓) = Authoritarian leaders /
   Produce or perish
- Hard on their workers
- When facing troubles, they blame others
2. Production(↓) people(↑) = Country club leaders
- Friendly atmosphere, not necessarily productive
3. Impoverished leaders (production & people ↓)
- Avoid getting into trouble → inactive and lazy
  ∴ No progress
4. Middle-of-the-road leaders
- Try to balance company goals and worker needs
- Ideal? No. Neither production nor people needs are fully met
5. Team leaders (most desirable)
- Production & people ↑ ∴ Effective & most productive

Listen to part of a lecture in a business class.

Professor: Well, let's move on to another behavioral leadership model, the "managerial grid." It uses two fundamental aspects, people and production, to define five basic managerial styles. In other words, this model categorizes leadership styles based on whether the leaders' concern is for relationships with other people or for production. Now, don't be confused. It's not about whether the leaders succeed in tasks or relationships, just about what they focus on more, okay?

Let's study the first type of leaders who have high scores in production and low in people. We call these task-oriented people "authoritarian leaders," or sometimes "produce or perish" style. They only concentrate on how to produce more and how to produce well, but they don't care about how to deal with people. I believe you guys fully understand that leaders of this type are hard on their workers. They expect people to do what they are told without any questions or debate. It means there is no allowance for collaboration, so it is difficult for subordinates to contribute to development. What's worse, when they face trouble, they look for who's to blame rather than the solution to or prevention of the problem.

Q11 🎧 Okay, next one... well, let's guess the title of this type of leader who has low scores on production and depends very highly on people at the same time. Guess what? They are referred to as "country club leaders." Well, I thought this was perfect name because these managers pay too much attention to the security and comfort of the employees. So the atmosphere is usually friendly, but not necessarily productive. It's because umm, they sometimes fail to employ coercive and legitimate power to accomplish goals for fear of jeopardizing relationships with other team members.

Now, we have the "impoverished leader" type, and this type of manager is not committed to either production or people. It is said that managers use this style to avoid getting into trouble. The main concern for this type of manager is not to be held responsible for any mistakes, so they look more like... um, inactive and lazy. I'm not judging them, but in this case, we could hardly expect that the business will progress.

Maybe you can guess the type in the middle. This type is called the "middle-of-the-road" style, and this kind of leader seems to try to balance between company goals and workers' needs. By giving some concern to both people and production, the leaders hope to achieve acceptable performance. So at first it appears to be an ideal compromise. There is a problem, though: when they compromise, they necessarily give away a bit of each concern so that neither production nor people needs are fully met.

Finally, we have the most desirable leaders a.k.a.

"team leaders." They have high orientation scores in both people and production, which means they stress production needs and the needs of the people equally highly. They encourage the workers to reach team goals as effectively as possible, while also working to strengthen the bonds among the team members. As a result, they usually form and lead the most productive teams.

03   pp. 172~173

12. Ⓑ   13. Ⓐ, Ⓒ   14. Ⓑ   15. Ⓑ, Ⓒ
16. Ⓓ   17. Ⓒ

Note-Taking

Intro_ Flowers in New Jersey - Fossilized!
; In an ancient marsh, 90 million years ago, 200 species

1. Rare findings because...
- Botanists don't expect to find them because flowers are too fragile
  Then, how? They were charcoalified = Burned (hard & waterproof)
      → washed into the marsh → mud hardened
      → fossils
- Size: quite small
  evolved into bigger ones or shrunk during fossilization

2. Importance - Insects inside
- Pollination: important in reproduction & evolution
  Because flowers have to attract pollinators & pollinators recombine
  ∴ Understanding of how they evolved together & driving force to diversity

Listen to part of a lecture in a botany class.

Professor: Let's change the subject for a bit and take a few minutes to talk about some flowers that were found in New Jersey a few years back. Now, finding flowers in New Jersey probably doesn't sound like a big deal to you. But these flowers are special because they were fossilized.

   They were, um, discovered in an ancient marsh that is now a clay pit and are estimated to be about 90 million years old. And amazingly, fossils from more than 200 species of flowers were found at the site... it's more than what has been found anywhere else on earth. Most of them are ancestors of the flowers that inhabit the earth today.

   Alright. These were really rare findings because umm... first of all, most botanists don't normally expect to find fossilized flowers... generally, flowers are considered too fragile to last that long. And since nobody was really looking for them, the fossilized flowers could easily have gone undetected.

Student: Q17 🎧 Excuse me, Professor? If flowers are so fragile, how did these ones become fossils? I mean, was it something special about the flowers themselves or was it the marsh that preserved them?

P: That's a good guess. But I have to say there is no difference between ancient flowers or marshes and those of today. Well, actually, the reason these particular flowers survived intact for so long is that before they were fossilized, they were charcoalified. That means they were burned by intense heat, most likely a forest fire, which turned them into charcoal. This made them hard and waterproof, allowing them to be preserved without rotting away. After the fire, they were probably washed into the marsh by rain, and sank to the bottom where they were preserved in the mud. Over millions of years, the mud hardened into rock and they became fossils.

   There is also another reason why fossilized flowers are so scarce. And that's their size. Ancient flowers were not like flowers we see growing today. They were quite small; some of them were actually no bigger than a tiny dot... unless you had a microscope, you might not even know they were flowers. We're not sure why they were so small... it may be that they evolved into bigger sizes later on, or that they simply shrank during the fossilization process.

   Anyway, an important, um... aspect of this discovery is that it included fossils of the insects that pollinated the flowers... as well as some of the pollen itself. Pollination is an essential step not only in the reproduction of plants but also for flower evolution. That's because flowers themselves have evolved to attract insect pollinators; moreover, the pollinators have contributed to... umm, evolution through genetic recombination within a dispersed plant population. Accordingly, the fossils found in New Jersey have given scientists a better understanding of the relationship between flowers and insects and... how they evolved together over time. In addition, we can assume that insects were a driving force behind the tremendous diversity of flowering plants.

# Practice TOEFL iBT Listening Section

01
pp. 176~177

1.   2. 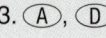 3.   4.   5. B

Note-Taking

Student teaching
; Helping Mr. Sullivan teach fifth grade class

Mr. Sullivan
- Asks a lot of questions, lectures not too long
- Curriculum with different topics → different activities
eg. astronomy class
    students: research → presentation → question
- Motivates & encourages students

Opportunities to lead the class? Not yet, but learning
(the story about the Roman myth and get attention)

His methodology is excellent topic! → prepare presentation

Listen to a conversation between a student and a professor.

[knocking sound is heard]

Professor: Oh, Steven! Hi! How's the student teaching going?

Student: Hello, Professor Ramirez. It's going great. Do you have a few free minutes to talk about it?

P: Sure. I was just getting ready to take a break from grading these papers. Have a seat.

S: Thanks. I was just on campus to take care of some errands, so I thought I'd drop in and let you know how things were going.

P: I'm glad you did. So... *[pause]* where are you working, again? Was it Hopedale Elementary?

S: That's right. I'm spending this semester helping Mr. Sullivan teach his fifth grade class. It's really been an eye-opening experience.

P: Tell me all about it.

S: Well, Mr. Sullivan has been teaching for almost twenty years, so he knows a lot of tricks to keep the students interested in his lessons. He asks a lot of questions, and never lectures for too long.

P: Yes. Children of that age have short attention spans.

S: Exactly. **Q5** 🎧 And he's broken the curriculum down into a series of units, each covering a different topic. He has the kids do a bunch of different activities related to whatever they're studying. Right now, for example, we're covering astronomy.

P: Oh, that sounds very interesting. Go ahead.

S: Actually, I never cared for it much in school, but Mr. Sullivan makes it really interesting. **Almost makes me wish I was one of his students instead of his assistant.** *[chuckles]* Anyway, each kid has been given a different planet, moon or star, and they're doing independent research at the library and on the Internet. Then next week, they'll each give a presentation, and all the other students have to ask one question on the topic. This way they're learning to be good speakers and listeners.

P: That's wonderful. I have a feeling you're going to have a lot to share when you rejoin the Education program this fall.

S: I sure am. I've really been impressed with the way he motivates his students. He can be strict, but he's always careful to encourage them.

P: That's very important. Has he given you any opportunities to lead the class yourself?

S: Yes, a few times. *[pause]* I'm mostly observing and helping out, but he's promised that I'll be pretty much in charge by the end of the term. *[laughs]* But right now, I'm content to sit back and learn, you know? It's the little things... like the way he'll bring up information from other units and relate it to what we're currently working on.

P: Hmm. I'm not sure what you mean.

S: Well... for example, I mentioned we were covering astronomy? Well, our next unit is mythology, so when we were talking about the planet Jupiter, he told them a little story about the Roman myth of the god named Jupiter. It really got their attention and it will make even more sense to them when we start the next unit.

P: Well, I really hope I have you in my elementary education class again next semester, Steven. I think Mr. Sullivan's methodology would make an excellent topic for our practical learning section. Regardless of whose class you end up in, you should really start thinking about preparing some material for a presentation.

S: Actually, I've already started. This is something I'd really like to share with my classmates... anyway, I've taken up enough of your time. I really should be going.

P: Okay, Steven. Stop by again soon with an update.

S: I will, Professor Ramirez. Bye-bye.

02

pp. 178~179

6. Ⓑ   7. Ⓑ   8. Ⓐ, Ⓒ, Ⓓ   9. Ⓒ
10. Ⓓ   11. Ⓐ

Note-Taking

Intro_ Medicinal plants
; Aloe Vera, ginseng, <u>garlic</u>

- longest known medicinal plant
  (eg. India, China…)
- what chemical is medicinal? allicin (causing odor)
- effects? lower cholesterol & blood pressure
            reduce cancer risk
            against bacteria and parasites
- allicin production: alliin → allicin (by alliinase)
  → defense mechanism: more crushed, more produced
- allicin is unstable → better to eat raw

Listen to part of a lecture in a nutrition class.

Professor: Medicinal plants have been used by humans for thousands of years. Can anyone name some kinds of plants that have been used for their medicinal qualities?

Student 1: Um, Aloe Vera plants are medicinal. They produce a juice that soothes burns, I think. And it's always listed as an ingredient in skin lotions.

P: Right. Aloe Vera is a great example of a medicinal plant.

Student 2: I think ginseng is another plant that's widely used for medicinal purposes.

P: That's right. Ginseng's another one. But today there's a different medicinal plant I'd like to talk about. Um, I guarantee you've encountered it before. Garlic.

S1: Oh, sure. I've heard about its medicinal qualities before.

P: Right. It's news to some people. Garlic is the kind of everyday spice that many of us take for granted. But garlic's actually one of the longest known medicinal plants. Records in Sanskrit tell us that garlic was used for medicinal purposes in India 5,000 years ago. Chinese medicine has been using garlic for 3,000 years. The Babylonians, Egyptians, Greeks, and Romans all used garlic for medicinal purposes. And during the World Wars, garlic was actually used as an antiseptic for its antibacterial properties. So, obviously, garlic's been around as a medicinal plant for a really long time.

S2: So is there a certain chemical in garlic that's mainly responsible for the medicinal properties of garlic?

P: Yes, you're right about that. An active component in garlic called allicin is responsible for the health benefits of garlic. It's actually responsible for that distinctive garlic odor too which some people love and some people hate.

S1: So… what are the medical effects of garlic, or allicin?

P: Well, there've been a lot of clinical studies about garlic. One of the recognized benefits of garlic is its lipid-lowering effect. I mean… garlic helps lower cholesterol.

Q10 🎧 Another health benefit associated with garlic is its antihypertensive effect. **Um, that means it lowers blood pressure.** Some studies have also suggested that eating garlic reduces the risk of stomach and colon cancer. And then there's also the antimicrobial power of garlic… it seems to have some effect against bacteria and parasites.

Q11 🎧 Okay, but getting back to allicin… um, it's important to mention that allicin actually isn't present in fresh garlic normally. It's produced under certain circumstances. I don't want to get into the chemistry of it… 'cause it's quite complex… but I'll give you the basics. There's a compound in garlic called alliin and an enzyme in garlic called alliinase. These components exist in different parts of the plant. But when garlic gets damaged or crushed, the enzyme alliinase alters alliin… alliinase changes alliin into allicin – the medicinal compound we've been speaking about. See, the production of allicin is the plant's defense mechanism. For example, if microbes attack the garlic plant, allicin will be produced and can end the microbial attack. This means that the more garlic is crushed or chopped, the more allicin is produced. But once it's made, allicin is somewhat unstable. It quickly changes into other compounds. Studies suggest that within one to six days, allicin becomes undetectable. Also… umm… due to allicin's such unstable properties, heating allicin causes it to degrade more rapidly. So if you're looking to get the most out of garlic, it's better to eat it raw.

03 pp. 180~181

12. Ⓓ 13. comets - Ⓐ, Ⓒ asteroids - Ⓑ, Ⓓ, Ⓔ 14. Ⓓ 15. Ⓒ 16. Ⓓ 17. Ⓑ

Note-Taking

Intro_ Small solar bodies
1. Comet
- long-period: long orbital period, originate in the Oort cloud (in theory)
  short-period: less than 200 years to orbit, originate in the Kuiper belt
- example: Hale-Bopp
- rock, dust, ice → nucleus
- coma & tail: near the sun comets melt

2. Asteroid
- star-like? No, "planet-like" because they orbit
- no coma & tail (made of metals or rock)
- in the asteroid belt

3. When asteroid enters atmosphere
- visibility: meteor
- object: meteoroid (pieces from asteroid)
- meteorite: lands on earth (cause impact craters)
  stone meteorites - common but rarely found because hard to distinguish from Earth rocks

Listen to part of a lecture in an astronomy class.

Professor: Okay. Today, we're gonna be talking about small solar bodies… like comets, asteroids, and meteors. Let's start with comets. They can be divided into two categories: long-period comets and short-period comets. Long-period comets are those that have a long orbital period. That means it takes them a long time to make a complete orbit around the sun. How long? More than 200 years. Up to 30 million years, actually. Q16 🎧 We believe that these comets originate in the Oort cloud. The existence of the Oort cloud hasn't been confirmed… but we theorize that it's a sphere-shaped cloud of rocks and dust that surrounds our solar system.

Anyway, short-period comets are ones that take less than 200 years to orbit the sun. And we think that they originate in the Kuiper belt. The Kuiper belt is a region filled with small objects orbiting the sun. It's out beyond Neptune's orbit. Okay. Has anyone in here ever seen a comet in the night sky?

Student 1: I have. I remember seeing the comet Hale-Bopp in 1997.

P: Great. Hale-Bopp is a great example. In spring of 1997 it was extremely bright, so very easy to see with the naked eye. I'm glad you got a chance to view that comet. It was quite a sight. Can you describe to the rest of the class what Hale-Bopp looked like?

S1: Uh, sure. It looked like a shooting star. Like a glowing ball with a long tail.

P: Thanks. A comet itself is really nothing more than a clump of rock, dust, and ice. That's the nucleus. Usually, it's less than fifty kilometers across. Okay. So what about this glowing ball you described? That's the coma. When a comet nears the sun, parts of the comet melt and turn into vapor. And that's what forms the coma. Comas can be much larger than the nucleus. Some are bigger than the sun. The tail of the comet is also caused by the effect of the sun – by the same reason as the coma's formation. The tail can be as long as 150 million kilometers.

Okay, now I'd like to move on to another kind of small solar body, asteroids. Q17 🎧 The word "asteroid" comes from the Greek for "star-like." **But, umm, in my opinion, "planet-like" is a more accurate term because they orbit the sun like other planets.**

Student 2: Oh, that sounds like comets as well… except the tails.

P: Yes. Asteroids don't have comas and tails. Why? Because they're not made of ice and dust like comets. Asteroids are made of metals or rock. And also they range in size and can be relatively large.

S2: Where can asteroids be found?

P: Many of them are in the asteroid belt that's between Mars and Jupiter. About 98.5% of asteroid orbits are in that region. Well, in the solar system, there're 1 to 2 million asteroids bigger than one kilometer in diameter.

S2: [surprised] Really? 1 to 2 million?

P: It's true. Impressive, isn't it? Okay, let's keep moving on. Can anyone tell me what happens when an asteroid enters the atmosphere?

S1: It becomes really visible.

P: Yes. The visibility is a result of the heat produced during atmospheric entry. This visual effect is called a meteor. It's from the Greek for "high in the air." But the actual object itself is called a meteoroid. Actually, a meteoroid is not a whole new thing – it refers to small pieces coming off from asteroids. A little bit confusing, huh? So, the meteoroid is somewhere between the size of a grain of sand and the size of a boulder.

Well, then do you know what a meteorite is? A meteorite is a meteoroid that makes it all the way through the atmosphere and lands on the Earth's surface. Sometimes they cause impact craters. In short, the actual object is a meteoroid and the visual phenomena is meteor; and when the meteoroid falls down on earth…

S1: That's meteorites.

P: Right. Well, the most common are stone meteorites. But ironically, the stone meteorites are also the rarest type of meteorites. It's because they are hard to distinguish from Earth rocks, and also erode more quickly than other meteorites. So, they are quite valuable and precious.